THE IMPOSTERESS RABBIT BREEDER

THE IMPOSTERESS RABBIT BREEDER

Mary Toft and Eighteenth-Century England

KAREN **HARVEY**

OXFORD
UNIVERSITY PRESS

OXFORD
UNIVERSITY PRESS

Great Clarendon Street, Oxford, OX2 6DP,
United Kingdom

Oxford University Press is a department of the University of Oxford.
It furthers the University's objective of excellence in research, scholarship,
and education by publishing worldwide. Oxford is a registered trade mark of
Oxford University Press in the UK and in certain other countries

First Edition published in 2020

Impression: 1

Published in the United States of America by Oxford University Press
198 Madison Avenue, New York, NY 10016, United States of America

British Library Cataloguing in Publication Data
Data available

Library of Congress Control Number: 2019947980

ISBN 978-0-19-873488-8

Printed and bound in Great Britain by
Clays Ltd, Elcograf S.p.A.

ACKNOWLEDGEMENTS

The idea to write this book emerged as I prepared to teach a module on Mary Toft to undergraduate students in the Department of History at the University of Sheffield. I had known about the case for some time, but in preparing the module I realized that there was not yet a book that examined the case from the perspective of women's and social history. This was the book I set out to write. Now it is done, my thanks go to the many students who took HST2002 between 2012 and 2017, and whose questions and contributions clarified my thinking and focus.

While teaching the module I began to research the case. For their assistance with this I am grateful to Laura Alston, Jo Birch, Simon Neale, and the inimitable Mary Clayton. Parts of the research were supported by the Department of History and the Faculty of Arts and Humanities at the University of Sheffield, a Wellcome Trust Small Research Grant (WT102487MA), a Distinguished International Fellowship at the Center for the History of the Emotions at the University of Adelaide, an Eveyln S. Nation Fellowship at the Huntington Library and a Professorial Fellowship at the University of Birmingham. At several institutions staff were unfailingly generous with their time and expertise: at the British Library, Godalming Museum Local Studies Library, Glasgow University Special Collections, Hampshire Record Office, the Huntington Library, The Library of the Society of Friends, London Metropolitan Archive, The National Archives, Northamptonshire Archives, Surrey History Centre, the Wellcome Library, Westminster Archives Centre and West Sussex Record Office.

Many colleagues have shaped this research. The scholarship of Lisa Forman Cody and Dennis Todd opened up the case of Mary Toft in new and significant ways. Others gave suggestions and answered my questions: Louise Falcini, Alireza Fazeli, Mark Hallett, Paul Halliday, Amanda Herbert, Nurul Akmal Jamaludin, Gwyn Jones, Ian Keable, David Lemmings, Allan Pacey, Ruth Paley, Nicola Phillips, Julia Reid, Martial Staub, Tim Stretton, Michael Stumpf, Mark Sullivan, Naomi Tadmor, Oliver Walton, and Andrew Wells. Formative discussions took place when I presented work at the universities of Adelaide, Birkbeck, Birmingham, Lancaster, Leeds, King's College London, Sheffield, St. Andrews, Sydney, UCLA, Uppsala, and York, at the Bedford Centre for the History of Women and Gender at Royal Holloway London, the Huntington Library, the British History in the Long Eighteenth-Century Seminar at the Institute of Historical Research, and the North American Conference on British Studies. In discussing Mary Toft with public audiences, at Fairfax House in York, Wellcome Collection in London, and a Huntington Library's 'Scholarly Sustenance' event kindly hosted by Lary and Mary Anne Mielke, I have learned from those with quite a different perspective on the case, including lawyers, doctors, midwives, and the many women who have shared with me their personal experiences of conception, pregnancy, and childbirth.

The anonymous readers for Oxford University Press gave insightful comments at various stages of the process. Parts of the research appeared in an earlier form in the journals *History Workshop Journal* and *Past & Present*, and the comments I received from the readers then also fed into this book. I am particularly grateful to John Beattie, John Broad, Steve Hindle, Tim Hitchcock, Nicholas Rogers, and Bob Shoemaker who took the time to read that early work. Helen Berry, Elizabeth Eger, and Amanda Vickery were inspiring companions (and convivial company) as I wrote in the sunny South of France. This trip, along with many others for the project, was made possible by unstinting support from Mike Braddick. And as the book took its present shape, I was supported by a dedicated group of brilliant colleagues who gave their feedback on individual chapters: Helen Berry, Lisa Forman Cody, Elizabeth Eger, Mark Knights, Alexandra Shepard, and Susan Whyman. I am mindful of the generosity of each of these colleagues, and of the many dear friends among them.

At Oxford University Press, Luciana O'Flaherty supported the project early on and her comments on the full manuscript made a decisive impact on the final shape of the book. The diligent efforts of the rest of the OUP team have brought the book into print and I thank them all for all their work.

Over coffee and cocktails, through dinners and dancing, I have been supported by the company of so many others while writing this book. Most especially, I thank Mark for all the love.

I dedicate the book with much love to my daughters Cora and Melissa, my joy and inspiration.

CONTENTS

LIST OF ILLUSTRATIONS

PRELUDE

From Guildford comes a strange, but well attested piece of News. That a poor Woman who lives at Godalmin, near that Town, who has an Husband and two Children now living with her; was, about a Month past, delivered by Mr. John Howard, an eminent Surgeon and Man-Midwife living at Guildford, of a Creature resembling a Rabbit; but whose Heart and Lungs grew without its Belly. About 14 Days since, she was delivered by the same Person, of a perfect Rabbit; and in a few Days after, of 4 more; and on Friday, Saturday, and Sunday the 4th, 5th, and 6th, Instant, of one in each Day: In all Nine. They died all in bringing into the World. Mr. Howard keeps them all in Spirits; and we hear, he intends to present them to the Royal Society. The Woman hath made Oath, That 2 Months ago, being working in a Field with other Women, they put up a Rabbit; who running from them, they pursued it, but to no purpose: This created in her such a longing to it, that she (being with Child) was taken ill, and miscarried; and from that Time, she hath not been able to avoid thinking of Rabbits. The said Woman has been deliver'd of 5 more Rabbits, in all 14. Mr. Molineux, the Prince's Secretary, is, we hear, gone thither by his Royal Highness's Order, to bring a faithful Narration of the Affair.

Daily Journal, Monday 14 November, 1726.

On 14 November 1726, the *Daily Journal* reported a remarkable event on its front page. A woman had started to give birth to rabbits in the town of Godalming, Surrey. The story had been gathering ground and news was spreading quickly, but this account was the first to give such detail about the case and the woman at its centre. The woman was Mary Toft. By the end of November, several leading doctors—some sent directly by King George I—had travelled to Surrey to examine her. Toft was soon moved to London, to be closer to the King and the doctors. By mid-December, she had been accused of fraudulently pretending to be a rabbit-breeder and taken into custody for the crime of imposture.

Mary Toft's unusual deliveries caused a media sensation in a burgeoning public sphere fuelled by new kinds of print, especially newspapers. People were genuinely curious to know what had happened and relished both the drama and the hilarity as the case unfolded. Her rabbit births were a test case for doctors trying to further their knowledge about the processes of reproduction and pregnancy. Yet the rabbit births prompted not just public curiosity and scientific investigation but also a vicious backlash. So much about this case prompts the question, 'why?' Why did it start? Why did she do it? Why did so many people believe her? Why was the King involved? Why was she punished? And why did people continue to discuss the case many years later?

This book answers these questions. It situates the case in the troubled local community of Godalming and trains light on the women who remained close to Mary Toft as the case unfolded. It considers the motivations of the medical men who came to examine Toft and the ideas that allowed them to countenance the claim that a woman might give birth to rabbits. It explores why Mary Toft's rabbit births attracted the attention of the King but also of several powerful men in government, following the progress of the case through the criminal justice system. It situates the case in the wider social, economic, cultural, and political contexts of early-eighteenth-century England, and shows what the case can tell us about this time and place. Amongst all this, the book tries to reconstruct the voice and experiences of Mary Toft, the 'Imposteress Rabbett Breeder', the woman who gave births to rabbits.

PART I
SURREY

CHAPTER 1

THE TOWN

'peaceable neighbours who are willing to live quietly'

There is no doubt that the events in which Mary Toft participated in 1726 were remarkable. Yet they were the product of the long-standing relationships amongst her local community in Godalming, a town lying forty miles from central London. To understand the case we need to understand how the town had transformed in the years prior to 1726, and how this had affected the people living there. In 1575 the inhabitants of Godalming were described as 'being in moste extreme ruine and decay'. Out of a desire to 'promote ye Towne to a better State', Queen Elizabeth granted a charter of corporation thus establishing 'the Inhabitants of the... Towne into a body Corporate & pollitiq', which could raise taxes and more effectively protect its economy. By 1725, Godalming was estimated as having a population of two to three thousand. Eighteenth-century towns were small by modern standards, with only around seventy having populations of more than 2,500. Godalming was therefore one of the larger commercial towns.[1] By the early eighteenth century it was an aspiring Surrey town, with a fine market place and genteel terraces. Yet it was also a town riven with the social divisions borne of profound inequality. A small town elite governed the population economically and morally through a series of institutions, while a group of poor labouring families became ever more impoverished. It was here that Mary Toft was born and died, and where the rabbit births began.

Eighteenth-century towns were the engine of social, economic, and political change. They were conduits of the new goods that were changing the face of English material life. They served as centres for new forms of commercialized leisure and sociability. An 'urban renaissance', as it is often called, led to new architectural spaces and an increasingly visible consumer culture in smaller English towns. Yet towns accommodated a range of social groups and in small towns and parishes throughout England there were increasingly marked divisions between the poor and an emerging 'middling sort' of office-holders, as well as between the poor and the landed gentry and aristocracy.[2] Godalming was a particularly poor area within the county of Surrey. In 1664 the town had one of the highest rates of exemption from the Hearth Tax (a property tax based on the number of hearths or stoves in the property) in Surrey—48 per cent of occupied households—suggesting a high number of small and relatively poor households in the town. In addition, the local landowner, Thomas Molyneux, handed out charity to 'severral poor people', and in 1719 by far the largest group on the list of recipients was the twenty-one people from 'The Towne', eight of them widows.[3] Though the woollen industry had previously brought prosperity to the town, the trade was in decline by the early eighteenth century.[4] The differences in wealth between the poorest and the richest were colossal. At this top end of the social scale in Godalming was the Duke of Richmond, who kept a house in the town. As the Tofts hunkered down for winter in September 1726, the Duchess of Richmond was dressing her servants in grey cloth and black velvet, purchasing a suit costing £1 12 shillings for the family's 'Black boy'—a curiosity for her guests to observe—as well as a new coat for the pet monkey, costing 12 shillings. At the other end of the social scale stood people like Mary Toft, who reported that she was paid a penny a day for her agricultural labour.[5] Stark social distinctions were also evident amongst those engaged in the struggling clothing trade. The will of a woollen weaver such as Robert Byde showed he had a house, workhouse, and garden to bequeath; the framework-knitter John Chitty owned two tenements in Ockford Lane, Godalming.[6] Unskilled clothworkers like Mary Toft's husband Joshua Toft—a group from whom no will survives—would have no property to leave.

Godalming certainly had its central Market House and shops. The Duke of Richmond's fine house in the centre of the town was a convenient stopping-off point between London and his country seat in West Sussex. Just two years prior to the case, in 1724, Richmond had refurbished this house on Church Street. The house was relatively modest in size, with four bedrooms and two main receptions rooms (the dining room and the drawing room). Yet the interiors were lavish:

Fig. 1.1 A detail from John Senex's map of Surrey (1729) [Copyright of Surrey History Centre]

the Duke's own room—with a yellow colour scheme—had cost £45, almost half of the total £103 18s 2d spent on refurbishing the whole Godalming house.[7] This architecture of gentility, sociability, and consumption characteristic of many burgeoning eighteenth-century towns stood almost back to back with the housing of the poor. Inequality and segregation was built into the spatial layout of Godalming. The poor lived in rented tenements on the eastern side of the town. It was there that several of the male power-holders in the town owned property. Heirs of Thomas Edsall, a juror on the manor's court leet in 1721, held the lease for one of the tenements known as Saunders and Emory's; Richard Tickner, Warden of the town in 1723, leased another; George Avenell, Warden in 1718, 1725, and 1731 and juror on the manor's court baron in 1726, also held a lease on one of the tenements known as Bridgors.[8] Several poor families were concentrated on Bridge Street. The families of William Chitty senior and William Chitty junior and John Toft (a separate branch of the Toft family) owned leases to properties on Bridge Street, the latter being 'the lowermost house in Bridge Street next to the Wharf'. The clothier Abraham Toft (no relation to Mary and Joshua Toft's family) owned 'the other a [sic] house in Bridge Street' next to the stream, which he appears to have subdivided and rented as properties and which on his death in 1728 were occupied by James Toft, Edmund Ayling, and Thomas Pinkett.[9] No surviving records confirm that this was where Mary and Joshua Toft lived. But by the nineteenth century it was deemed common knowledge that it was amongst the crowded tenements of Bridge Street that the rabbit births had taken place.[10]

The 'chief inhabitants'

Eighteenth-century towns saw the sharpening of divisions between the labouring poor and the rest of the urban population. At the same time, poor families were increasingly subject to the regulation and intervention of local governors. In London, the twin systems of poor relief and criminal justice had set the poor apart and identified them as a social problem.[11] But similar processes were in train in smaller towns and rural parishes. Within the town of Godalming alone, the Toft family were subject to no less than four formal systems of governance. First, life in Godalming was regulated by the Corporation and its office-holders (such as warden and bailiff), the self-styled 'principal

Inhabitants'. The oath for those newly elected into the Corporation bound these men 'to uphold and maintain every Lawfull Liberty & constitution made for the benefit of the corporation'.[12] These mens' governance took different forms. Godalming's town clock was typical of the way in which towns regulated the everyday life of their labouring inhabitants: the clock was so 'apprentices, servants and workmen' could keep 'fit hours'.[13] The Corporation also upheld strict rules of conduct through its several meetings and its court, as in other European towns, all recorded carefully. Intersecting with the Corporation was the second form of governance, the estate of the local manor owned by the family of More and More-Molyneux of Loseley. The manor also had its own courts: the court leet or frank pledge (for peacekeeping in the jurisdiction of the Sheriff) and the court baron (which included free and customary tenants of the manor as well as civil disputes). These courts comprised tenant jurors who enforced by-laws relating to rent, property, and crime, but also regulated the behaviour of the tenants which might disturb the peace of the manor or bring the reputation of the Lord into disrepute. These courts were still playing an important role in monitoring community behaviour well into the eighteenth century; indeed, urban manor courts in towns such as Godalming were more active in policing unruly behaviour than the rural courts.[14] Third, was the court of the Godalming Hundred. Godalming was divided into nine tithings, each consisting of a group of ten householders governed by tithingmen who sought to maintain good conduct. The court of the Hundred comprised these tithingmen (and by the eighteenth century this overlapped with the manor).[15]

The fourth form of regulation was through poor relief from the parish and other sources. The parish provided relief for the poor in the form of regular pensions or irregular dole (often in kind), but receipt of such relief required parishioners' conformity not just to formal rules (about settlement in a particular place, for example) but also to expectations of appropriate behaviour. No records survive for the overseers of the poor or the parish vestry for Godalming. Just prior to the hoax, in August 1726, however, there was, 'lately Erected [...] a Workhouse and Dwelling place for the poor', an institution that would have served as an instrument of social control over the parish's poor.[16]

In a town the size of Godalming, these forms of governance were enacted not by anonymous institutions but by the familiar faces of neighbours. The men who staffed these ostensibly separate institutions rotated offices within their narrow group and even served the different institutions at the same time. Though the particular network of governing institutions was different in each town, the urban magistracy of Godalming took the form of a classic urban oligarchy. While each institution had its own particular focus, they converged on the issues of maintaining the peace and disorderly behaviour. When the governors could not keep the peace using the town's institutions, these men drew on forms of authority outside the town in order to discipline disorderly residents. In 1724, many of these men styled themselves the 'chief inhabitants' and petitioned the Surrey Quarter Sessions about the Godalming resident Stephen Boxall. He had, they reported, 'threatened to Incite or otherwise trouble & molest Severall persons [...] as disorderly and abusive to him'. The forty-two signatories to the petition attested that those persons were in fact 'quiet & peaceable' and that it was Boxall who was to blame, being an 'Envious, Turbulent, disorderly man'. The 'peaceable neighbours', the petition insists, 'are willing to live quietly', if Boxall 'would let them alone'. The signatories to this petition included many of the official governors of the town who policed the town for its economic and moral well-being. They were also the same men who gave considerable sums of money in a subscription to raise funds for repairs to the market house and who were wealthy enough to pay taxes and be classed as the town's independent 'householders'.[17]

The men in this group were linked personally as well as professionally. They were connected by both marriage and friendship.[18] Nicholas Edsal (on the manor court leet) and Abraham Toft (again, no relation to Joshua and Mary) the framework-knitter (signatory to the petition against Boxall) were brothers-in-law, married to the sisters Margaret and Elizabeth.[19] The mason George Chitty, who died in 1728, was father to John Chitty (on the Corporation jury in 1733 and subscriber to the Market House in 1729), and father-in-law to John Shrubb (also a Market House subscriber).[20] The daughter of the vicar of Godalming, Anthony Warton and his wife Mary, was married to Abraham Toft junior (a clothier and son of Abraham Toft the framework-knitter). In her will of 1719, Mary Warton named William Chitty junior, malster (a subscriber to the Market House and on the Corporation jury from 1733, and later elected as Assistant to the Warden) as trustee to her daughter Elizabeth.[21] William Chitty junior, alongside William Chitty senior

(Warden in 1720), also witnessed the will of the widow Joan Freeman in 1719.[22] To John Shrubb and Abraham Toft junior, clothier, Freeman left a ring that she had wrapped up in paper and marked with their names. Her cousins included Charity Toft, daughter of Abraham Toft, Jane Ticknor, wife of Perrier Ticknor (on the town jury of 1726 and Market House subscriber) and Abraham Toft stockingmaker.[23] Governing the inhabitants through an intricate web of institutions, the power of this network of governors and chief inhabitants from the established middling and upper sort was consolidated by social and familial ties.

In contrast, a group of poor labouring families became ever more impoverished by the declining cloth trade in the region. And it was into this group that Mary Toft was born on 21 February 1703 to John and Jane Denyer. In 1720, aged seventeen, she married the eighteen-year-old Joshua Toft.[24] As a cloth worker Joshua was a member of the unskilled poor and one certainly affected by the depression in the trade. Though the records are patchy, it appears that the Tofts were part of the town's persistent poor. A John Denyer, perhaps Mary Toft's brother, was admitted to the Godalming Hospital or almshouses, run by the Company of Carpenters for poor men of the town, in 1725.[25] This relief was limited, though, and in 1734 residents of the almshouses complained to the Company that they 'could not subsist without having further releife And that the parishes would not maintaine them without going into the Workhouse'. The Company answered that the men would get no more provisions and if they could not subsist then they should leave and enter the Workhouse.[26] Seven Tofts died in the workhouse between 1729 and 1757. In such circumstances, the poor turned to the support of kin and neighbours.[27]

Mary Toft's family were not simply poor but, as we might expect, part of the Godalming population that stood apart from the governing chief inhabitants. Though we are severely limited in our efforts to reconstruct Toft's family and local community, two exceptional documents give a clear indication of the Toft network. The first was a recognizance generated at the Guildford Quarter Sessions in July 1726, not long before the rabbit births. It lists the men who appeared at the Sessions, charged with trespassing on the pond of James Stringer. Amongst the thirty-eight names is that of Joshua Toft clothworker, Mary Toft's husband, who is recorded as admitting to the offence.[28] This first document allows us to reconstruct an occupational network for Joshua Toft and get some indication of the family's place in Godalming society. Only six of the names on the 1726 recognizance appear in lists of Godalming governors or householders, suggesting little overlap between these two groups. Thomas Underwood, stockingmaker, was churchwarden, named as a chief inhabitant on the 1724 petition against Boxall, and served as juror on the court baron in 1726. The office of churchwarden was an honourable one, typically fulfilled by someone of middling rank, often a craftsman.[29] A Caleb Tickner might be the man of the same name listed as a subscriber to the Market House repairs three years later. It is certainly likely that the Timothy Grover, cordwainer, Jonathan Painter, clothier, William Pincot, clothier, and Richard Stedman, weaver, were the same four men listed elsewhere as householders or rate payers.[30] Overall, then, the correlation of those on the Sessions recognizance with the lists of governance, chief inhabitants, or householders is very weak when compared with the correlation *between* those other lists. Unsurprisingly, the group of men bound to appear at the Sessions were poorly represented in the town's governance and relatively unconnected to networks of power.

Wills from Godalming reinforce this picture and help us place the men who took part in the trespass in terms of wealth and social status. Eight of the names listed in the 1726 recognizance also appear in wills from the Archdeaconry or the Commissary Court of the Bishop of Winchester in the Archdeaconry of Surrey (though not in those from the Prerogative Court of Canterbury, the court which dealt with wills of the relatively wealthy). Two of these names—Thomas Woods and George Chitty—are very unlikely to be the men in the recognizance as they are either the wrong profession or age.[31] We can be more certain that the six remaining names from the recognizance that also appeared in Godalming wills did refer to the same men. The first, Timothy Grover (cordwainer in the recognizance), may have been the brother-in-law to James Finch (dyer). In his will of 1730, Finch left his sister Margery £25, adding, 'I forgive my brother Timothy Grover what he owes me'.[32] James Toft (stockingmaker in the recognizance) and Thomas Pinkett (clothier) may have rented property owned by the clothier Abraham Toft of Godalming, and were mentioned as tenants in his will of 1728.[33] The fourth man, Caleb Tickner (stockingmaker), was likely to have been a witness to the will of his neighbour, the carpenter, John Costen, in 1709 (proved in 1723).[34] The final two men, John Hayes and Richard

Stedman, named as stockingmaker and weaver in the recognizance, were witnesses to the will of Edward Bonner, a labourer of Godalming, in 1701.[35] Stedman—a householder in the town— left his mark on the will, rather than signing it.[36] Bonner's daughter-in-law was Margaret Edsall, wife of Thomas Edsall of Godalming, linen weaver, and perhaps the same Thomas Edsall who served in the manor court leet in 1721. If this was the case, then this link between Edsall, Bonner, and Stedman, together with the presence of Thomas Underwood the churchwarden and perhaps Caleb Tickner, are the only—and very tenuous—links between the group of men in the recognizance and the network of governors. Moreover, three of the men with whom Mary Toft's husband trespassed on James Stringer's pond may have served as witnesses to wills and three more may have been referred to in a will; but none of these men either left a will or received any bequests. The men from Godalming who were brought before the Sessions accused of trespass were tenants without property. The same was also true of Joshua and Mary Toft, and their branch of the family, who are never mentioned in a will. Perhaps the only exception is the will of William Ray, cooper, of 1720, in which Ray leaves to his daughter his half of five houses in the occupation of four people including '(widow) Toft'.[37] It is a tantalizing possibility that this might have been Joshua Toft's mother Ann, or Mary Toft's mother-in-law. Yet it is impossible to say.

In addition to the recognizance for trespass, a second document allows us to reconstruct a narrower network of the Tofts' neighbours. In December 1726, a major landowner in Godalming, Baron Onslow, was tasked to investigate the case of the rabbit births locally. The depositions he obtained from six individuals close to the Tofts were published later in 1727. Edward Costen (framework-knitter), Mary Costen (widow), Mrs Mason, Mary Peytoe (wife of John, husbandman), Richard Stedman (weaver), and John Sweetapple (currier and Quaker), each reported their eye-witness accounts of what had taken place in the Toft household. They were called upon because they knew or lived nearby the Tofts, or had been involved in the affair. We will consider what this document tells us about the case in a later chapter, but here it is important to note the presence of both women and men. The three women deponents cannot be traced in the historical record.[38] Richard Stedman—the weaver named on the recognizance who was also a tax-paying householder in the town—appears again, as does another textile worker, Edward Costen. This second document hints that the Toft network may have been consolidated not just by proximity or occupation, however, but by faith. The deponent John Sweetapple was identified as a currier and a Quaker. He is distinguished as a Quaker in the depositions because Quakers could not take oaths; thus Sweetapple 'solemnly affirmeth' (rather than 'maketh oath' like the other deponents).[39] John was likely to have been related to Benjamin Sweetapple, also a currier and a Quaker of Godalming. Benjamin signed a formal apology to the Friends' Monthly meeting at Guildford in July 1729, admitting that 'I did goe out to a priest to take my Wife, contrary to the good order established among friends', perhaps suggesting his comfort in the Anglican community as well as his commitment to his fellow Quakers.[40] Benjamin Sweetapple seems to have been well integrated with Anglicans and was one of four witnesses to the will of Henry Woods in 1714.[41] This was typical. Under Charles II the population of Godalming was 'very largely nonconformist' (somewhere around a half), though by 1725 the number of Dissenters was relatively few. By the end of the seventeenth century, Quakers were well integrated into local communities, with non-Quakers buried in Quaker burial grounds and testators choosing non-Quakers as executors of their wills.[42]

There is no concrete evidence that the Tofts were themselves Quakers, though no historian has yet located a record of Mary and Joshua's marriage in Anglican records (which survive well for this period). Yet the presence of Quakers in the Toft network—one was a Quaker and two were clothing artisans—may well have been significant. Quakerism and its antecedents have long been associated with industrializing or proto-industrial areas, and in particular the clothing industry. Road networks and communications linked disparate cloth industry areas and allowed radical ideas to spread, such that seventeenth-century clothiers were more likely to own books than other occupational groups in some areas.[43] Both communities were associated with dissent. This underscores the Tofts' exclusion from the networks of power in the town. Indeed, it is only Richard Stedman who appears in the network of the Tofts' neighbours, the occupational network in the recognizance and amongst the chief inhabitants. Mary and Joshua Toft—and almost all the people connected to them—were part of Godalming's poor and excluded entirely from the governing network of the town.

Order and disorder in the town

Local communities—particularly the parish—were bound by a strong sense of belonging. Yet this did not mean internal cohesion. Given the two relatively disconnected networks of the Tofts on the one hand and the governors and chief inhabitants on the other, we might expect Godalming to be a town starkly divided into two opposing factions. In fact the group of chief inhabitants themselves showed considerable variation in terms of occupational identity and wealth, though most were drawn from the trades and crafts rather than the wealthy land-owning or professional middling sorts. Shopkeepers, butchers, and husbandmen all featured amongst the 'chief inhabitants'.[44] Some of these individuals left considerable sums of money to the poor of God-alming. On his death in 1725, the clothier James Shrubb (signatory to the petition against Boxall) left land and buildings in several parishes, as well as paying to the poor of Godalming £20, 'to such of them as me Executors shall think fitt'.[45] The financial security of these men could not be assured, though. The list of recipients of the Lord's charity in 1719 included several people from the local governing families, such as Widow Edsall, John Chitty, William Chitty, and William Chitty junior. Also on this list were John Stedman, William Pinket (or Pinquet), and William Musgrove. Musgrove and Pinket appeared together before the local county Quarter Sessions court accused of the trespass in the summer of 1726, where they were listed as labourer and clothier respect-ively.[46] Stedman was to become bailiff to the Godalming Corporation in 1725, and a juror for the town the following year. By 1729, at the age of sixty-two, he was sufficiently established to contribute to the repairs to the Market House building in the centre of the town. The range of men receiving charity in 1719 and the apparently different paths they later took reflects both the consolidation but also the precariousness of the eighteenth-century middling sort.[47]

Such divisions may have been behind the open conflicts among the governors. The Stephen Boxall who was the subject of the petition to the Quarter Sessions in 1724 was apparently the same 'S. Boxall' serving as a juror on the frank pledge court just two years later.[48] William Chitty junior, the son of a long-serving Godalming office-holder and himself the holder of several town offices, was fined twice by the Corporation: once for not appearing when called by the bailiff and once for not serving the position of Assistant to the Warden to which he had been elected. On the first occasion on 2 January 1727, Chitty had been summoned by the men of the Corporation, 'the principal Inhabitants', but he had 'refused'. They used the powers given them by the corporation charter and fined Chitty for contempt, three shillings and four pence.[49] William Chitty senior had died in the autumn of 1726, and his son was described in the papers of the manorial court as 'his next heir & of full age', though it seems that William was reluctant to take over his father's town responsibilities.[50] Two years later, in February 1729, Chitty was again chosen for office, once again refused, and was once more fined by the Corporation.[51]

In the treatment of both Boxall and Chitty junior we can see the town governors seeking to reinforce the public authority of civic office. The higher authority of the county Quarter Sessions could also be called upon to reinforce this. In 1725, for example, a letter was sent to the Surrey Quarter Sessions calling for two men to be bound over for failing to recognize the authority of the current High Constable of the town. John Chitty and Thomas Keen, labourers of Godalming were accused of, 'scandalizing Jo:ⁿ Garrald of Godalming & threatning to do him some bodily Harme [and] Divers other breaces of ye Peace (£20 each)'. John Garrard was not only a 'Gent[leman]' but was also High Constable for Godalming, along with a cordwainer and a framework-knitter. Thomas Keen was a bricklayer who the Corporation had paid to carry out work in the town. Chitty in particular had clearly made an error of judgement. A letter was soon sent to the Sessions, explaining that Chitty 'has an unfortunate difference with John Garard high Constable of the same town where in he is no offender [...] for he only refused to takes Thomas Keen into custody without any Just reason as he conceived nither did he no John Garard was any peace officer.'[52] Given Chitty's familiarity with the Corporation it seems odd that he did not recognize Garrald as a town office-holder; it is tempting to see Chitty's action as one of knowing defiance. Whatever the truth of Chitty's testimony, the case bespeaks the fragile authority of office-holders and a concern to use the power of the county courts to ensure that this was upheld. Perhaps this unease explains why, in 1724, the Duke of Richmond had invested a tidy sum to improve security at his Godalming house, repairing gates, window bars, and doors.[53]

Social relations in the region

Throughout the region, in Surrey and the bordering counties of Berkshire and Hampshire, local landowners were exerting an ever-tighter grip on their property and thus over the lives of those who lived and depended on the land. Increasingly tough measures were encroaching on the customary rights to the land long held by the poor. Property laws were extended that slowly privatized previously common goods and increased the punishment for encroachments on this private property. This was just one aspect of the growing emphasis on a fundamental belief in the primacy of property and rights to it. Part of this was the redefinition of some animals as property rather than game, the effect of which was to reclassify the taking of these animals a crime of theft rather than one of poaching; the crime of theft was subject to increasingly harsher punishment over this period.[54] Activities which had previously been the legitimate customary exercising of common rights were now trespass and theft. Historians have debated the character of this 'criminal' activity in the early eighteenth century. Some see it as an example of 'social crime': not regarded as criminal by the perpetrators or their community but defined as such by lawmakers.[55] Others see poaching and wood-taking as acts through which the rural worker resisted the encroachment on their customary rights, challenged landed authority and the concept of property ownership enshrined in the law, and acquired agency through resistance. Social historians have developed an approach to crime that sees some crime not as an act of the socially deviant but instead as a social practice that grew out of custom and that could be seen by its participants as legitimate protest. This situates such activity in the context of labouring *mentalities*. Seen through this lens, these were not crimes but protests. The clearest example of this was poaching, an activity often organized by large and violent gangs. Though it would be wrong to see all such activity as either self-consciously criminal or political, much of it took place within the wider context of a breakdown in social relations.[56]

Not all regions in England experienced the same degree or type of activity, and responses to criminal activity against the private property of landowners differed from place to place.[57] During the 1720s, though, direct social conflict began to emerge within Royal Forests, originating in the area around the county borders between Berkshire, Hampshire, and Surrey. Known to contemporaries as the 'Blacks' because they acted in disguise, often by blackening their faces, these groups of poachers are associated with deer-hunting, though their activity took other forms that included the breaking of fishponds. E. P. Thompson's examination of these events in *Whigs and Hunters* (1975) characterized the crimes of the poachers as protests, ones directed at the property of the ruling Whig elite (a party drawn from the aristocracy and landed gentry) as well as royal rights and prerogatives. It was the violent group actions of these men, or perhaps more generalized fears of a threat to the regime, that caused the Whigs to seek to protect their own property by extending the list of capital crimes against property with the Waltham Act (or 'Black Act') of 1723.[58] The press also played a key role, stoking anxieties into moral panic that would lead to more draconian legislation.[59] In the early 1720s, the unrest in this region to the south-west of London was, in the minds of contemporaries, connected to the wider social order.

For decades the Surrey constituency had seen bitter battles between the Whigs and opposing Tories for the two parliamentary seats of the county. The major landowners, the Whig Thomas, 2nd Baron Onslow (who later took the depositions from Toft's neighbours) and Thomas More-Molyneux, had struggled to retain power in the area. There had been long-standing grievances against the Onslows, not least for their apparent ability to control the second seat. The 1720s were an unsettling time for the Onslow family. The only break in their almost continuous hold on one of the seats was between 1722 and 1727, when no Onslow candidate was available.[60] Moreover, Thomas Onslow was one of those Whig landowners in the southern counties who had experienced attacks at the hands of the Blacks. And he had personal experience of violence. In September 1723, an attempt had been made on his life, 'by a Fellow with a Gun on his Shoulder, ready cock'd'.[61] Edward Arnold was found guilty and sentenced to death, but perhaps as a result of Arnold's plea of insanity, Onslow interceded and the execution was prevented. Arnold's prosecution under the Black Act transformed its application. The Act was originally intended to prosecute men who were both armed and in disguise: Arnold was not in disguise and this successful prosecution for an incident on Onslow's land thus extended the application of the Black Act far beyond its original remit.[62] An equally significant detail of the case is that Edward Arnold claimed he was using the gun to shoot Onslow's rabbits, but had instead accidentally shot at the Lord. Arnold reportedly explained that, 'Lord Onslow and King George had got all the money, so that he could get none'.[63] A lower-ranking man had sought to justify his shooting at the rabbits—or perhaps at the landowner—while voicing disaffection about his lot.

Fish, rabbits, and protests

At the heart of this area of the Berkshire, Hampshire, and Surrey county borders was the small but divided town of Godalming. The town appeared to escape the notorious protests seen in other places, but there is evidence that politically driven unrest reached Godalming. The evidence comes from the case of trespass in which Mary Toft's husband Joshua was involved in the summer of 1726. This case involved thirty-eight men charged 'for a trespass in entering the ground or pond of James Stringer Covered with water with an intent to steale fish'. Such a large group was almost certainly an organized protest.[64] While these men were unconnected to the governors or chief inhabitants of the town, neither were they drawn primarily from the labouring poor. Alongside Joshua Toft 'clothworker', the group of men included labourers, bricklayers, gardeners, and a carpenter. Listed separately are another group of men with occupations such as clothier, fishmonger, cordwainer, weaver, malster, carpenter, and gardener.[65] Straddling the River Wey, Godalming had many ponds and their contents were to be defended. James Stringer, the proprietor of the pool, had previously been an appraiser for the Hundred of Godalming, protecting the fish belonging to the lord of Godalming manor's, Thomas More-Molyneux. A later case of poaching from a Godalming pond also reached the Sessions. In November 1727 John Balchin confessed that he and John Charriot had stolen nineteen carp from the pond of John Walter, Esquire, divided them between them, and which Balchin had intended 'to eat in his family'. For his part, Charriott confessed to having stolen twenty carp, taking his share and selling on five.[66]

Rabbits were also an object of theft and a focus for protest. The meat and fur of rabbits had long been a rare commodity and a symbol of elite status, and this continued into the eighteenth century even as private commercial warrening was established.[67] But landowners' rabbits encroached on common land to eat the food of the sheep and cattle upon which commoners and tenants' livelihood depended. Disputes over warren rights were violent and long-standing on Cannock Chase, for example. As with deer, the legal status of rabbits changed from wild game to enclosed animals, thereby being redefined as private property.[68] The Black Act thus referred to 'Conies or Hares', as well as deer, cattle, and fish.[69] Rabbits were a focus for social tensions because in the sandy areas suited to warrens, rabbit farming was a direct replacement for dairy and arable farming as the prices of wool and grain declined from the late seventeenth century; the decline of the clothing trade in some areas thus went hand in hand with the growth of commercial warrening.[70] Due to its suitably deep sandy soil, Godalming possessed large rabbit warrens. A large new commercial warren was laid out in Godalming in 1671–73, on a 260-acre site that had previously been used for sheep pasture, though the large warrens in the area were still in the hands of the local landowner, Thomas Onslow.[71] Stealing the rabbits in Godalming could conceivably have been another protest against Onslow, though this is not the explanation that Mary Toft gave. Instead, Toft claimed in her early report to the first London doctor to examine her, Nathanael St André, that she had chased the rabbits because she, 'being very poor and indigent cou'd not procure any'.[72] Toft's claim was strikingly similar to Edward Arnold's explanation for firing shots at rabbits on Onslow's land, shots that flew perilously close to the baron's head. Moreover, Mary Toft's statement that she was taking rabbits because she was poor and could not afford to buy them was tantamount to an admission of theft. This was a highly provocative statement in a context where the theft of animals was not only punished harshly but could be seen as a threatening expression of protest.[73]

The events that were to follow Mary Toft's chasing of the rabbits—the rabbit births themselves—have been understood partly in the context of Toft's poverty. The remarkable deliveries were, perhaps, intended to generate an income.[74] Yet there are scarce few references of any money changing hands in this case, and only Cyriacus Ahlers (another doctor who examined Toft) himself reported that he gave Toft money.[75] Instead, we might interpret the rabbit births as an appropriation of the rabbit as a traditional symbol of elite privilege in the manner of other protests. Perhaps the births were a 'ritual of insult' used by the powerless in resistance to the powerful.[76] Certainly, early-eighteenth-century plebeian culture provided ample resources for the ritual parody of elite power. And others have noted the role played by women in later protests against enclosure.[77] A poor woman unable to buy or catch rabbits who then began to reproduce her own would have been an eloquent upending of the stark disparity in exclusion and privilege that characterized a town such as Godalming. It is a tempting interpretation, though one of which we cannot be certain. But on the eve of the rabbit births and at precisely the time of the Blacks' activity in the region, Mary Toft's husband took part in a large-scale protest. Both the rabbit births and the fishpond trespass were disorderly actions involving highly disputed animals that did not, or should not, belong to the protagonists. Both would disrupt a town that was already starkly divided both socially and politically and in which the keeping of the peace and the authority of those in power was closely guarded. Only one would arouse the interest of the press, the public, and the King.

CHAPTER 2

THE WOMEN

'they workt for me'

In his later account of the rabbit births, the doctor Nathanael St André described how he had interviewed Mary Toft shortly after the rabbit births began. His account of her is brief: 'She seem'd to be of a healthy strong Constitution, of a small size, and fair Complexion; of a very stupid and sullen Temper: She can neither write nor read.'[1] The description of Mary Toft in the *Oxford Dictionary of National Biography* is an obvious paraphrase of this: 'Mary, an illiterate, was of small stature, with a healthy, strong constitution, and a sullen temper.'[2] We can add a great deal to this short description, though. Mary Toft was born in 1703 and was seventeen when she married the eighteen-year-old Joshua Toft (below the average age of twenty-four at first marriage). Mary was the second, and the eldest girl, of John and Jane Denyer's five surviving children. Joshua Toft, just two or three months older than Mary, was the sixth of twelve children. Their first child, Ann, was born on 27 March 1723, though was buried in July of that year. Mary was soon pregnant again and their son James was baptized on 8 July 1724.[3] Mary Toft's maternal family is almost entirely absent from records of the case, which mention only once her brother, John Denyer, with whom she and Joshua were reported to be living at the time of the hoax.[4] Toft was thus a young married woman who had left her natal family and was now legally part of the Toft family. The absence of her family, and particularly her mother, from all the accounts of the events that took place in 1726 is striking because mothers were commonly closely involved in their daughters' reproductive lives. Instead, it was Mary's husband's family that was closely involved in the case. Joshua's mother, Ann Toft, was a key figure in the whole affair. The rabbit births began in the intimate setting of a three-generational family and a group of female neighbours, and documents disclose the critical role that kin, neighbours, and especially the women played at every stage. Indeed, one of the notable features of the case of Mary Toft is the continuous presence of a group of women in close physical proximity to Mary during the affair. This began when Mary first saw rabbits while she was working alongside other women, and continued for some time. Her life, as was common at the time, was lived largely in the company of other women. The Tofts may have been excluded from the governing networks in the town, but Mary was not isolated. On the contrary, a tight-knit group of women huddled close to her at almost every stage. To understand her life, we must therefore place Toft in the context of the lives of women in early-eighteenth-century England.

Labouring women's lives

Fig. 2.1 Mary chases the rabbit with a fellow worker, a scene from the broadsheet *The Doctors in Labour, or A New Whim-Wham from Guildford* (1726) [New York Public Library]

The past lives of the poor are always more difficult to reconstruct than those of the educated and the wealthy; the lives of poor women in particular have left a relatively feint trace in the historical record. Our evidence of the life of Mary Toft is patchy. The newspapers that reported the births from October 1726 and a number of printed pamphlets written by some of the men involved in events, and which began to appear in December, provide some important detail about the case and Toft's experiences. They even claim to include statements from Toft herself. These are, of course, all filtered by the authors' concerns as they addressed a public audience. But the richest documents are the three surviving manuscript statements given by Mary Toft in early December 1726. In some ways, these are also the most problematic because they are retrospective statements produced in the context of the criminal investigation that followed the rabbit births. These documents have been labelled by contemporaries, archivists, and historians alike as 'confessions', though this is not quite accurate. Nevertheless, these three statements constitute the only surviving account of events from Mary Toft's perspective. They are also rare and valuable evidence from a labouring woman of the early eighteenth century.

In drawing these sources together we can build up a fairly detailed picture of Mary Toft's life at the time of the rabbit births. The earliest newspaper report of the case described how three women, all pregnant, had been working in a field when they chased the rabbit, though only one had since given birth to 'something in the Form of a dissected Rabit'. This was soon reinforced by Mary Toft's own accounts. According to the first newspaper article to give her version of events, she had given an oath that she was 'working in a Field with other Women' when they chased a rabbit'.[5] And as she explained to St André, 'as she was weeding in a Field, she saw a Rabbet spring up near her, after which she ran, with another Woman that was at work just by her'. Some months later, Mary reported, she experienced heavy bleeding and passing other substances— the onset of a miscarriage—until one day she was again at work and she reported milk coming from her breasts, 'in the beginning of *September*, as she was working in the Hop-Ground'.[6] In the first of her later statements she added that it was in the hops garden that she had experienced more bleeding or, as she put it, 'a flood[in]g'. This episode marked the onset of the intense period of the miscarriage. In pain, she began the short journey home. But she only just managed to make it out of the hop garden before she was forced to crouch down as 'another substance came away'. The journey home that followed was understandably a difficult one. She stated that her walk home took two hours, 'tho it was not above a quarter of a mile I was in so great pain'.[7]

Mary Toft contributed to the family income by working as an agricultural day labourer, undertaking seasonal work as many poor women would do. Though men and women did sometimes work alongside one another, they undertook different tasks: hops drew heavily upon female labour for weeding and harvesting, whereas they might be limited to gleaning with other crops. Women's work was ubiquitous in eighteenth-century England and in the first half of the century the participation and productivity of labouring women in agriculture was taken for granted.[8] As a young mother in a poor family, Mary Toft's work made a crucial contribution to the household economy. Poor households at the time practised an 'economy of makeshifts', reliant on a collection of often unstable sources of income gathered together to make ends meet. In England, the economy of makeshifts comprised a broad range of tactics (including poor relief).[9] For poor families in rural environments, or those who could migrate, one important strategy to keep destitution at bay was the limited opportunities afforded by seasonal and/or casual work. Everywhere, much of this work was performed by women, and not just by single women. Records of wages suggest that the majority of the women who carried out casual work for daily or weekly payments, in contrast to these engaged in more stable work on annual contracts, were married. Tasks such as gleaning were performed predominantly by women—particularly married women— in some counties.[10] Indeed, the casual nature of women's and children's agricultural work meant they were the ones to benefit from the common rights to the land (that is the customary right, for example, to graze animals on or take wood or turf from common land), converting this labour into the marketable items—food, fuel, handicraft products—to generate income. Their reliance on common land meant that women played a significant role in opposition to enclosure (and thus removal of common land) in the second half of the century.[11]

Women performed a broad range of work in this period. They were paid wages for some tasks but they also engaged in the informal economy. The more formal records of women's paid work suggest that much of this work was an extension of the ordinary domestic or housewifely duties of childcare, cleaning, cooking, and washing. Yet incidental references to women's work in court records shows that this may have accounted for almost as little as 10 per cent of women's activity.[12] Women were therefore employed in a broad range of economic activity outside the sphere of the domestic and to take account of the different ways in which women contributed to the household economy requires a very broad definition of 'work'. In some areas, declining opportunities led women to resort to criminal behaviour. For the poor, theft was a tactic, with periods of hardship seeing higher levels of property crime.[13] The line between women's making shift and crime became blurred. In selectively granting poor relief to women and their children as they sought to manage the growing burden of poor relief, parish overseers and increasingly the vestry effectively policed procreation and women's reproduction role. But the eighteenth-century poor were becoming adept at negotiating institutions of criminal justice and social welfare and some women manipulated the Poor Law system with fraudulent claims for relief. They also used deception to get other forms of charity. One woman was found begging while pretending to be blind.[14] In using deception as a strategy, as did other marginal individuals, poor women sometimes used their child-bearing capacities. In the year that Mary Toft began giving births to rabbits, for example, one Mary Cossens was brought before the Guildford Quarter Sessions for extracting 'Great Sums of Mony...under Prentence [sic] of her being near Labor of Child bearing'.[15]

Surrey was one of the southern counties where agrarian capitalism was developing particularly quickly and this relatively fast transformation caused dislocation and distress amongst the most vulnerable. Given the declining textile trade in Godalming, the combination of long-term economic transformation and short-term seasonal cycles would have had a pronounced impact on the poor in the town. The detail of agricultural cycles is important to the case of Mary Toft. Mary was undertaking daily paid weeding in a field in April. Yet once springtime was over, the three summer months (June, July, and August) saw the highest risk of unemployment for agricultural labourers. Mary managed to find some work in the hop garden during harvest time in September, but her work was about to dry up. The rabbit hoax took shape as work opportunities for Mary, and perhaps also for Joshua, became scarce. The first delivery to take place with witnesses happened, finally, on 27 September. This was the day before Michaelmas, the traditional time when farm servants would be hired at the local fair.[16] The hoax became public knowledge just as the Tofts and their poor neighbours were about to sell their labour to local landowners. The narrative of the rabbit births was tied to the fortunes of poor workers in agricultural communities.

The narrow glimpse of the world of female agricultural workers offered by Mary Toft's 'confessions' or statements suggests that this group could work together in solidarity. Her story of the onset of her miscarriage in her first statement described how the women covered for Mary's absence. '[T]hey that were w[i]th me workt their dinner hours that I might goe sooner'; 'otherw[ise]', she said, 'I had lost a penny for they workt for me.'[17] This description suggests that her fellow workers covered the part of her shift that she missed so Toft herself could take the full pay for the day. Perhaps these women felt sympathy towards her, given what might have been her clearly pregnant state and certainly her pain and distress. Yet these women may have also had something to gain by covering for Mary's absence because women were more likely than men to be paid as part of a team. Mary's early departure from the hop garden may have threatened them all with a lower wage. And Mary's statement suggests a very low wage indeed. Women's pay for a day's agricultural labour remained fairly constant for the seventeenth and eighteenth centuries at 6 pence per day, around one third to one half of the rate for men's day wages. The wages of these casual female workers, always lower than men's, were increasingly falling behind the sums paid to both casual male workers and women who were paid annually.[18] Toft's reference to 'a penny' may have been a casual reference to a nominal figure or to a piece rate for a portion of the day. Or perhaps her experiences reflect the fact that wage levels were set against other factors such as levels of poor relief or the family arrangements of the worker, as well as being only one component of a workers' entitlements that might also include payment in kind, such as food and drink. Poor families were heavily reliant on credit (including from employers) rather than cash.[19] Nonetheless, if one pence was the pay for her day's labour, then Mary Toft was engaged in very poorly paid work indeed.

Mary may have relied on other women during the miscarriage. Two weeks after the episode in the hop garden, she was going past the Market House in the centre of the town when, she explained, she was taken 'with such a pain that I was forced to goe into [a] Shope till it was over'. This may have been the shop and bakehouse of Mary Hart located close to the Market House, on Church Street.[20] Not all women who worked were engaged in unskilled poorly paid labour; Hart was a businesswoman from the 'middling-sort'—those in the trading, commercial or professional middle ranks of society without land or title. Shops were certainly a place where friends socialized, especially women.[21] There was certainly another woman supporting Toft every day she went out to work in the fields. No record refers to Toft's eighteenth-month-old son James being with her in the hop garden, nor as a babe in arms in the field earlier in the year. Irregular seasonal agricultural work and work on the common land was arguably best suited to the responsibilities of motherhood, allowing mothers to bring small children with them. Yet the silence in the records suggests that Toft was adopting another strategy sometimes used by the poor, calling on female kin or neighbours to watch children while they worked outside the home. Wives and mothers struggled to keep working, in contrast to other women and men; childcare was crucial if women were to retain a foothold in the labour market.[22] We do not know who was looking after James while his mother went out to work, but his childcare was one further component of the support that women provided for one another, as well as the unrecorded labour of another nameless woman in the town.

The women close at hand

Many aspects of women's lives were conducted in 'homosocial' women-only environments. Women did not only work together but created enduring and effective networks for care, community, and camaraderie. They forged relationships of friendship and alliance that were important given the wider context of a profoundly patriarchal society. There were powerful expectations that women would form enduring friendships with one another, predicated on their perceived greater capacity for care and feeling. And many women enjoyed mutually sustaining bonds that provided practical and emotional support, bonds that came to define a particular model of feminine identity forged in collective social contexts. The very social force of these groups of women was reflected in the ambivalence towards female-only sociability evident in men's

Fig 2.2 'The Doctors here and Midwives all Consult', a scene from the broadsheet *The Doctors in Labour, or A New Whim-Wham from Guildford* (1726), showing St André speaking to two women and three men [New York Public Library]

whose 'usual prate is about their husbands, complaining of some vice or other in them'. Women's speech could be disruptive, publicly calling into question the honour of anyone in the community.[23]

Mary Toft was supported by working women—fellow labourers in the fields, women providing childcare, and perhaps Mary Hart the shopkeeper—but she was also surrounded by women in her home as the miscarriage transformed into the monstrous birth of rabbits. The doctors refer to these women throughout their accounts, even as they fail to note the women's names. Shortly after arriving at the house in Guildford, where Toft was now staying, St André noted, 'the Nurse who attends the Woman' came to call for John Howard, a doctor based in Guildford. This nurse, we learn in the subsequent publication of the witness depositions, was the widow Mary Costen, who explained she was hired as a nurse for Mary Toft until she went to London.[24] St André entered the room to examine Toft, where she was 'dress'd in her Stays, sitting on the Bed-side with several Women near her'.[25] In an effort to underscore his account as an accurate description, St André also included a number of oaths given to the then mayor of Guildford, Joseph Burtt, at the end of his pamphlet: Olive Sands swore in an oath that from 11am to 3pm on Sunday 20 November, 'she was constantly in the room' in Guildford. Another doctor who subsequently wrote about the case was Cyriacus Ahlers, surgeon to His Majesty. He showed that these women had considerable license: although the door to Toft's room in Guildford was 'well fasten'd, and to suffer no body to come in: Nevertheless, a little while after, several Women went in and out, as they pleased'. Women were still present when the doctor Richard Manningham arrived at Guildford on 28 November. His pamphlet stated that on his first examination of Toft there were at least three doctors present, together with 'several Women and Midwives'. On a later visit, Manningham noted that the strong jerks and movements of Mary's body were so violent that, 'as I sat on the Bed in Company with five or six Women, it would sometimes shake us all very strongly'. Once in London, Mary Toft was nursed by her sister-in-law.[26] The image of Manningham sat on a bed with a group of women is a striking one. It was precisely this proximity to women's bodies that stirred doubts about the unseemly motivations of male surgeons operating as 'man-midwives', and who were increasingly involved in childbirths at this time.[27]

These printed sources appeared once Mary Toft had been moved to London and the hoax was about to or had already become public knowledge. But the clearest picture of the women around Toft in the early stages of the affair emerges from the manuscript records of her three statements from early December 1726. It is striking that these documents pictured women at every turn. In the first statement, Toft explained that following the first sighting of rabbits, she passed 'a substance as big as my arm ' which, she said, her mother-in-law, Ann Toft, handled: 'My mother opend it.' Five or six weeks later, after she had left the hop garden and passed 'another substance', Mary asked her husband to fetch his mother again because she was in such pain. Another woman was also present at this early stage: Mary Gill gave Mary Toft a pot into which she delivered the first animal parts. By this time, a group of local women had assembled, and the contents of the pot were shown to 'all the women who were not able to make any thing of it'. Unable to make sense of what they saw, these women sent the parts to the Guildford doctor John Howard. Before he arrived, though, Ann Toft had already delivered her daughter-in-law of further strange parts.[28] A group of female kin and neighbours were gathered close around Toft from the very beginning of the hoax and she was accompanied by these and other women throughout the affair.

Though the births were strange, this gathering of women was quotidian. Communities were sustained by cooperation between neighbours of similar social rank. Women relied on the neighbourliness of those who lived and worked close to them for support, neighbours often being 'the first port of call' in an emergency.[29] The role that female kin and neighbours played in the intimate lives of women is reflected in Mary Toft's description of events as the rabbit births got underway. Moreover, the communal, sociable, and public character of Mary Toft's deliveries was typical of childbirth at this time. Deliveries were supposed to take place in a dark, quiet, secluded, and domestic space, but the process was always a social one. For poorer women in particular, who were likely to share rooms and beds with other family members, experiences of birth often lacked privacy. As historian Laura Gowing has noted, childbirth was 'a public affair however privately it took place'.[30] Birth was also public because the health and good order of the body politic relied on the health and good order of the bodies of the community. The reproductive body was thus of public concern. Women's bodies, and birthing bodies in particular, were scrutinized, managed and controlled. The identity of the fathers of poor illegitimates was demanded by parishes so that these men—rather than the parish—could be required to maintain the child, while in landed and royal families certainty of an infant's legitimacy was necessary for purposes of inheritance and succession.[31] Yet the practical publicity of birth was also circumscribed. For centuries, the matter of pregnancy, labour, and childbirth had been the business of women; the 'lying-in'—the period of birth up until women were 'churched' in a ritual that marked their readiness (and cleanliness) for re-entry to the church congregation—was generally female-only. Men, particularly husbands, were sometimes closely and sympathetically involved in women's reproductive health and care, as they could be in all manner of domestic medicine.[32] Nonetheless, the idea that birth and reproduction were matters for women remained dominant in the early eighteenth century.

Formidable women

Through their management of this crucially important process of reproduction, women claimed considerable authority. This was particularly evident in the status of the midwife. Though reproduction was being redefined as a subject for empirical medical knowledge associated with male scientists and practitioners, the historic authority that midwives had held over the processes of reproduction remained. Midwives learned their skills through practice. With statements of support from local medical practitioners, elite women they had served, or already licensed midwives, a woman could apply for a midwife's license issued by the Diocese. Midwives could even act as instruments of the patriarchal state, compelling unmarried women in the throes of labour to name the father of their child so that he would bear the costs of the child's upbringing. Not all women who served as midwives were licensed or played these formal roles, though they were often highly regarded members of their communities with considerable occupational status. Midwives derived this authority largely from their experience of labour, either their own or that of the women they had attended in childbirth. This experience was consolidated and expressed through the midwife's touch: her skill and knowledge lay in her hands.[33]

In her practice, a midwife used her experienced touching to exert authority over younger and less experienced women. Court records from the sixteenth to the nineteenth century show that for centuries, the pregnant and birthing bodies of women were controlled and surveilled by other women, particularly by those who were older, married mothers or who had formal status as midwives. A birthing women was required to defer to the knowledge and experience of the many women around her; the very presence of neighbours and kin at the labour was considered unquestionable and something she was unable to deny.[34] In this context, as in many others, there were power dynamics at work in female-only groups: women were competitive as well as cooperative.[35] Toft's accounts reveal these power dynamics at work, casting her centre stage as the younger inexperienced woman surrounded by authoritative women who exercised power over her and her body. Early in her first statement, Mary Toft described her mother-in-law as 'a midwife' in her first statement. This was confirmed by St André's earlier published description of Ann Toft as 'a Midwife, and a neighbouring Woman'. This description of Ann Toft as a 'midwife' is significant. There is no record of Ann Toft being issued with a bishop's license as a midwife, nor is she one of the three women listed as midwives in the parish registers.[36] Many women practised as midwives on an informal basis, though.[37] Ann Toft certainly had extensive experience having had twelve children over twenty-three years, and most likely attending many other deliveries in Godalming. Mary Gill, a local woman, had taken the pot containing the parts that Mary Toft had delivered first and 'shewed it to my mother Tofts who shewed it to all the women'.[38] Mary Gill must have been regarded as particularly expert as Ann Toft sent for her before she called for John Howard. And Ann Toft here appears as a figure of authority for Gill, taking control of the all-important pot to request other women's opinions. Whether or not Toft's description of her mother-in-law as a midwife described Ann Toft's informal occupation or reflected Mary Toft's vision of her mother-in-law as a figure of authority in the matter of birth, Ann Toft appears as a formidable woman.

It was not just midwives who exercised authority in these situations. In her second and third statements, Mary Toft was also careful to describe other women and their status. In the final statement taken on 12 December, Betty Richardson was described by Toft as 'a silkstokg M[r.] wyfe' (a silkstocking-maker's wife); Mrs Mebbin was described as a 'a gentle w[oman]'.[39] Their status as middling-sort women conferred upon them direct access to Toft's body. Toft's careful description of these women's social status was not designed to give credence to her story: by this final statement the game was well and truly up and she had admitted that the rabbit births were not real. Instead, these references suggest that Toft was acutely aware of these women's social status, its significance, and its relative elevation compared to her own. Growing economic and social divisions within communities were weakening the traditional culture and obligations of neighbourliness. Historian Keith Wrightson even suggests that the sorts of phrases used by the governors of Godalming to distinguish themselves—'the chief' or 'the principal inhabitants'—were one index of these increasingly divided communities.[40] Mary Toft's experiences show how these divisions might be enacted in the birthing room. Clearly important to her account of events, these hierarchies between women shaped Toft's experiences of events.

While women could be friends, allies, confidantes, and colleagues, they were also antagonists and adversaries. Reproduction was itself closely policed by female kin and neighbours; perhaps Mary Toft had not yet fulfilled her reproductive purpose. In spring of 1726, Mary Toft had already lost one child aged three months, had a son rising two years, and had then experienced a long miscarriage of a third pregnancy. Neighbours—even female ones—were not always supportive. Such fault lines could be seen amongst women as well as the wider community of Godalming. Mary Toft's own stories about the hoax, coupled with observations from the doctors, also suggest that women played in an important role in the affair. The young Mary Toft was surrounded by female kin and neighbours who exercised their authority over her body. It was these women who stayed close to her throughout the rabbit births and at times appeared to have directed the affair. But it was when Ann Toft sent for the Guildford doctor, John Howard, that the affair moved out of the women's circle. The question of how and why others believed them so readily is the one to which we must now turn.

CHAPTER 3

THE BIRTHS

'a Fact of which there was no Instance in Nature'

From the first newspaper reports of the case, it took seven weeks for the rabbit births of Mary Toft to be declared false.[1] This was despite intense investigation by several senior doctors. In exploring why this was the case—why these educated and experienced professionals did not admit the deceit sooner—we need to appreciate how people understood the female body and pregnancy. Scientists, anatomists, and physicians had at their disposal robust methods for examining the body, subscribing to standards of empirical knowledge that we would now recognize. But knowledge about the body was limited by the opacity of the body itself. The eighteenth-century body—whether male or female, young or old—did not give up its truths easily. The internal workings of the live human body were impossible to observe. Only through dissection after death could knowledge of the body's structures and processes be seen. External symptoms were therefore crucial to diagnosis, as was a patient's own narrative. If we explore precisely how people went about investigating the case of Mary Toft, we can expose the range of ideas about reproduction, both popular (or lay) and learned medical knowledge. For some, the rabbit births could be explained by long-held theories about pregnant women, though for others these ideas were already contested. The case of Mary Toft would become a test ground for old and new ideas about pregnancy. Yet this case is not just about ideas and knowledge. Mary Toft's rabbit births were not genuine, to be sure, but she did experience a series of real physical events. This experience was profoundly shaped by a shift in control, away from a group of authoritative women, and into the hands of a group of educated men claiming to serve the advancement of scientific knowledge.

What the men saw

The first doctor to witness the rabbit births was John Howard. Howard was a wealthy doctor based in nearby Guildford. By the time of his death he owned five properties in the town which he divided between his three children, leaving his son the further bequest of his books, surgical instruments, silver-hilted sword, pistols, and horses.[2] In 1726, Howard already served the medical needs of some of the chief inhabitants in Godalming. He had been in Godalming in early October, conducting minor surgery on the neck of John Chitty, the current High Constable of Godalming, writing a note on 4 October excusing Chitty from his duties at the court of the Surrey Quarter Sessions.[3] It may have been on the same visit to Godalming that he first visited Toft. We do not know if it was Howard who first got news out to the press, which was reporting the case from 22 October. But it was certainly Howard who wrote a series of letters to 'Persons of Distinction in Town [London]', thus initiating contact with the first London doctor who would travel to Surrey to observe the case for himself, Nathanael St André. He had already received reports that John Howard had delivered eight rabbits by the 6th November, and when he arrived in Guildford on 15 November Mary Toft was on the verge of delivering the fifteenth. St André rushed to the room above John Howard's house, where she lodged, and waited for her labour pains to grow stronger. Fresh pains brought on the delivery of the torso of a rabbit, skinned, with the heart and lungs intact and which St André estimated was around four months grown. A few hours later, Toft's nurse delivered the lower half of this rabbit, with its reproductive organs and bowels still intact. That evening, short intense labour pains result in the delivery of a rabbit's head, this time with the fur still on.[4] When Nathanael St André released his pamphlet on the case of Mary Toft, he vowed to include an account of the delivery of the eighteenth rabbit in a subsequent appendix, as soon as that rabbit appeared. He for one was convinced that he had seen a woman giving birth to rabbits.

Cyriacus Ahlers arrived at Guildford a few days later, on the morning of the 20 November. His first contact with the rabbits was a piece of skin—'very fresh, like the Skin of a wild Rabbet, just stripp'd'—that Toft's nurse showed him. Ahlers could not understand how a rabbit could be skinned in the womb, and Howard's assertion that it was caused by the violent pressure of the uterus against the pelvic bone did little to reassure him. Shortly afterwards Ahlers delivered the hind part of a rabbit, skinned but with both flesh and bones remaining. Ahlers' account of this episode is the most graphic description of the birthing process we have. Having ordered Toft to sit in a chair, Howard positioned himself in a chair directly opposite. Ahlers' description clearly implicates Howard in the deception of the rabbit births: 'He made her put her Legs between his, and with his Knees he press'd hers close together'. The light from the fire was dim and Ahlers was unable to see clearly, 'and in particular to mind the Motions of Mr. *Howard*'s right Hand'. The two continued in this intimate pose for some time: 'Mr *Howard* continued all the while to keep her Knees close together; and holding his Head against hers, he took her Hands into his, while she stooping with her Head forwards, push'd her Back against the Back of the Chair with such Violence, that I was forc'd to hold the Chair to prevent its going over.' In Ahlers' account, Toft comes across as a consummate performer: writhing, twisting, squalling, and roaring while keeping her knees pressed tightly together; 'she knew best', he stated, barely disguising his suspicions, 'what Posture was the most advantageous for her singular Delivery'. Significantly, he reported how Toft 'laugh'd very heartily' twice during his visit, something which he considered extraordinary for a woman in her situation.[5] The strange actions of Howard combined with the staged response of Toft allowed Ahlers to suggest their unlikely partnership in orchestrating the births.

Arriving at Guildford on 28 November, Richard Manningham did not witness the delivery of such large animal parts but merely a piece that he described as 'like a piece of Bladder'. This was removed from Toft by Howard, though Manningham soon removed another piece himself, which he described suspiciously as, 'like a piece of Hog's Bladder'. At this point, Manningham might have roundly denounced the monstrous births as fictitious. Instead, and quite remarkably, he secured the piece of hog's bladder that he had removed from Toft's body into his pocket book, storing it for safekeeping until he could display it to several men back in London.[6] In fact, all three of these men carefully transported specimens of the rabbits that came from Mary Toft's body back to London for display and thorough investigation. The actions of Howard, Toft, and the people around her—often dramatic performances—did not lead these men to immediately discount the affair as fraud. Instead, all the men subjected this case of purported monstrous births to careful investigation.

Ambiguous knowledge

Imposture and pretence were familiar to this society. All manner of beggars, tricksters, and quacks claimed fraudulent identities. This makes it all the more surprising that the rabbit-birth deception was sustained for so long. Yet Toft's case was distinct from these more quotidian frauds because the rabbit births appeared to take place in the realms of either the preternatural (a very rare occurrence that worked within natural laws) or even the supernatural (an event that was not possible within the laws of nature and was therefore necessarily caused by another force).[7] Both were considered possible and the excitement among the doctors in particular lay in determining which, if either, it was. Knowledge about the female body allowed for a belief in monstrous births. Women's bodies, like all bodies, harboured secrets. The processes of those bodies, and particularly the processes of conception and gestation, were hidden from view and shrouded in mystery. Conception, pregnancy, gestation, and childbirth provoked the determined interest of both male and female experts in print, and naturally men and women generated considerable practical experience, but thinking on these topics was marked by metaphor, debate, and ambiguity. From medical treatises to erotic poems, women's bodies were presented as unknowable. Creating new life was glorious. But at the same time women's mysterious reproductive power could be terrifying. This underpinned the often blatant misogyny which so often shaped attitudes to the female body.[8] Mary Toft's case was part of this broader landscape of shifting and undetermined knowledge.

Understandings of the body were dynamic and varied. Specialized medical knowledge was developing within the broader context of the scientific revolution, and in particular the elevation of empirical knowledge based on observation and experiment. Yet the distinctions between popular, lay, educated, and professional medical knowledge remained blurred. The widespread credulity in the face of Mary's Toft's rabbit births was possibly precisely because there was so much overlap between the views of the uneducated poor and professional medical men.[9] The world view of Mary Toft and those around her had enough in

common with the doctors' beliefs that those men could be convinced—
or at least curious—of the 'facts' of the case. The principal idea at the
heart of this shared knowledge was the theory of the maternal imagination. According to this theory, what a woman saw or felt when
pregnant could make such a mark on her as to pass through her
sensorium to make a literal impression on her mind that was then
physically imprinted upon her foetus. An old idea found in the works
of Aristotle, Galen, and Pliny, the theory was founded on two more
general principles about the body and the natural world. First, the
human body itself was part of the environment, each made from the
very same elements. Changes in the environment had a direct effect on
individuals such that the outside world and its stimuli could enter and
be embedded in the body. These processes were invariably ordinary and
unremarkable. It was a fact that illness could be prompted by the
weather, for example, as well as by emotions of grief or distress.[10] The
second key principle was an understanding of the natural world that
saw no clear division between the material and immaterial. This meant
that the physical and emotional, body and mind, were intimately linked
and indivisible. Emotions were substances and thoughts became shapes.

These mechanisms underpinned the theory of the maternal imagination. In his landmark book on skin diseases, De Morbis Cutaneis.
A Treatise of Diseases Incident to the Skin (1714), the surgeon and physician
Daniel Turner explained how marks on children's skin could be a direct
result of the mother's imagination during pregnancy. He explained the
mechanisms that allowed this to work: the soul was moved by an
external object, causing us to feel a passion—such as joy, sorrow, or
anger. That movement of the soul then stirred the spirits that were
carried through the nerves, and that in turn caused other physical
changes such as an increase or restriction of the circulation of the
blood and the other humours, affecting the body's organs. A series of
examples of reported monstrous births were marshalled to prove 'how
great an Empire, the Phantasy of the pregnant Woman has over the
Blood and Humours together with the Spirits of her Body, and how by
their Ministry she is able to give not only monstrous Shapes and
Figures to that of the more tender Fetus, but to communicate Diseases
also'. This mechanical system led Turner to a popular conclusion:
women's strong feelings of shock, fear, and frustrated desire—'disappointed Longings'—could be imprinted on the unborn. Turner

produced an enlarged second edition of his book in 1723. Then in the following year, John Maubray—establishing himself as a man-midwife in London—published *The Female Physician, containing all the Diseases incident to that Sex, in Virgins, Wives and Widows* (1724). Maubray enveloped several pages on the imaginative faculty within this work, explaining even more clearly than Turner how the imagination worked in the mind to move the soul and the body of both mother and child. 'I very well know', he wrote, 'that when the *Soul* is elevated and inflam'd with a fervent IMAGINATION, it may not only *affect* its own proper *Body*, but also *That* of Another'.[11] The publication of the third edition of Turner's *De Morbis Cutaneis* in 1726 underlines the traction of the theory by the time of the Toft affair.

Yet the idea that the thoughts or imagination of a woman triggered by her environment would affect not just her own mind but the form of another separate body was unsettling, to say the least. According to the literary scholar Dennis Todd, this unease arose from a philosophical impasse about the nature of the relationship between body and mind: a stand-off between the mechanists who saw the body as a machine and the metaphysicians who saw the body as matter that could be moved only by the immaterial soul.[12] Toft's monstrous births seemed to represent the extreme of the mechanistic view: that the imagination could affect the body and distort the self—or another self—into a monster. It was a terrifying prospect: that the corporeal body—and a female body at that—might trump all reason. Thus, people wondered about the effect on expectant mothers of the sight of maimed or deformed beggars.[13] Yet no doctor had yet seen proof. This was one reason that Toft's case was so exciting for doctors. She explained her monstrous births were the result of her chasing rabbits in the fields. William Pountney, a friend of John Howard, had even heard that the following day she had returned to the field, lay upon the ground and 'clap'd her heart upon ye little turf where one of ye rabbits Satt' in the hopes of finding him. The vision of this seen but lost rabbit had entered her mind and imprinted itself on the form taking shape in her womb. But more than this, the process was still going on. Mary Toft's rabbit births promised to constitute the first live evidence that the pregnant woman's imagination was so powerful as to transform a human foetus into something monstrous. As Nathanael St André put it, he visited Toft in order to be, 'convinced personally of a Fact of which there was no

Instance in Nature'.[14] This was why the doctors so swiftly applied their scientific strategies of medical investigation to the bodies of both Mary Toft and the rabbits. In the autumn 1726, the classical theory of the maternal imagination appeared to have moved from the status of hypothesis to that of observable scientific fact.

Observation and enquiry

Though events were initially dominated by the women around Toft, these women were slowly joined—and ultimately pushed out—by a steady stream of men. It was the men who created the network through which the hoax became public. According to Toft's first statement, Ann Toft (her mother-in-law) first sent the animal parts to the Guildford doctor, John Howard, who then came to observe for a few days. It was then Howard who wrote to the King's anatomist, St André. Two further letters followed; the third of 9 November was reproduced by St André in his pamphlet on the case published in late November. By this time, Toft had been moved from Godalming to Guildford. Howard said that he had moved her 'for better Convenience'. Toft admitted that she allowed herself to be moved to Guildford because, 'I thought my selfe in a very desperate condition in hopes of relief.'[15] Perhaps she was seeking an escape from Godalming. But the move made her more accessible to the men who were beginning to come and view her. St André then visited Samuel Molyneux, secretary to the Prince of Wales, who then accompanied St André to Guildford on 15 November. He visited a second time on 23 November. Ahlers, on the other hand, who had been in Guildford from the 20 November, wrote himself that he had been sent by the King. St André was also in contact with the King, and claimed to have displayed some of the preserved rabbit parts to him on 26 November, after returning from his second visit to Toft. St André subsequently wrote to Richard Manningham, on the suggestion of his Majesty at Kensington. So keen was Manningham to see more of this case that he stayed up until St André and Limborch (another doctor) arrived at his house between 3 and 4am, and they all travelled to Guildford in the very early hours of 28 November.[16]

These men made considerable efforts to investigate the case and each of them rushed into print. Yet the few days that set them apart were crucial. The pamphlets of St André, Ahlers, and Manningham were completed just a week apart. St André's was completed on 29 November and announced in the newspapers on 1 December 1726, just before the deception was exposed on 5 and 6 December. Preserved for posterity in print was St André's attempt to demonstrate the truth of the monstrous births; the print was barely dry and the book presumably still on display in booksellers as the deception was exposed. His notice that he would insert an account of the delivery of the eighteenth rabbit as an appendix to a later edition immediately appeared positively absurd. In contrast, Cyriacus Ahlers' and Richard Manningham's works were completed after the pretence had been uncovered. By the time they had signed off their manuscripts on 8 December, laid down their pens, and taken the bundle of papers for printing, the truth was already out.[17]

As we might expect, then, there are important differences between these pamphlets. Of all the doctors, it was St André's account that could be accused of sensationalizing the case, announcing itself as *A Short Narrative of an Extraordinary Delivery of Rabbets*. In a more restrained register was Manningham's work, *An Exact Diary of What was Observ'd During a Close Attendance Upon Mary Toft*, which began with a pared down description of Manningham's journey to Guildford without any preliminaries to establish the remarkable nature of the case. Ahlers' title, *Some Observations concerning the Woman of Godlyman*, was positively uninspiring, though the subtitle alluded to the sensationalism by insisting that the book would 'prove her extraordinary Deliveries to be a Cheat and Imposture'. Yet regardless of these differences of style, all three men subscribed to similar standards of investigation and proof. From the opening of his *A Short Narrative*, for example, St André's emphasis was on the truth as he observed it first-hand: he vouched to present only 'the Facts that I saw' after he began to 'enquire into the Truth of such an Extraordinary Event', and would only only recount the parts with which he was 'actually concerned'. As if to remove any vestiges of doubt from the readers' minds, he firmly distinguished his own narrative from those 'flying Reports and Conjectures' that have been available about this or earlier cases. Ahlers, too, separated himself from other accounts (notably St André's), insisting that he would present only '*what* I can take upon me, *and what I my self saw, heard, or transacted*'.[18] It was important that the evidence they presented was empirically sound. All the doctors were careful to underline that they had *seen* and *observed* Toft.

Fig. 3.1 'Dr John Howard and Mr St André in Consultation upon Mrs Mary Toft, Guilford in Surrey. 27 November 1726' [Wellcome Collection]

As a result, Toft was kept under almost constant observation. The repeated references to women or nurses suggests that they were always in attendance, and St André emphasized that he was also ever-present: 'I constantly stood before her', he insisted. Committed to presenting all the evidence for the reader to assess for themselves, St André even included details that seemed to demonstrate that the births were entirely fraudulent, such as Mary's intact and blood-free vagina following a delivery. Such judicious presentation of all the evidence went hand-in-hand with his credentials. The title page announced his role as 'Surgeon and Anatomist to his Majesty' and after examining the case he underscored the truth of his findings with the hint of royal approval, reporting that 'All these Facts were veryify'd before his Majesty, on *Saturday Nov.* the 26th.' His text is burdened with attempts to underline the veracity of his account. Witnesses are described as 'a Man of known Probity, Character, and Capacity in his Profession'. The letters that tempted him to Guildford are exchanged between 'Persons of Distinction in the Town'. St André even included several simulacra of the handwritten manuscripts in his printed pamphlet, rooting his printed narrative in oral evidence: a type-set letter from Howard, a signed statement affirming St André's account from Samuel Molyneux and no less than five oaths or witness statements, including one by Mary Toft herself, signed or marked by the deponents and witnessed by the current and a previous mayor.[19] St André, or his publisher, was sure to use all the techniques available to indicate that his account was grounded in first-hand accounts.

Once he was in the presence of Mary Toft, who was now lodged in an upstairs chamber at John Howard's house in Guildford, St André immediately set about undertaking every reasonable scientific enquiry. His hands-on attention was focused as much on the rabbit parts as Toft herself. His first delivery was of the trunk of a rabbit. His companion, Mr. Molyneux, took part of the lung and put it in water. The fact that it rose to the surface indicated that it had been outside Toft's body as part of a living and breathing creature. St André also found what appeared to be fishbones in the gut of a later delivery of a cat, and others reported on the faeces found in the intestines. Such evidence one would expect to be dead giveaways of the deception. But the births could not be dismissed as false because when St André examined her breasts he found 'Milk in one of them'.[20]

Ahlers claimed not to have found milk in Toft's breasts. He was also careful to state that he was the first doctor whose suspicions were aroused in Guildford on Sunday 20 November. Yet he nonetheless bookended his account with a five-page 'Anatomical Description of the several Parts of the Sixteenth Rabbet', parts which he took to show His Majesty.[21] The forensic detail of this account underlines Ahlers' commitment to scientific examination of the evidence and a reluctance to deny the monstrous births without it. Manningham did report finding a thin substance 'like *Milk*' when he examined her breasts. Though he was careful to state that he suspected fraud, he nevertheless admitted that the movements of Toft's body and especially her belly were genuine and unlike anything he had seen before. In contrast to St André and Ahlers, for Manningham the truth of the matter was to come from his thorough examinations of Toft's body, not those of the rabbits. On his first visit he went about methodically assessing her apparently pregnant body. Having looked at her external signs (her breasts and her belly), he 'diligently search'd the whole *Vagina*'. He examined the cervix and from within the vagina used one hand to try to assess the contents of her uterus, detecting 'something of substance' inside. With his free hand, he pressed on her abdomen and again felt something inside and particularly on the lower right side. This was a rational and thorough examination and characteristic of the several examinations Toft was to undergo under Manningham's hands. The evidence he gathered led Manningham to the view that nothing had come out of her uterus and therefore that the monstrous births were simply impossible. Her cervix was closed, 'in such manner that it would not receive so much as the point of a Bodkin into it's Orifice', let alone part of a rabbit. He coupled this with his subsequent assessment of the animal parts: the membrane that was suspiciously like a hog's bladder, he reported, 'never came out of the *Uterus*'. With the benefit of hindsight, Manningham's pamphlet glossed his evidence as pointing to 'a Fraud'.[22]

Fig. 3.2 The doctors examine Mary Toft's breasts and abdomen, from the broadsheet *The Doctors in Labour, or A New Whim-Wham from Guildford* (1726) [New York Public Library]

It remains striking, though, that all the doctors were compelled to demonstrate that they had taken proper care in investigating the case. They went about their investigations methodically, examining the physical evidence before them—both Mary Toft's body and the animal parts that emerged from this—subjecting all this to a series of tests based on physical touch and visual scrutiny. As Lisa Forman Cody has demonstrated, all the doctors remained wedded to applying an empirical method to test the veracity of Toft's story. There was certainly scepticism during the whole affair and 'very warm Disputes' between the doctors, as Manningham put it.[23] Yet no doctor publicly rejected Toft's story until the deception had been uncovered by other means. Perhaps more striking was the fact that none of the doctors subsequently claimed that they had rejected the matter out of hand all along. Instead, they worked hard to demonstrate that they had taken the case seriously enough to subject the animal parts to rigorous scientific experiment and Mary Toft to repeated physical examination.

The prestige of being the doctor who could claim for himself these real-life births as proof of the maternal imagination was the principal factor driving these men from the beginning. It is curious, then, that none of the doctors used the maternal imagination as an explanation for the rabbit births. St André did not, unlike some of the newspaper articles, lead with the story of Toft's chasing rabbits in the field. Instead, he devoted several pages to the physical evidence of the case, suggesting that unusual fallopian tubes may have somehow caused the gestation of rabbits. Ultimately, St André only went so far as to say that the nature of the animal parts on which he conducted experiments, 'proves in the strongest terms possible that these Animals were of a particular kind, and not bred in a natural Way'. When he did refer to Toft's maternal imagination as the cause, he was reporting her claims of 'longing' for the rabbit and not his own opinion on the case.[24] Richard Manningham is much clearer and simply never alludes to the maternal imagination, while Ahlers gives the theory no credence whatsoever. The doctors' careful investigations into the case were thus predicated on the theory of the maternal imagination, though none of them explicitly refer to it. Other than St André, there is little evidence that any of the doctors involved in the case set much store by the theory of the maternal imagination. The idea was already losing purchase in some parts of the medical world, though it remained the topic of vociferoud debate and never died out. In a burgeoning medical field on reproduction, foetal development, and infant anatomy, it was as important to prove falsehood beyond all doubt as it was to prove the truth.

The route to truth appeared to run through Toft's body. Mary Toft increasingly became subject to a series of painful examinations by both women and men. The word that Toft uses to connote an examination was 'touch': for her, this word communicated not gentleness or care but coercion. Initially, these experiences of touch ended with an animal part being painfully extracted. As events progressed, she described a series of men beginning to 'touch' her as part of their investigation, with apparently little concern for her comfort or well-being. Manningham acknowledged the damage that the experience had wrought to her uterus, vagina, and cervix, causing her 'violent bearing-down Pains', yet like all the doctors he treated the pains as an indication of an imminent delivery and thus an invitation to examine her.[25] In her second statement, for example, Toft describes a series of internal examinations being carried out in quick succession by four men: Howard, St André, Molyneux, and Ahlers. According to Toft, instead of removing the piece of animal inside her, Ahlers 'punched it further'. When Howard asked Ahlers why he did not remove the piece, Ahlers apparently explained that he needed Toft to experience a pain—perhaps because he thought the pains were forcing the expulsion of the parts—and when she did Ahlers finally removed the piece. Toft then begged Howard to remove any remaining parts, 'because that gentleman hav[e] put me to a great deal of pain'.[26]

The doctors saw pain as the principal index of the hidden and remarkable processes of Toft's mysterious body. Yet this understanding of pain also made manifest their disregard for her suffering. For the doctors, Toft's body was a cipher for their furthering of medical knowledge, either by proving or disproving the incidence of monstrous births and the veracity of the maternal imagination. The debate amongst the doctors had been vociferous and the doctors continued to battle over the restoration of their reputations. Nathanael St André was an easy target. Already quickly discredited in the pamphlets of Manningham and Ahlers, the surgeon Thomas Braithwaite produced a thirty-two page critique of St André's ill-fated pamphlet in which he demanded to know why St André had prevented more suitably qualified surgeons—himself, William Giffard (a famous man-midwife) 'and

Fig. 3.3 St André, dressed as a fool, is left isolated as Mary Toft is escorted away, the hoax having been revealed, in the broadsheet *The Doctors in Labour, or A New Whim-Wham from Guildford* (1726) [New York Public Library]

several of the Profession'—to enter the bagnio. St André pedalled backwards fast. Just days after the announcement of his book in the *Evening Post*, the same paper announced that he would shortly publish a new book titled, 'An Account of the Imposture of Mary Toft, the Godliman Woman, with the Derections [*sic*] of her pretended Deliveries, and the several Stratagems She employ'd to effect the Fraud'.[27] All this was to no avail. St André, Manningham, Ahlers, and the many other men who came to investigate this apparent medical wonder were ridiculed in newspapers, poems, books, and caricatures for their faith in a scientific method that had seemingly blinded them to the deceitful activities of the Tofts and the people around them.

A widely shared knowledge of the maternal imagination had been the context for Mary Toft's rabbit births. The story of her chasing the rabbit in the fields was reproduced by Toft and Nathanael St André, and echoed in newspapers. The affair had taken form within the group of women around Toft some time after she had experienced a traumatic miscarriage. Yet by late November 1726, the case of Mary Toft was becoming uncoupled from the fortunes of the theory of the maternal imagination. As James Douglas subsequently commented of his own motivation in investigating the case, his aim was 'to come at a speedy Discovery of the Imposture, by plain, sensible, and undeniable Facts, of which all the World might be Judges, and not Physicians and Anatomists only, who were capable of determining the Matter upon other Principles'. The context for Toft and her remarkable deliveries was no longer wonder but determined and thorough investigation. As the context for the case shifted, those women who had claimed authority over events and stuck close to Toft in the early weeks began to retreat into the shadows and an ever-expanding group of men assembled. Whatever power the Godalming women had exercised over Mary Toft now evaporated as control transferred resolutely to the men involved in the case. To investigate the case properly, these men needed easier access to Toft. And so, as she herself later confirmed, it was 'resolved to bring the Woman to Town'.[28]

PART II
LONDON

CHAPTER 4

THE BAGNIO

'several persons of distinction'

On Saturday 3 December, 1726, a short notice appeared in the London essay-paper *The British Journal*, announcing Mary Toft's arrival in London on 29 November:[1]

> The Rabbit-Woman of *Godalmin* near *Guilford*, so much talk'd of, is brought to this City, and lodged at the *Bagnio* in *Leicester-Fields*, and is bringing forth more and more Rabbits: A fine Story![2]

Though bagnios could serve as brothels, a reputation they still struggle to shrug off, most functioned more as places for refreshment, recuperation, medicinal bathing, and other treatments. They were multipurpose spaces where customers came in search of food, lodging, and a range of services promoting the health of the body. As such, they functioned as comfortable and convenient meeting places, especially for the elite men whose business involved meeting other men in town. As disturbing as the details of the rabbit births is the scene that quickly developed in the bagnio in Leicester-Fields (or Leicester Square). Here, Mary Toft was kept under constant watch for nine days, surrounded by a group of elite men who together embodied some of the principal pillars of patriarchal power in this society: the law, the medical and scientific establishment, and the propertied aristocracy. It is extraordinary that these men had such close encounters with a woman like Mary Toft. Whatever role Toft herself had played in the affair was now eliminated, and the influential circle of women rendered superfluous: the scene in the bagnio reflected the women's utter powerlessness in the company of such men, and instead brings home the authority of the learned and of the law. In the move to the bagnio, Mary Toft was catapulted from the intimate circle of family, kin, and neighbours to the heart of the power structures of eighteenth-century Britain.

Leicester-Fields and London

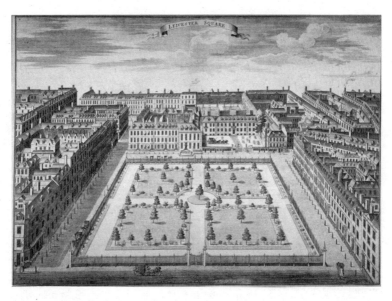

Fig. 4.1 Sutton Nicholl's engraving of Leicester Square, *c.*1720, showing the Prince of Wales' residence at the top and Roger Lacy's bagnio on the right

Leicester-Fields was a broad open space at the heart of the genteel and fashionable West End. In 1720, the cartographer John Strype described it as 'a very handsome large Square, enclosed with Rails, and graced on all Sides with good built Houses, well inhabited, and resorted unto by Gentry'.[3] Its population was varied. Along one row was a property owned by the Earl of Leicester and in 1726 occupied by a wig maker and then a tallow chandler. In contrast, the large building at the north end of the square Leicester House was used as a royal residence from 1717 until 1727: it was the site of the house of the Prince of Wales.[4] The location of the Prince of Wales' house in Leicester Square is a clue to why Mary was brought to this location in London: it mean that the Prince and Royal Household could be easily kept abreast of the case as it developed. At no. 27 Leicester-Fields was the bagnio run by Roger Lacy. The bagnio in Leicester-Fields was a respectable establishment in an expensive property measuring 200 foot by 22 foot. Before Lacy, the house had been occupied by Lady Margaret Watson; before Watson it had been occupied by the Earl of Rockingham. The neighbour at no. 28, in a building owned by the Earl of Rockingham, was Sir Christopher des Bouverie, a director of the South Sea Company.[5] Visitors to Lacy's bagnio thus rubbed shoulders with wealthy country families, the titled, and the royal.

Roger Lacy claimed to have been brought up in a bagnio. He was described as a 'cupper', someone who drew blood by applying a heated cup tightly on the skin, suggesting that he himself provided medical services. But Lacy was also a businessman; 1726 was to be his most eventful year yet. Having run his own establishment on Suffolk Street, in December 1725 he set about establishing a bagnio in Leicester-Fields. Lacy rented the property from Catherine Roos (a widow from Kentish Town), and signed a lease for twenty-one years at the rate of £130 a year. In order to transform the building into the well-appointed bagnio he intended, Lacy had to carry out extensive renovations on the property and install all mod cons. The property already comprised, 'a Room proper and Convenient for a Bagnio two Bathing Rooms and five Coolling Rooms with Cisterns [and] Vessels'. On signing the lease Lacy had determined to demolish 'the Backhouse' and replace it with three new rooms including 'a Cooling room usuall and fit for a Bagnio'. At the same time he would create a passage from the front of the property (in Leicester Square) to the back door of the house, through the Stables and into Castle Street at the rear. The 'New Bagnio' was announced to the public on 8 March 1726, offering sweating, cupping, and bathing 'perform'd after the best Manner'. It was equipped with a range of up-to-date 'Conveniences', 'good Lodging-Rooms', and a discreet back-door entrance away from the square. So extensive were these changes that Lacy later claimed to have invested more than £1,200 'Erecting a Bagnio and other substantial Improvements' on the property.[6] Over that door Roger Lacy hung his own name.[7]

This financial outlay was to take its toll. By autumn 1726, Lacy was struggling with financial difficulties and was in dispute with his landlady. When he began renting the bagnio in 1725, a William Conyngham had provided Lacy with personal security. In return he would provide bail for Conyngham should Conyngham not be able to pay his creditors. Months later, Conyngham's creditors did indeed come to call. Lacy alleged that his landlady Catherine Roos and two other men had colluded in extracting £50 for a false bill that would ostensibly release Lacy from the bail he had agreed to provide for Conyngham, thus enabling Lacy to pay his rent to Roos. When Lacy then refused to provide bail to Conyngham he became 'greatly Exasperated and Enraged against your Orator [Lacy] and threatened to arrest him'. Lacy was, he said, 'greatly terrifyed'.[8] His financial situation perhaps jeopardized further by the demands of catering to Toft, her family, and the growing number of visitors she attracted, Lacy thus brought a Chancery case against Roos and the other men. On 5 December 1726—with Toft in his bagnio—Lacy made his complaint against Roos, a day which would also mark a critical turning point in the case of Mary Toft.

It was also on 5 December that a Justice of the Peace entered the bagnio to question Mary Toft. While Lacy had been in conflict with his landlady, he had also been providing space and catering for some remarkable gatherings around the person of Mary Toft. Indeed, the two might very well have been connected. Lacy was under pressure to find money and he may have calculated that Toft would bring him business. It most certainly brought people through the doors. In addition to her family members (her husband and sister-in-law), she was joined by a group of women and midwives, at least five doctors (several of them in the pay of the King and the Prince and his wife), the Justice of the Peace, and around fifteen further men named in the reports made by Manningham and Douglas. By the time Douglas arrived he reported there being 'a good Number of Gentlemen' alongside St André and his companion, Mr Amyand (or Amiand).[9] To these individuals we must add the steady stream of 'the public': just as 'most of the People at Guilford' had been to see Toft, so 'Every creature in town, both men and women' attended in London.[10] The bagnio was becoming a destination, a place to witness a most remarkable performance. Joining the Surrey poor and the local women who had accompanied Mary were the elite landowning men who represented the expanding English state and justice system, the doctors jostling for authority and consolidation of their reputations, as well as a disparate group from the fashionable elite.

In this upmarket bagnio with a prestigious address were brought together an eclectic group of people who came to look—and to touch—the rabbit woman.

The doctors

Fig. 4.2 Detail of the manuscript 'An Account of the Rabbets &c' [Wellcome collection]

Late on the 29 November 1726, Mary Toft was brought to Roger Lacy's new bagnio. A newspaper reported that this was 'by Order of his Majesty', and that she was accompanied by the doctors Manningham, St André, and Howard.[11] Along with the King himself, these doctors played a key role in her move to London, competing for the credit of bringing her from Surrey. Richard Manningham implied it was he who had brought Toft to London. But Nathanael St André claimed this credit for himself. He did so in a letter to Sir Hans Sloane. Sloane was president of the Royal College of Physicians, secretary of the Royal Society and editor of its *Philosophical Transactions* (becoming president of the Society in 1727). His commitment to new knowledge is palpable in his extensive collections (a principal part of the founding collection of the British Museum) and the huge numbers of letters he exchanged on matters relating to medicine, science, and natural history.[12] A letter to Sloane would launch the case into his extensive networks and might raise the discovery of rabbit births to the status of respectable scientific headline, but a visit from Sloane would stamp his *imprimatur* on the case. St André wrote:

> Sir,
>
> I have brought the Woman from Guilford[sic] to ye Bagnio in Leicstr Fields, where you may if you Please have the opportunity of seeing her deliver'd Wednesday morning.[13]

There is no record of Sloane accepting this invitation. But with Toft now in London, St André began to invite more men to visit her and publicize his apparent success in discovering this live specimen of a monstrous birthing woman. At midnight on 29 November, St André wrote almost the same note to James Douglas:

> I have brought the Woman from Guildford to ye Bagnio in Leicester fields. She now has a Live Rabbit in her and I Expect shortly a Delivery: you will infinitely oblige me to deliver her your Self.

St André wanted to move fast and Douglas responded immediately.[14] The urgency is palpable.

These doctors, some of whom had been present in Guildford, were in control of the bagnio for the first few days of December. Toft was now some distance from her local community in Surrey, as well as being removed from the house of John Howard, who had controlled events in Guildford. Now, it was the London doctors who assumed management of her body and people's access to it. Which doctor was in control was the subject of some debate. On Douglas' arrival, St André gave him the impression that he was the one managing events and controlling access to Toft: St André even apologized that he must let Manningham see Toft before Douglas, because the King had expressly asked Manningham to be included. Richard Manningham's pamphlet gives the distinct impression that the control soon lay in his hands, while James Douglas' account records his negotiation with both St André and Manningham and their acceptance of his conditions for his examination of Toft. Their printed records present them each in turn as the hero of the hour, and reflect the tussles over power that took place around Toft's bed during these early days of December. This was a serious game. The reputation of the doctors already hung in the balance: no one wanted to be counted amongst 'our Country conjurers of D[oct]rs', as one letter-writer described them, but instead to be judged one of 'the Great Physicians [who] have all steer'd clear of it & never gave it the countenance of any Inquiry'.[15]

The competition amongst these men arose partly from their different origins and status. Richard Manningham had been educated at Cambridge, licensed by the Royal College of Physicians in 1719 and knighted by George I in 1722; by 1726 he was a well-regarded physician and man-midwife. By the end of his life in 1759 he had acquired five houses and a personal collection of portraits of himself and his wife, his mother and father, as well as the Duchess of Richmond and Queen Anne.[16] James Douglas was a highly regarded Scottish anatomist and man-midwife who had trained at Edinburgh, Utrecht, and Rheims and had been made an honorary fellow of the Royal College of Physicians in 1721. Cyriacus Ahlers was a German surgeon attached to the King's German household, while Phillip van Limborch was singled out by Manningham as 'the German Surgeon and Man Midwife'. In contrast, Nathanael St André was a Swiss émigré who had trained in anatomy and surgery in the house of a London surgeon, building up his practice and reputation in Westminster until, in 1723, he was appointed surgeon and anatomist to the Royal Household.[17] St André in particular had swiftly risen in status to acquire his position from the King; despite this royal connection he, like Ahlers, was an outsider. These men's interactions must have been tense. Yet for all their competition, these men operated within a network of expert professionals. Though in print they were keen to distinguish themselves from one another, they relied on each other's good opinion. Having welcomed Douglas to the bagnio, St André continued to write notes to Douglas, presumably in an attempt to persuade him of the truth of the monstrous births. His note of the 3 December urged Douglas to respond: 'I must need speak with you as soon as you can.' The piece of membrane like a hog's bladder that Manningham had taken from Guildford to London in his pocket book, he showed to Douglas immediately on his arrival at the bagnio and asked for his opinion.[18] It is striking that the doctors rarely worked alone but instead always brought someone, usually another doctor, to accompany them. These drew on the well-established medical community of which they were a part, though there was clearly a pecking order amongst these men. Douglas refers to the 'List' of medical practitioners that St André and

Fig. 4.3 St André shows the rabbits to two fellow doctors, from the broadsheet *The Doctors in Labour, or A New Whim-Wham from Guildford* (1726) [New York Public Library]

Manningham had composed, and to which he wished to add further names, though they resisted.[19] Having one's opinion seconded by another was one way to verify evidence, and signals the operation of these men within a sociable and scientific context.

The bagnio was a site for jostling between the doctors, but it was also a place for genuine scientific enquiry. The network of trained medical men intersected with a respectable gentlemanly culture of scientific enquiry. Scientific disciplines were still in their infancy and, as an occupation, science was legitimately practised by both those who had formal university training and those who had the resources and networks to develop the requisite skills and knowledge. Expert credentials were underscored by aristocratic patronage and membership of academic societies, rather than a university post.[20] So while the physicians and surgeons were in the largest number in Guildford and during the early days in the bagnio, they were often accompanied by other men who took a keen interest in the natural world. For these men, Toft was a potential medical wonder. The men in this group included Samuel Molyneux, secretary to the Prince of Wales, who had travelled to Guildford with St André. It may also have included Hans Sloane, who received more than one letter about the case. James Douglas himself exemplified the broad interest in the natural world possessed by such men. His interest in Toft sat alongside his interest in the anatomy of elephants and fish, about which he wrote to Sloane.[21] Some of these men were undoubtedly driven by career-building and even a search for fame. But their printed works suggest that many of them—trained physicians or not—were genuinely committed to furthering the bounds of natural knowledge by the application of empiricism. For them, the bagnio was a place of formal observation and experimentation.

The several rooms of the bagnio not only allowed for the movement of large numbers of people but also provided additional spaces for further debate and discussion. Mary was kept in a lodging room while the doctors would gather in a nearby dining room to view some of the animal parts.[22] The rabbits were of considerable interest and a focus for experiment, yet it was in the bagnio that interest began to turn to Toft's own body. Initially those present simply watched, but physical examinations soon began in earnest. Manningham stayed up with her for her first night in the bagnio but does not appear to have examined her until the morning of the 1 December. Douglas conducted his first internal examination on the same day, during which he observed 'a Fullness and Constriction of the *Vagina*, occasion'd', he believed, 'by holding in her Breath'.[23] These examinations stepped up as the days progressed. By 4 December the bagnio was crowded and Mary had been kept under observation with repeated examination for days. At three in the afternoon, she was examined in turn by four men: Manningham, James Douglas, Maubray, and Limborch. These doctors undertook their own examination of Toft, but they also invited and monitored examinations conducted by others. When Manningham became expectant of a delivery—to be the first in London—and realizing that the room was very full, he announced to the 'many Persons of Distinction' in the bagnio that 'if there was any Person present willing to examine her, that they would do it then while her Pains were upon her.' Having issued his open invitation he added, 'Accordingly, several Persons did examine her'.[24] These are unsettling descriptions of multiple examinations over which Mary Toft appeared to have little or no volition.

Intimate power

Fig. 4.4 James Douglas' dated copy of William Hogarth's engraving Cunicularii (1726) [Glasgow Special Collections: MS Hunter D321/2]

The bagnio was now thronged with men. In addition to the doctors already present, a journalist reported that 'Great Numbers of the Nobility' came to see her on Thursday 1 December and 'many Physicians' on Friday 2nd, 'in order to make a strict Search into the Affair; another Birth being soon expected'.[25] These men's proximity to Toft's body is astonishing, given both her poor status and the fact that she was apparently still giving birth. William Hogarth's engraving Cunicularii, or the Wise Men of Godliman in Consultation (1726) brilliantly captures both the drama and the trauma of these astonishing circumstances, as a string of doctors sought to investigate the case. Published in late December, the title of the print was a suggestive pun that brought together 'coney' or 'cony' (a colloquial term for rabbit) with 'cunny' (a slang term for vulva), and references to 'coney-warren', 'coney-skin', and 'cunny-peepers' abound in pamphlets about Toft. Set in Roger Lacy's bagnio, it is those 'peepers' that Hogarth wishes to expose. The scene shows Toft surrounded by a small crowd, a family group comprising her husband Joshua and sister-in-law Elizabeth on the left, and a collection of doctors and other men on the right. The room is a crowded scene, and even though she is fully clothed, Hogarth conveys effectively Toft's exposure in what quickly became a bustling and semi-public space. Mary Toft's head is wrenched back in agony as she raises her wide-open and panicked eyes heavenwards. No one looks directly at her; she is alone with her pain. Her contorted left arm clutches at her belly. The well-developed forearm was a sign of the labouring ranks, and Toft's forearm is formidable, ending with noticeably rough and ungenteel fingers. Her right arm is cradled by her sister-in-law, while her husband looks aghast at the men streaming in to observe his wife. With her strong and large body, Toft is set apart from those fashionably dressed and somewhat effete men crowding near the door. John Howard surreptitiously obtains a small rabbit from the man at the door. In a posture that reflects his previous job as a dancing-master, Nathanael St André grace-fully steps towards Toft with his hand outstretched. In the background, John Maubray raises his eyes to the heavens in delight at the imminent birth of a 'sooterkin', a small creature birthed by women of whom Maubray had recently written. Maubray was another doctor and man-midwife who visited Toft, on 4 December, and who in 1724 had pub-lished a book that described how a woman's 'strong IMAGINATION' of a disagreeable thing 'quickly impresses the *Imaginary Idea* of *That* thing heard off, or the *Shape* and *Form* of *That* thing seen, upon the FOETUS'.[26] With Toft at the centre of the image is the man who is 'searching into the Depths of things', Richard Manningham. He bends towards Toft, engaging his entire frame with apparent effort, and he also exposes a muscle-marked forearm with a barely disguised powerful shoulder outlined by his clothing. This physically powerful man leans into the space created by Toft's open legs.

Hogarth's is a fanciful depiction. The print captures only a small number of the people who entered the room in which Toft was held, for example. It does, though, convey the tenor of the treatment Toft received at the hands of the men around her. No expression of sym-pathy by these men for Toft survives in the historical record. This was not because emotional expressiveness was unfamiliar to them; the surviving love letters to their wives written by two of the men involved (the Dukes of Montagu and Richmond) are positively effusive. But as a poor woman, a mother of a monstrous birth, and then a suspected criminal, Toft was precluded from such emotional responses and she was instead regarded with distance, disdain, and even cruelty. There are general statements referring to her sorry state, such as the surgeon Thomas Howard's (brother of John), description of Toft as 'the poor miserable Woman *Mary Toft*'. This contrasts with an almost complete lack of interest in Toft's discomfort or pain by the men around her. St André comments on her 'exquisite torture', though he does nothing to alleviate it.[27] We might expect the doctors at least to have been sympathetic given the increasing importance of empathy to the practice of man-midwives and its role in legitimizing male-midwives' growing control over the process of birth (a hugely significant change to the lives of both birthing and working women).[28] Instead, it sometimes appeared that the men wished to see Toft's discomfort. Olive Sands, one of the women who attended to Toft in Guildford, swore under oath that Ahlers had offered Toft a pension, 'on his seeming satisfied of the Misery the Woman underwent'.[29] For the doctors, pain was not an emotional state but was evidence (the only evidence they had) of the hidden events taking place inside Toft's body.

The lack of interest in Toft's emotional and mental state is also puzzling because it might have been used to gauge the truth of the matter. Already a woman's guilt or innocence at trial could be judged partly on their emotional responses, and mental incapacity, including that caused by childbirth, could be used as grounds for a defence of diminished responsibility in cases of infanticide.[30] Women in trials for both murder and infanticide were judged partly on their display of feelings, and women and the poor were often regarded as having little control over their stronger emotions, or passions. Only one person in the entire case appears to have considered emotional response as a form of evidence: this was the nurse to Mary Toft in London, Mary Costen, one of the witnesses whose statements were delivered to Baron Onslow. She suspected Joshua Toft because he showed insufficient concern for his wife: 'this Deponent never saw him dejected, or any ways concerned for his Wife's Misfortune: And also saith, That during her attending the said Mary Toft, she never heard her or her Husband desire that any Minister might be sent for to pray by her'.[31] Those investigating the Toft case were not interested in Toft's genuine feelings. The theory of the maternal imagination should have placed Mary Toft's emotions central stage in this story, but paradoxically she was treated as incapable of feeling.

Officers of Justice

Hogarth's engraving is a satire at the expense of the doctors who became embroiled in the hoax. It is an artistic snapshot of events, most likely those taking place on 4 December, as the doctors awaited the delivery of rabbits and what would be the first delivery in London. Still at this point, doctors were open to the idea of the rabbit births. James Douglas arrived on 4 December and reportedly 'cd scarce believe his own senses' as he examined Mary Toft.[32] It was later that day that the deception began to fall irreparably apart. Suspicions had already been aroused as soon as Toft arrived at the bagnio, at least as the subsequent reports of Ahlers, Manningham, and Douglas suggest. The deliveries were drying up and observers were beginning to ask difficult questions of both Howard and St André. First, through the thin walls of the bagnio, the conspirators were overheard. One constable reported, 'an odd Sort of Conversation he heard pass between the said Mr. Howard and Mary Toft, thro' a Partition at the Bagnio in Leicester-Fields'. Then the porter of the bagnio, Thomas Howard (no relation to John Howard) spoke up: he had 'been sent to Market with all imaginable Secrecy, to buy the youngest Rabbit for her he could get', and had passed this information on. He described a rabbit that Toft 'had clandestinely procured by his Assistance'.[33] This was a critical step and clear evidence that the rabbits were not being delivered from her body but smuggled through the back door of the bagnio. A Justice of the Peace was called, to whom Thomas Howard would make a statement.

If the doctors had initially managed the situation in Lacy's bagnio, control now shifted to the men responsible for law and social order, mostly men from the landed class who occupied positions of state. A large group of men were involved: one report on the discovery of the hoax noted that a group of 'several Noblemen have been very active therein'.[34] In Godalming and Guildford, the investigation had been advanced by Thomas, 2nd Baron Onslow, the local landowner in Surrey who had been shot by Edward Arnold in 1723. Thomas himself had connections to Leicester Square through his cousin, Sir Arthur Onslow,

Speaker of the House of Commons, who was named on several of the property leases.[35] But it was in his capacity as Lord Lieutenant for Surrey that on 3 and 4 December Thomas Onslow interviewed six witnesses at his large country seat, Clandon House: Edward Costen, Mary Costen, Mrs Mason, Mary Peytoe, Richard Stedman, and John Sweetapple. These interviews confirmed beyond doubt that the rabbits were not monstrous births. Costen, Stedman, and Sweetapple deposed that Joshua Toft had come to them to ask to buy rabbits, Stedman noting that Toft killed the rabbits he bought before he left Stedman's house and Sweetapple that he had removed the rabbits' entrails before Toft took them. Sweetapple described how Joshua Toft had come to him both before and after his wife had been moved to Guildford and insisted he buy Sweetapple's rabbits, however small they were.[36] Toft lodged at Mason's house in Guildford and Peytoe deposed that Joshua Toft also bought rabbits from her; Costen was nurse to Toft during the births. There are no commentaries on these interviews, though Onslow's cousin later commented that while he was a principled man of humanity, Thomas' 'behaviour, conversation, and dealings with people were generally distasteful and sometimes shocking'.[37] Whatever the nature of these encounters, the outcome was clear, and late on 4 December Onslow himself sent a letter Hans Sloane:

> The report of a Woman's breading [sic] of Rabbits has almost alarm'd England and in a manner perswaded Severall people of sound judgm:ᵗ of that truth; I have been at some pains to Discover the Affair, and think I have Conqeur'd My poynt [sic]; as you will se [sic] by the Deposition taken before me, which shall be published in a Day or to [sic].[38]

This was the second letter Sloane had received from a man boasting success in the case of Toft, this time claiming to have evidence that the rabbit births were false. With the porter's disclosure and the depositions from Guildford all delivered by 4 December, the case was poised to topple.

In London, three other men were instrumental in the progress of the case: the Dukes of Richmond and Montagu, together with the sixth Baron Baltimore. The respective positions of these men in the Royal Household suggests that they may have been sent by the King, though Manningham implied he himself had sought these three out as a group on 30 November to discuss with them the hog's bladder.[39] Of this group, the Duke of Richmond, Charles Lennox, present during Mary Toft's first interrogation, was most likely to be affected by the case. His house in Godalming was conveniently placed between London and his country seat in West Sussex, Goodwood. In 1724 his steward recruited the services of the carpenter Joshua Keene (carpenter) for seventeen days in order to undertake a large number of repairs, many of which were concerned with house security, perhaps a recognition of the tense social relations in the town. Duke since 1723, he had recently been installed a Knight of the Garter; as the case died down and following the accession of George II, he was appointed High Constable of England (a post overseeing criminal justice at Quarter Sessions) and made a Gentleman of the King's Bedchamber. Richmond was therefore at the beginning of his stewardship of the Dukedom and in the process of building a career as an aristocrat close to the monarchy and Whig party elite.[40] Like the other men, he possessed wealth, title, and power.

The Duke of Richmond, who sometimes met acquaintances in a St James' bagnio just a short walk from Lacy's, had been in London for most of October, and was there again from 25 November to 6 December, as payments to his several male servants Charles Venturing, Walter Steers, William Manning, and Thomas Girdler attest. Payments were incurred for horses used for journeys between London, Goodwood, and Godalming, and the Duke also travelled within London. The twenty-six-year-old Duke dressed well and may have been wearing the blue velvet suit with silk and shagreen lining, along with the 'fine bever hat', all ordered earlier in the year. He was certainly taking full advantage of the commercial opportunities of London in the autumn, ordering—on the day before Mary Toft made her first confession to Clarges and the noblemen—'a Broad Cloath Sute 3 Shirts & a p^r of hose' for £5 8s 4½d from the mercer George Harris.[41] Records do not reveal if Richmond remained in the bagnio as the interrogation of Mary Toft began, though he is likely to have been one of the 'several of the Nobility' in the room.[42]

Lord Baltimore and the Duke of Montagu were certainly both present on the day that Mary Toft was made to talk. Baltimore had a house at Epsom and had contested the seats of Surrey in 1722 and Guildford in 1728 (against Arthur Onslow, Thomas Onslow's cousin), both unsuccessfully, before gaining the seat of Surrey in 1741. He was in London at the time of the hoax petitioning the Privy Council with the nomination of his brother to the Governorship of Maryland.[43] Alongside him stood John, second Duke of Montagu. Montagu was Master of the Great Wardrobe (a sub-department of the Royal Household) and Knight of the Order of Bath. Montagu was already in London. His house in Blackheath was being prepared for the shortest days of the year, with deliveries of several household items including large quantities of tallow candles, while Montagu was taking care of his own legal business in town.[44] But Montagu may have also had a special interest in a case such as this. He was intrigued by the curious. On a trip to Europe he reported back to his wife details of the curious appearance of women he saw, attaching two sketches. He was also in contact with an enslaved African man, Job, who was introduced at court and whom Montagu, along with several others, had provided with money to help the slave buy his freedom and return home.[45] The monstrous births and Mary Toft were perhaps another focus for Montagu's curiosity. As a recent father who had also experienced infant loss, the case of Toft may have also touched upon Montagu's personal experiences of becoming a father. A son, born in autumn 1725, prompted effusive congratulations:

> May y^r grace long live in all felicity, & behold with encreasing joy this y^r illustrious progeny going on to excel in all ye united vertues of his great progenitors.

Montagu was still paying a woman for nursing a child in May 1727, though the boy appears to have died soon after.[46] These elite men had sadness in their own lives, then. And Montagu was himself capable of expressing deep emotion, often signing off his effusive letters to his wife, 'I am dear dear Angel for ever yours.' He could also be supportive of those in need, using his considerable power to assist others. In June 1726, for example, he had to the Lord Chancellor recommended a man called Thomson, 'with the caracter [sic] of an honest but unfortunate man, and I believe is a very Great object of charity'.[47] We do not know whether he treated Toft with such magnanimity, though it seems unlikely. We do know that he was one of the men who 'in a most particular manner exhorted' Toft to give a full confession to Thomas Clarges.[48]

It is difficult to exaggerate the social distance that held these titled men apart from the likes of the Tofts. The House of Commons settled £800,000 on King George in 1726, though the allowance for the Prince of Wales for the year was a mere £50,000. The amount given to the departments of the Wardrobe, of which Montagu was Master, was increased by £10,000 in that year alone.[49] A few months after the hoax, Robert Walpole, the First Minister of His Majesty's government, maintained Thomas Onslow's status as one of the four Tellers in the Exchequer (the men who received payments into His Majesty's Exchequer) in August 1727, setting down his ability:

> To have, hold, Exercise and Enjoy the said Office together with all Fees, Wages Rewards, Diets, Allowances, Liveryes [sic], Houses and Profits whatsoever thereunto belonging, or any wise appertaining to himself, or his sufficient Deputy or Deputies during our Pleasure, in as large and ample manner and form to all Intents and Purposes.[50]

The privilege and wealth is startling. And like the doctors, these men formed a tight network. Montagu and Richmond in particular knew each other well.[51] It is striking that in their surviving letters neither Montagu nor Richmond discuss the case of Mary Toft. Instead, the records of these men show their concerns above all else to be the Whig government and the royal court (and their place in both). Mary Toft had found herself in the midst of the political oligarchy of early Georgian England. Historians have tended to concentrate on the doctors, but they were part of a larger group of men. In Lacy's bagnio Mary Toft was confronted by a formidable group of elite men who represented the authority of learned scientific knowledge based on enquiry, the power of office-holders of the state, and the pre-eminence of landed wealth.

Central to this group was Sir Thomas Clarges, the London Justice of the Peace (JP) who played the critical role in the escalation of events. JPs were powerful local officials with wide-ranging powers and a considerable degree of discretion in applying the law. They also formed the vanguard of the state in the regulation of the poor. Clarges was the JP to whom the porter, Thomas Howard, made his statement. He was accompanied to the bagnio by Nicholas Paxton, deputy solicitor to the Treasury. Clarges and Paxton were steeped in the prosecution of crime in Surrey and London, including the actions of the 'Blacks', those groups of men believed to be conducting violent actions against the property of the Whig elite. Paxton prepared the government's cases against the Blacks, including the first use of the Waltham Act against the Hampshire Blacks in 1723.[52] Clarges was one of two JPs who took evidence in a notorious case of deer-hunting in Surrey on the King's 'Endfield Chase' in Middlesex in July 1725. More recently, Clarges had committed to jail a man who had created worrying chaos in Leicester-Fields, escaping capture for a shooting and instead entertaining crowds of 'several thousand' 'near the Prince's Palace' by running over the rooftops of houses in the square for an afternoon in March 1726.[53]

Soon after Clarges' arrival at the bagnio, the *Daily Post* reported that on that day—5 December—'some odd Discoveries' had been made, that Toft had been taken into custody and that the matter was now under 'strict Examination'. This word 'strict' is often repeated in commentaries on the interrogation of Toft, and reveals something of the tone of the exchanges. Toft initially denied the truth of the porter's report. Two events then took place that clearly frightened Toft. First, having already 'strictly examined' Toft, Clarges 'threaten'd her severely, and began to appear the most properest Physician in her Case'. Manningham's chilling description alludes to Clarges ill-treatment of her, and he adds that Toft remained quiet after Clarges' threat. Newspapers reported that Toft was initially put under the care of the High Constable of Westminster for two weeks, because of the 'leniancy' of Clarges, though as was also reported in the newspapers, Manningham explained that he had interceded 'After some Difficulty' on Toft's behalf and persuaded Clarges to let her stay in the bagnio.[54] Then, Manningham himself began to put Toft under pressure. He urged her to confess, and told her he knew she was an impostor but that in her capacity to get rabbits into her uterus he believed her body was different from other women. He made preparations 'to try a very painful Experiment upon her', but promised that if she confessed he would request leniency from the noblemen present. Ultimately it was Manningham's threat that made Mary Toft talk. Having been given a night to consider her predicament, she relented on the morning of 7 December 1726. A newspaper reported that having refused to name her accomplices until she was assured of the King's pardon, she had delivered a 'Confession taking up several Sheets of Paper'.[55]

The affair was about to withdraw from the bagnio. For Roger Lacy, the episode ended much as it began, with a court case about money. This time Lacy was in dispute with St André over the costs of Toft's upkeep at the bagnio. In May 1727, Lacy brought a trial against St André to the Court of Common Pleas, over his failure to settle the bill of charges owed to him from 'the Affair of the Rabbet woman, for Lodging and Money laid out on that Occasion'. The jury found in favour of Lacy, valuing the damages at the significant amount of £56 14s 10d.[56] St André's very public failure had been Lacy's success. And as the owner of the bagnio, Lacy was perhaps the only winner. Toft and her family may have shown tenacity, and the interest that they generated for the case managed to draw the great and the good into the room with them, yet in the end it is hard to see what they gained. Mary Toft herself only suffered. Her repeated physical examinations reflected the power that other people held over her and her family. Surrounded by these rich and titled gentlemen, Toft's poverty and status was all the more stark. The intimate power that was exercised around her poor body opens up a world of starkly unequal social relations in early-eighteenth-century England. But nor did the doctors or noblemen stand to gain. Their education, wealth, and connections had counted for very little in the face of this poor family, and their credulity when dealing with the hoax had put their reputations at risk. Events had moved on considerably since Toft had arrived at the bagnio on 29 November, surrounded by eager doctors in search of a medical wonder. There was no longer any expectancy of the delivery of an eighteenth rabbit. The concern was not for the truth of a purported monstrous birth but instead an identification of the culprit. The women had receded into the background and many of the men virtually banished by Clarges. Mary Toft was now brought before two representatives of His Majesty's justice.

CHAPTER 5

CONFESSION

'I was loath She should touch me'

It had been a week since Mary Toft had been brought to Lacy's bagnio.[1] There, at three in the afternoon on the 4 December, everything changed. Richard Manningham witnessed such violent pains in Toft that he announced to the busy room that a delivery was imminent. But what would have been the first delivery in London simply evaporated: 'vanished on the sudden', as Manningham put it.[2] The delivery of rabbits was over. It was that evening that the porter of the bagnio, Thomas Howard, gave his statement to the JP Thomas Clarges in which he described rabbits being smuggled into the bagnio. Upon hearing the evidence of Howard, Toft 'was taken into Custody'.[3] Once in the bagnio, Clarges took charge from the doctors. They could now attend only in groups of three or more, rather than individually or in pairs: Clarges deemed them all possible conspirators. The presence of Clarges, acting as one of His Majesty's JPs, had transformed the bagnio from a sociable space of enquiry into a court of law.

Mary Toft was made to talk. And her words were recorded for posterity in three remarkable documents. They are perhaps the richest sources of evidence we have about the case. Brief reports of Toft's early version of events had appeared in newspapers, but the three 'confessions' or statements contain a wealth of detail about how and why the case developed. These thirty-six pages of Toft's statements are rough notes and are now kept in the collection of the doctor James Douglas, who served as amanuensis to Thomas Clarges. These documents were never published. Present at the first interrogation and keen to publicize the news of the hoax, Richard Manningham published a short summary of the first confession in his pamphlet, *An Exact Diary*, which was subsequently reproduced in newspapers.[4] But most of the content of the confessions was kept out of circulation. They were first copies of which Douglas probably intended to submit tidied versions to the court of the Westminster Quarter Sessions as evidence. And as Douglas himself explained, the documents were the property of the court: the case 'does not belong to me nor any private person', he explained, but was in the hands of a magistrate 'to whom she has delivered her Confession under oath'.[5] Douglas was merely the note-taker working under the authority of Clarges. Mary Toft had spoken publicly about the hoax before. The very first newspaper account published in the *British Journal* on 22 October reported a shorter version of events that she was later reported to have made under oath, and St André's pamphlet reproduced a later statement Toft made under oath on 5 November, beneath which she placed her mark '‡'. But the three statements given in early December marked the decisive shift of the case from a medical to a criminal context.[6]

Interrogation

The actions of Clarges towards Toft were remarked upon by several contemporaries. Already, prior to her first official statement, she had been 'strictly examined' and threatened by Clarges. Once the interrogation was in progress, one particularly ominous description noted how his presence inaugurated a 'stricter Inquisition'.[7] Likening the interrogation of Toft to the Inquisition, a process that sought out behaviour that contravened Catholic doctrine, conveys both the force of the judicial action against Toft and the view that her alleged crime was moral as well as criminal. The first statement was extracted in the bagnio on 7 December. The pressure that she had been under—from Clarges and Manningham but also from a week of round-the-clock observation and examination—is palpable in the first of her words to be recorded: 'I will not goe on any longer thus I shall sooner hang myselfe.'[8] Some of her words are visceral and almost audible. One poignant moment comes near the very end of the first statement, when she declares 'she is most heartily sorry for' the whole episode.[9] This first interrogation then ended with one final question:

I asked if her fits were real or counterfate
She answ: she had been subject to fits all her life to a greater degree.[10]

Mary Toft here reported that she had suffered with fits all her life, though she may well have been making excuses for her repeated performances of labour. She had been coerced into speaking and she had many reasons not to tell the truth. There is no doubt that— as Clarges also knew by the time the first confession began on 7 December—she was lying about the monstrous births of rabbits. Parts of the confessions suggest that she was trying her best to answer the questions of Thomas Clarges and bring the affair to an end. So the documents are certainly shaped by Toft's attempts to tell a story that would deflect blame away from herself, and onto others. And by 7 December, Mary Toft would have been exhausted and was most likely very poorly. Her words and her memory may have been coloured by this, too.

There is another reason we need to be cautious when using these documents: they are extremely difficult to decipher. Douglas' writing sometimes disintegrates as his hand hurried to keep up with the pace of Clarges' questioning and the urgency of Toft's responses. The speed of events partly explains the awkward syntax of the written words and the sometimes confused narrative structure. Douglas' writing is littered with corrections, erasures, and crossings out. Deciphering where the truth lay in Toft's words was difficult for Clarges. It is even more of a challenge for us because we cannot witness her speaking her own words. Instead, we have a version of her account recorded in haste by one man (Douglas), an account that was already shaped heavily by the aggressive questions of another (Clarges). These layers obscure the voice of Mary Toft.[11]

Mary Toft's voice is submerged but by no means effaced. That voice is framed by the questions of Clarges and the recording of Douglas. Douglas was a thorough amanuensis, though, who applied a system of note-taking that distinguished questions, interruptions, and his or Clarges' commentary on what Toft said from her own statements. We can pick apart these different elements in the documents and recon-struct the exchanges between Toft and the men involved in the inter-rogation. The belligerence of Clarges is felt in the abrupt breaks in the flow of Toft's statement and the insertion of questions. These breaks are recorded by Douglas in the form of a large 'X' and a horizontal line scored across the page.[12] Sometimes Douglas had time to record Clarges' questions, such as 'has not your mother got it' and 'I think you have not got them all', as well as Toft's responses (in this case, 'she saying she had not he had examined and brought away the foot him

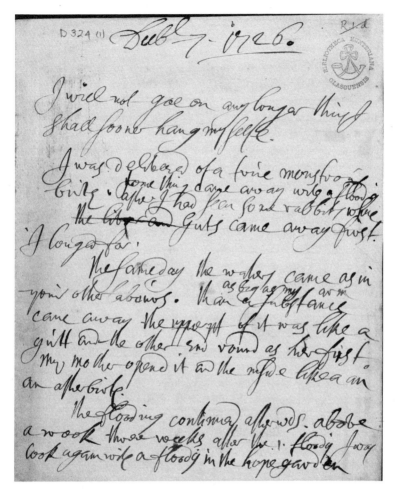

Fig. 5.1 The first page of Mary Toft's first confession [University of Glasgow Special Collections: 7 December 1726, MS Hunter D324].

S[elf].').[13] But the speed of the encounters meant that Douglas usually only had time to preserve Toft's responses, rather than the questions themselves. Written in his hand, they contain sometimes barely legible scrawl from Douglas as he struggled to record the exchanges.

Everything about these documents—the abbreviations, the symbols, the messy handwriting, the notes in the margins—indicates the urgency of the interrogations.

We can be confident that the three statements provide a fairly good account of what Toft herself said, though, if we can compare them to two other documents that are preserved in Douglas' papers: two tidied copies of the first confession. The first of these copies—the 'Fair Copy of Mary Toft's Confession'—has retained many of the details in the original, though several changes have been made. All evidence of the breaks in the interrogation, the questions, and her direct responses to these have been removed. Some small grammatical changes have been made: the 'Fair Copy' includes the phrase 'my Brother, who liv'd with me', rather than 'who did live with me' which appears in the original.[14] There are some changes to the content, too. The mysterious woman who urges Toft to undertake the hoax says she must go through with it 'now I had begun, but that she have/some of the money'.[15] The second clause about the money is not in the original, however.[16] The third version of the first confession—'An account of Mary Toft's first confession'—adds more new details. It includes judgements that are clearly those of Douglas, Clarges, or one of the other men present. The nameless woman comes 'upon a frivolous pretext', for example; she is 'the strange Woman'; and 'the poor Woman [Toft] having with some deficiency consented the experiment was accordingly try'd'.[17] These are missing from the first draft. Perhaps most strikingly, the 'Fair Copy' restructures the order of events quite considerably, a structure that is then summarized in 'An Account'. These changes do not alter significantly the basic events as told by Toft in the original statements, but they do show how those originals are a relatively less mediated account of the questioning and get us as close as possible to the words of Toft herself.

Toft's story

When the first statement began, the game was well and truly up on the hoax. Yet initially Toft denied all knowledge of a crime and insisted that she had experienced 'a true monstrous birth'. She had begun to pass strange parts and 'a woman whom I don't know if I was to be put to death' suggested a way she could make money by inserting animal parts into her to continue with false deliveries. Asked further questions about this woman, Toft elaborated: she was 'a woman whose husband is a knife and shooes grinder' and who travelled around the country.[18] Clarges must have been frustrated because Toft could not give firm details on how or where to find this woman: the best she could do was to suggest they ask a shoemaker in Godalming who the woman had mentioned. Still wanting information on a named perpetrator, Clarges appears to have asked her directly if named individuals had been involved, and her response was revealing: 'She clears her mother in law, her husband, her sister and every body besides that woman from knowing any thing about this cheat'.[19]

Clarges was clearly not satisfied and so he returned to the bagnio for a second interview on 8 December. Toft now told a different account. She began by denying all knowledge of how the rabbits entered her body, at the same time that she started to implicate her mother-in-law and John Howard. Clarges' annoyance at her claims to ignorance are visible in his interruption of her, to which she gave the clearest account yet of culpability: 'She is of the opinion that if the Rabbits did not breed in her that her mother-in-law and Mr Howard must have put them up for nobody else came near her.'[20] Toft was now charged with imposture. Officially in the custody of the Quarter Sessions, but unable to pay her bond or to find anyone to pay on her behalf to secure her release on bail, Clarges committed Mary Toft to the local house of correction, the Westminster Bridewell, later on 8 December. He wasted no time in pursuing the case and (along with Nicholas Paxton, deputy solicitor to the Treasury) visited Toft in Westminster Bridewell on the afternoon of Friday 9 December, 'to examine her farther about that wicked Imposture'.[21] There is no record of this, the fourth exchange between Clarges and Toft, though presumably Clarges was applying considerable pressure to make Toft confess so that he could bring the case to a close. Following a break over the weekend, Clarges returned to the house of correction on Monday 12 December, when the third and final 'confession' was taken down. Toft had held up to questioning with determination. She removed Howard from suspicion, explaining 'if he did mistruste that it was a trick he never said any thing to me about it'.[22] It was only now, in the fifth interrogation, that she gave Clarges what he wanted: an admission of the hoax together with a single named perpetrator. Faced with Clarges' opening question, 'Who first put you upon it or who first contrived?', Mary Toft answered, 'Ann Tofts My Husbands mother'.[23]

Having doggedly resisted Clarges questioning, giving different accounts of what had actually happened across the three statements, Toft finally gave him a satisfactory answer. The objective for Clarges had always been to identify the perpetrator of the hoax. Following Thomas Howard's statement, Clarges knew that Toft had been lying. He openly dismissed her initial claims of a monstrous birth, cutting her off when she used the word 'monster' to describe the rabbits.[24] In this context, what is remarkable about Toft's statements are her insistent repetition of details about the events that were clearly irrelevant to Clarges, prompting him to interrupt several times and demand that she keep to the point. There are remarkable consistencies in Toft's account that are entirely superfluous to the investigation and point to truths in her false account, truths concerning her feelings and the actions of some people around her.[25] As in witch trials, claims of false events or strategic and dishonest statements are always framed in beliefs and contextual details that are firmly grounded in the real world.[26] Most of us would now consider as untrue an accused witch's claim that she flew with the Devil, but we would nevertheless accept that this untruth was upheld by contemporaries' genuine belief that the Devil intervened in the temporal world. In her statements, the false aspects of the hoax were folded into a story about the whole affair from April to December 1726 that Toft insisted on telling and retelling. This story was full of incidental detail about the people around her, what they did, and how she responded to them. While these documents do not offer direct access to the events of 1726, they do present Mary Toft's personal truth about her physical and subjective experiences, as well as her experiences of the people around her.

The real deliveries

The monstrous rabbit births were a deception; Mary Toft did not gestate rabbits in her uterus. Yet there were real deliveries during this affair, and though he may have not wanted to hear about them, it was these that Mary Toft was compelled to speak about in all three of her statements. In fact, she suffered two distinct traumatic physical experiences. The first event was a prolonged miscarriage. The description in the first statement is frank and detailed. After she saw some rabbits 'whc I longed for', she said, 'Some thing came away with a flooding.' In her three statements, Toft repeatedly describes this heavy bleeding, her body being 'open' and passing fleshy objects. The descriptions are immediate and powerful and share features of other contemporary descriptions of miscarriage, notably 'flooding', a word that recurs in many other accounts from women.[27] Toft's reports that during this process 'the waters came as in your other labours' and 'My body was so open as if a child had just come away' also showed Mary drawing on her experience of her previous pregnancies, rendering the ordeal comprehensible to herself and others. This bodily experience was similar to her other deliveries in this regard, yet the language Toft used to describe what came away from her body rendered it both familiar and strange. The large piece that she passed early in this process, she said, was like 'an afterbirth'.[28] Toft's words describe neither a recognizable infant nor a frightening monster, but instead deployed simile to communicate to her interrogator what was inexplicable and unusual.

Miscarriages can be prolonged events lasting several weeks, and this is what Mary Toft appeared to have suffered in the weeks leading up to the pretended rabbit births. She claimed she was five weeks' pregnant when she first saw the rabbits. The miscarriage began around seventeen weeks later (twenty-two weeks into the pregnancy, towards the middle of August), at which point, St André explained, 'she was taken with a Flooding and violent Cholick Pains, which made her to miscarry of a Substance that she said was like a large lump of Flesh'. She continued to bleed heavily and three weeks later, in early September, she experienced further 'flooding' and great pain as she was working in the hop garden. It was at this stage that during the long journey home she was forced to stop, fell to her knees, and passed a substance which, 'without observing I was forced to throw away'.[29] Toft was clearly experiencing a traumatic event and here implies that she could not bear to look.

The miscarriage finally came to an end, though Toft, as she reported to St André, continued to exhibit 'the Symptoms of a breeding Woman', with milk coming from her breasts. Yet this pregnancy was different: 'as she had Children before, she thought she felt very differently from what she used to do', she told St André. On 27 September, she was taken very ill and sent for her mother-in-law and 'voided' what she described as parts of a pig. John Howard, perhaps already in Godalming to treat John

Chitty, was called and a few days later he delivered some parts of a rabbit, the guts and the liver she described at the start of her first statement. Two weeks later she reported being 'churched' in the Anglican Church's ritual of cleansing following a childbirth, noting that her husband had not lived with her since the miscarriage began and thus absolving him from any role in the conception of the rabbits. It was finally at this point, she said, that she 'thought all was over with her'.[30]

Mary Toft insisted that the miscarriage was the prelude to the monstrous births. She told and retold this story: it featured in the newspapers in October and November and then again during the interview with St André given in November. Subsequently, in her first statement to Clarges, when asked to explain how the whole affair started, she gave a full account of the miscarriage with the same details and chronology. This was the story she had told for weeks, and the one she wanted to tell. It was a distinct phase in her story, but in Toft's mind it was the trigger for the events that followed. Precisely how the miscarriage was the trigger is impossible for us to know. It is perfectly possible that Mary Toft thought that chasing the rabbits in the field had caused her to miscarry. What she saw during her miscarriage may have caused her to believe that what she was carrying was not human. Women could not observe the interior of their own pregnant body. The body of the infant was therefore also a mystery. The invisibility of the unborn child was a theme of many texts. Anna Laetitia Barbauld's poem *To a Little Invisible Being Who is Expected Soon to Become Visible* (1825) is a moving example, in which Barbauld's 'infant bud of being' is an unknown stranger. Barbauld's poem certainly envisaged her unborn infant, if not fully visualized her, and other such poems expressed not just fear and apprehension but also love.[31] Yet no eighteenth-century woman could be certain what her growing pregnant belly contained.

There are other possibilities. Toft may have been experiencing either a remaining papyraceus foetus—a partially formed body of a twin left behind following an earlier pregnancy—or a molar pregnancy: the large parts she lost during the miscarriage, together with her symptoms of bleeding, swelling, and passing substances for a long period, are consonant with the clump of cells that form a hydatidiform mole. Another possibility is that Toft had experienced a very rare form of tumour, a uterine teratoma, which can possess some of the features of an infant mammal, such as skin, hair, teeth, bones, and other internal organs.[32]

These would now almost certainly be detected with ultrasound scans, but in Toft's case they would have either remained in her body or been lost in a spontaneous miscarriage. It is also entirely possible that Toft or someone close to her might have simply thought the lost parts looked rather like rabbits: a foetus lost during a miscarriage at this stage does not take the form of a full-term child in miniature. Whether or not Toft was pregnant, the distress of the suspected miscarriage and the apparent loss of a pregnancy may have sparked the insertion of animal parts into her body as a response on the part of Mary or even a family member. Contemporaries understood that pregnancy and birth caused emotional turmoil for women and we can easily imagine that such a late and prolonged miscarriage would have been destabilizing for Toft, at the very least.[33]

Whatever the reality of Toft's physical experiences, the second event and the main subject of the three statements was the series of rabbit births that followed. Concerning these rabbit births, each of her three statements give a different account. Yet Toft was again consistent on several details as she told and retold the story. What is evident is that Mary Toft did experience a series of real deliveries: animals were placed inside her vagina (even, according to one doctor, inside her uterus) and they exited her body.[34] This would have been an extremely uncomfortable if not excruciating process given the size and nature of the animal parts. One piece of rabbit consisted of, 'the entire Trunk, strip'd of its Skin, of a Rabbet of about four Months growth'. On another part, 'The Nails of the Paws were most of them exceedingly sharp.'[35] Such parts, and many others like them, were hidden in Mary's body over a period of several weeks. Many of the physical symptoms that puzzled the doctors—the abdominal swelling, high temperature and physical discomfort—were likely not feigned but were the result of inserting freshly dead rabbits into Mary Toft's vagina. She must have become perilously ill.

One of the clearest indications of the physical trauma experienced by Mary Toft are the repeated references to pain in all three of her statements. These were all made retrospectively: by the time these statements were taken down the deception had been exposed. Yet Mary Toft was still insistent that these experiences had caused her extreme discomfort. She felt 'gt pains all that day' or was in 'pain in pain/all that time'. Remarks such as, 'then in great pain' and 'being in gt pain' may have been designed to court sympathy, yet their sheer number seems to outstrip this motivation.[36] Her interrogators did not want to hear how difficult the affair had been for her personally; they wanted to know who had instigated the hoax. Yet Toft persisted. Expressions of pain reflect both the physiological experiences of discomfort, but they also reflect the cultural conditions in which those experiences are set.[37] Several of Toft's references to pain naturally associate it with the process of passing the rabbit parts. Many of Toft's pains are reminiscent of classic labour pains, such as 'a great forcing down that I could scarcely bear it'. She described pain like 'the tearing of brown paper' and discomfort like 'a pricking of bones'.[38] Mary Toft's insistence on giving such vivid details to her interrogators suggest some compulsion on her part. These are not the subject of the investigation for which she was being held, but they were evidently crucial components of the story she wanted to tell. In telling and retelling this story Toft was giving form and meaning to the events she had experienced. She made sense of the events by transforming them into a narrative of trauma that imposed order on experiences and perhaps wrested control over a situation that, as she told them, had been directed by others.[39] In each interrogation, the story permitted Toft no volition over her body but instead ascribed agency to others.

Sinister women

Toft's descriptions of pain and suffering underline her powerlessness; they are also clues to how the hoax took shape. Her descriptions of the later stages of the affair stressed the agony that the men caused as they removed the rabbit parts. Women removed parts, too. The gentlewoman Mrs Mebbin removed two rabbit feet from Toft's body, though Toft says Mebbin would not believe it was a monstrous birth.[40] Suffering with rabbit parts inside her, the stocking-maker's wife Betty Richardson was 'forced to take it out again'.[41] What is more striking is how women inflicted pain not just by removing parts, but by inserting them. According to Toft, two women were instrumental in devising the hoax and forcing her to go through with it. First was the nameless wife of the knife grinder, on whom Toft blames the hoax in her first confession. Following her miscarriage, and the passing of several strange parts, Toft explained how this stranger suggested she undertake the hoax with parts of dead animals. After seeing Toft in pain and being told what was happening, this woman suggested the hoax to Toft: 'I told her such a thing would not be done. She sayd it could and desired to try.' The woman had assured Toft that the plan would 'get so good a living that I should never want as long as I lived'. The woman wanted her share, though, insisting 'she must have some of the money'. The details about this woman are illuminating. As the wife of a knife grinder, she was connected to a suitably intimidating occupation and wielded a knife with which she could cut the dead animals. Unlike the other women Toft describes, this anonymous woman was not a neighbour: she and her husband travelled 'about the country'.[42] Toft described a shadowy and ominous figure who is entirely unknown and unconnected to her.

The second female figure was Ann Toft, Mary Toft's mother-in-law. Toft is clear that Ann is involved in the affair from the start, delivering or examining her during the miscarriage. Already in the first confession, Toft had described her mother-in-law as an authoritative woman and a midwife. It was on the following day, 8 December, that Toft began to implicate Ann. Toft at first denied any knowledge of how the rabbit births happened: 'She protests she know of nothing being put up her body but that they came from me she was but too sensible.'[43] James Douglas had placed a large 'X' after this sentence, though, noting that she had been interrupted. This moment marks the critical turning point in her story. Clarges must have expressed his utter disbelief in her suggestion that she did not know how the animal parts were placed inside her body. In admitting that someone must have put them there, Toft blamed her mother-in-law and John Howard, the Guildford doctor: it was they who 'must have put them up her'.[44] By the third statement, taken on 12 December, Toft responded to the direct opening question by admitting that the whole affair was orchestrated by Ann Toft.

The details that Toft gives about Ann in the subsequent exchange with Clarges is revealing about the dynamics between daughter and mother-in-law. As in the previous two statements, Toft has gone back in time to events in the hop garden, but a horizontal line in the document marks a question along the lines of, 'why didn't you tell the truth about your mother in law?' She responded, 'I was very unwilling to tell the truth because it light upon she: when I have told the Tr[uth] God knows if ever I shall be the clearer for it'. Toft seemed to be saying that she had tried to protect Ann Toft, and now wondered if it was in fact too late for her interrogators to believe her. It was Ann, Toft deposed, that 'told me that I would do it and goe thro' I should get a good living'. Like the knife grinder, Ann had apparently promised money for Toft. Ann was also intimidating: she had 'persuaded' and 'ordered' Toft and told her 'be ruled by her and not tell of her'.[45] Toft's plaintive report in the final confession is evidence how frightened she was of Ann: 'I was loath She should touch me.'[46] In contrast, Mary's own mother, Jane Denyer, was entirely absent from all the accounts of the events of 1726. Mothers commonly tended to their daughters at times of childbirth and were likely to be heavily involved in other aspects of their reproductive lives. Jane's absence from the records suggests Mary's isolation. In her final statement, Toft described how she was 'in a most violent Rack and torture.'[47] This followed a long, gory description of the jagged pieces of a rabbit skull that her mother-in-law had put inside her body. This metaphor powerfully conveyed Mary's view that agonizing pain was being intentionally inflicted upon her.

We might see Mary's shift of blame from the knife grinder's wife to her mother-in-law as a *volte-face*. But there is an alternative interpretation. The theme of suffering at the hands of a sinister woman is consistent in Mary Toft's narratives about the hoax. What changes is that the shadowy nameless wife of the knife grinder is replaced by the figure of her mother-in-law. Both women were figures of fear for Toft. Women were sometimes frightened of childbirth and of monstrous or abnormal births, but Toft was frightened of the people around her.[48] She uses the figure of the knife grinder's wife to symbolize menacing women and the violence they could carry out. Using symbolic elements in a story to express visceral emotions and real trauma was something women did in other court settings. In witchcraft trials, for example, women expressed obliquely the conflicts they had with family and neighbours by dramatizing these as battles between good and evil, while the pain of the loss of children was conveyed in mythical stories about fairies.[49] In Toft's statements, she described the actions of her mother-in-law and the fear this produced while at the same time trying not to reveal her identity. She did this by creating a mirror image of Ann Toft: a stranger, unconnected to family, kin, and neighbourhood, whom Mary Toft was simply unable to identify. This woman carried out the very same actions that Toft ascribed to her mother-in-law, putting pressure on her to undertake the hoax for money. In the final analysis, determining where the blame lay is impossible. Yet even if Mary Toft was not 'telling the truth' about Ann Toft's instrumental role in the hoax, it was nevertheless remarkable that she had implicated her mother-in-law to the JP Thomas Clarges. This fact alone provides evidence that relations between these women were fraught: Ann was the most senior woman in the family and lived in close proximity to her son and daughter-in-law. In this context, the most convincing interpretation of the events of autumn 1726 is that they were orchestrated by one or more authoritative women who forced Mary Toft to serve as protagonist.

Mary Toft's experiences show how the female-dominated environment of reproduction could be marked by coercion rather than comfort. Yet this was no ordinary birth. In this exceptional instance of delivery, the women were perhaps punishing Toft for not fulfilling her reproductive duty, or perhaps it really was an attempt to make money by putting Toft's body to work. Relations between the women suggest a different reason why one woman, or perhaps a group of women, might organize such an event. Mary had reported that on 23 April, she was weeding in a field with other women when she chased a rabbit and 'this set her a longing for Rabbets, being then, as she thought, five Weeks gone with Child'.[50] The woman who chased the rabbit with her, according to Mary, had 'charged her with longing for the Rabbet they cou'd not catch, but she [Mary] den'y it'.[51] This accusation by the other women indicates the way in which women—and all neighbours—watched and policed one another, but it was also perhaps an allusion to poaching. Poaching was the focus for protests, including those concerning deer, fish, and rabbits. Mary Toft's own husband had been involved in a protest at a fishpond in the summer of 1726 with another thirty-seven men. Perhaps the rabbit births represented a related hoax, but one initiated by women. Women were actively engaged in politics as petitioners to Parliament, as producers of print, in debating, writing, networking, patronage, and philanthropy. Much of women's public political activity arose from the springboard of the family and traded in ritualized performance and the use of fans, feathers, and embroidery.[52] The body was itself used as a tool of political expression, even becoming a site of resistance for some women.[53] Mary Toft's rabbit births might have been a political response to poverty and social dislocation by the women in the town, rooted in women's preeminent knowledge of the reproductive power of the female body.

Regardless of a possible political imperative, the disempowerment of Mary Toft in this affair belies any rosy visions of women supporting one other. According to Mary Toft's accounts, only in the fields, when the women worked to cover her absence during the miscarriage, was she offered any assistance by the women. The actions of the women who crowded around her during the births bore an altogether more sinister tone. As she described them, Mary Toft's experiences were those of a victim of female kin and neighbours exercising their authority over her body. This is an uncomfortable vision of a young woman who had already experienced a painful and distressing miscarriage being exploited by the older women around her. Punishments, rivalries, and dysfunctions amongst women played out in cases of witchcraft and violence, and it seems that this was precisely what had happened in this case.[54] In the traces left in her three statements, we can hear Mary Toft's plaintive descriptions of suffering and her increasingly insistent incrimination of her mother-in-law. Over the several interrogations, her admission that the monstrous births were a hoax inevitably and irreparably transformed the affair.[55] Just weeks after the public had been notified of the rabbit births in the newspapers, the deliveries were now confirmed as false. The response was swift and severe. Having been committed to the Westminster Bridewell, where she was reportedly kept at hard labour, all efforts quickly turned away from discovery to the pressing matter of punishment.[56]

CHAPTER 6

PUNISHMENT

'an Abominable Cheat & Imposture'

A rabbit-breeding woman hardly posed a major threat to the power-ful men who surrounded her in the bagnio. Yet the strong reac-tions provoked amongst early-eighteenth-century law-enforcers, and their determination to administer punishment, is testament to the danger she was believed to represent.[1] The hoax demonstrated that the illiterate poor could take events into own their hands and dupe the intellectual elite. It showed that the dispossessed might express dissatisfaction with the status quo loud and clear. And it revealed that a poor woman could come very close to making a fool of the King. The disturbance generated by Toft and her family had tugged at the deep roots of anxieties about social order. These were stoked by the growing number of printed reports and particularly visual depictions of Mary Toft which subjected her to public scrutiny. They presented her char-acter as criminal and her person as worthy of punishment. The effect was the determined efforts of the men—often described as aggressive and angry—to convict Mary Toft and her accomplices.

Fear and loathing

1720s London saw a perfect storm of conditions in which Mary Toft's hoax would trigger a powerful reaction amongst contemporaries. Toft's reproduction of rabbits associated her with a new form of property crime at precisely the time when violent conflicts around the question of property had erupted in England. But there was also wider national disquiet about disorder and crime in the 1720s. Protests in the streets and panic in the newspapers were matched by a virulent application of the death penalty. The decade witnessed a crime wave. Women were especially prominent: a much higher proportion of women were being prosecuted in London, for example, especially for prostitution and property crimes. At the same time female criminals were becoming more visible in growing numbers of printed accounts that showcased their actions, often in sensational accounts that played on the unease of readers and the suspicions about unruly women. Poor women represented an identifiable social problem and the result was a determination on the part of men to bring such women under control.[2] Mary Toft conformed to the emerging stereotypes of such women and her actions triggered a potent mix of deep-seated misogyny and a fear of social disorder. The attitudes of the doctors, landed gentlemen, and particularly the officers of the law were a direct expression of their distaste for the poor and of poor women in particular. Toft's misfortune was to come to the attention of these men when they were acutely sensitized to the social problems of crime, order, and protest.

Just as we might now think it should have been obvious to the doctors that Toft's monstrous births were impossible, it seems equally remarkable that she was taken into custody for pretending to give birth to rabbits. This is one of the enduring puzzles of the case. Nothing had been stolen or damaged and no harm had come to anyone, though several rabbits had died in the process. Nonetheless, at the bagnio on 5 December Toft was taken into custody for the crime of imposture, removed to the Westminster house of correction on 8 December, and ultimately proceedings against her were to come before two London courts: the Westminster Quarter Sessions and the King's Bench. Eighteenth-century England had a private system of criminal prosecution, in which a prosecution had to be pursued by an individual, usually the victim of the alleged crime. Ordinarily, Thomas Clarges would have been acting for the person prosecuting the case. Unusually, though, the Westminster Sessions documents from the Toft case do not provide any clues about who was prosecuting the case. This means that we cannot be sure how the case first reached the Westminster Sessions. The case may have originated from a disgruntled resident of Godalming or Guildford. We know that neighbours in these tight-knit early-modern communities policed themselves, often in collaboration with officers of the law, and often focusing on women's behaviour.[3] It seems more likely that the prosecution was generated from amongst the group that had gathered around Toft in London. The most likely explanation is that the notoriety of the case had attracted the attention of the JP Clarges and he was himself advancing the case, or had been encouraged to prosecute by someone else. Either way, Thomas Clarges was clearly driving proceedings.

Mary Toft had been charged with an 'Abominable Cheat & Imposture'. John Howard, the Guildford doctor, was charged with conspiring with Toft 'to impose upon the World the said Mary Toft's being delivered of Seventeen Rabbets [sic] at Seventeen Severall times'. Toft's husband, Joshua, was bound to appear as a witness against Howard for his role in the hoax. Elizabeth Williams (Joshua Toft's elder sister) was also bound over to appear, 'to give Evidence ag[ains]t Mary Toft for a Cheat and Imposture'. She was also later bound to give evidence at King's Bench against Toft. A fifth person, Thomas Howard, the bagnio servant where Mary Toft was being kept in London and who had called time on the hoax, was also bound over to give evidence against Mary Toft. The Sessions records are sparse, but newspapers fill in some of the gaps. Toft was brought before the Westminster Sessions on Saturday 7 January. There, she and John Howard entered the court to give their pleas: Toft was remanded back in custody at the house of correction while Howard was entered into a fresh recognizance.[4]

The case against Howard was subsequently moved to King's Bench. King's Bench was the highest court of common law in England and Wales. The case would have been moved from the Westminster Sessions to King's Bench by writ of certiorari (the order that directs a lower court, in this case the sessions, to send a case to a higher court for a review). Such a procedure was costly, as was a King's Bench case itself. In keeping with these higher costs, when Howard was bound over to appear at King's Bench it was for the huge sum of £400 (one newspaper reported the sum to be as large as £800) in contrast to the customary £20 at the Sessions. The expense of both the writ and a King's Bench case suggests that the wealthy Howard may have moved the case himself, wanting to question the procedures of the Sessions and perhaps scupper the case.[5] He stood to lose his reputation and livelihood, after all. His treatment at the hands of the local and metropolitan authorities may have left him disgruntled, leading him to change his political allegiance. Howard had voted for the local Whig landowner Onslow in the Guildford Borough election in 1720 but had defected by 1734. Alternatively, someone was determined enough to put their support behind a very costly prosecution. A newspaper report that a prosecution at King's Bench had been 'ordered to be carried on' implied some direct institutional or state involvement.[6] Notes that survive in the papers of James Douglas and who recorded the principal evidence for the trial (the three statements given by Toft) also strongly suggest this, referring variously to the 'proper Magistrate' and the 'Kings Evidence', or the 'Civil Magistrate' and 'his Majesty's Evidence'. The government was certainly becoming increasingly proactive in prosecuting criminal cases against private citizens during the second quarter of the century. Nicholas Paxton, who had accompanied Clarges on all except the first of his visits to question Toft, had himself managed several of these trials as deputy solicitor to the Treasury during the mid-1720s.[7] Paxton was also instrumental in regulating the content of newspapers. The full power of George I's government may well have been behind the case against Howard.

It was not just members of King George I's government who were involved in the case, but also those serving the Royal Household.[8] Concerns about unruly women and the disorderly poor aside, once the rabbit births were revealed as a hoax the apparent humiliation of the Royal Household would surely have been compelling motivation for determinedly prosecuting the case. Cyriacus Ahlers was surgeon to the King's household in Germany and Nathanael St André was surgeon and anatomist to the Royal Household in London; James Douglas was also developing links with the King and Queen, later becoming physician to Queen Caroline, who herself was pregnant at the time of the hoax. Samuel Molyneux, who visited Toft in the bagnio, was secretary to the King's son, the Prince of Wales. These men reported back to the King and his courtiers during the case. Henry Davenant, a courtier of George I, had visited Toft in Godalming even before St André, and was kept up to date in the ensuing days by John Howard. On returning to London having seen Toft at Guildford, Ahlers immediately made a report to the King and showed him part of a rabbit extracted from Toft. And on Toft's arrival in Leicester-Fields, the newspapers had broadcast loudly that her move had been commanded by George I.[9] Though they never met Toft, the King and Prince of Wales had been involved in her case from the beginning.

The Westminster Bridewell

As the case moved slowly through these London institutions, Toft remained locked up in the Westminster Bridewell or house of correction at Tothill-Fields. No one was forthcoming to pay her bail and so there she remained until the trial began. At this point, women were the majority of inmates in the Westminster Bridewell.[10] These inmates were kept at 'Work and Labour', but were also provided with access to a room for rest and a room near a pump for washing. Nonetheless, the main concern of the governor of the Westminster house of correction was not the comfort of the inmates, but the security of the jail. One inmate—'Delap a madman'—had recently broken through a door. A palisades barrier had been blown down. And after an inmate had climbed over the garden wall in October 1726 it had been decided that this had to be raised higher. Repairs were needed to several battered and broken features of the Westminster Bridewell, most intended 'for the better Strengthening the said prison & securing the prisoners committed'.[11] Like other inmates, Toft was reported as being 'kept at hard Labour' in the Westminster Bridewell. And as for many others in the house of correction, her time in the Westminster Bridewell was characterized by uncertainty as she awaited trial. One newspaper reported on 14 January that, having been charged as a cheat and imposter, she was brought again before the Westminster sessions. She was then remanded back to the Westminster Bridewell to await trial at the Surrey Assizes, which were due to meet in mid-March. On the same day another paper reported that in fact the sessions case had been 'referred to Sir Thomas Clarges, Bart. to continue, Bail, or Discharge'.[12] The case did not go to the Assizes and Toft remained in jail.

Mary's experience was nevertheless different from the majority of inmates. She did not enter the Westminster Bridewell alone. Instead, the list of those committed to the house of correction shows that she was initially joined there by her husband Joshua, possibly because she was so unwell. There must certainly have been a pressing reason for his presence given that Joshua was also a witness against Howard, his wife's alleged accomplice. Joshua later left the Westminster Bridewell but was, one reporter noted, 'strictly search'd' when he came to visit. Generally Toft appears to have been kept in isolation: the same reporter claimed that only the Keeper's wife could go in to see her. This did not deter people from trying to catch a glimpse of Toft and may have sparked even greater curiosity. A well-developed culture of celebrity would develop in England later in the eighteenth century, in which performers—actors, actresses, singers, and musicians, alongside writers and sportsmen—were prominent. But in the earlier decades a rapidly expanding print culture fed the creation of notoriety, and often of the criminal.[13] For the spectators, the rabbit affair was perfectly consonant with a developing culture of spectacle and celebrity, but the level of interest in Toft was nevertheless remarkable. One newspaper reported on 'the infinite Crowds of People that resort to see her' in the Westminster Bridewell, even though they were 'not being suffered to approach near her'.[14] Toft had already attracted hordes of visitors to the bagnio, and they now followed her to the Westminster Bridewell. The attraction of this particular spectacle, involving a woman's body in an astonishing but confected reproductive process, also tapped into the increasing publicity of reproduction, mediating between the public sphere and intimate family life as this previously women-only process was slowly transformed by the presence of male midwives. One woman, prosecuted for shoplifting, claimed to have been going to see the 'Rabbit Woman' with a friend on 10 January, when the friend stole some linen.[15] The spectators seemed to come from a range of social groups for whom Mary Toft was apparently a distraction—or cover—as they went about their everyday lives.

The face of a criminal

It was during her time in the Westminster Bridewell that the public became interested in the person of Mary Toft. It is striking that the volume of newspaper articles about the case increased once the case was exposed.[16] Following the Christmas vacation, the case was again underway when the business of the courts resumed in early January. The coverage of the case against Toft and Howard during the early weeks of 1727 was such that one paper reported on 4 February that for 'grub street' writers (or hack journalists), 'The Diversions of the Town, the Affairs of *Europe*, and of the Rabbit Woman, have found them constant Employment and comfortable Subsistence'. The *Daily Journal* reported that a prosecution had begun in the Court of Arches at Canterbury, 'against Mary Tofts the pretended Rabbit-breeder'. Soon afterwards,

Mist's Weekly Journal reported from the Westminster Sessions that 'the famous Rabbit Woman of Godalmin' had appeared and entered her plea, 'for a late mysterious Piece of Iniquity'.[17] Once referred to as 'the Woman' or 'the poor Woman', Toft was now given the moniker of notoriety that she would carry long after her death. The image of Toft was transformed for posterity; she had become 'the rabbit woman'.

As such, the public—or at least the press—was no longer interested in the hoax and the possibility of a medical wonder but in the punishment of Mary Toft and John Howard. Brief articles repeated that Toft was to be prosecuted for being an 'infamous Cheat and Impostor', in so doing contributing to the characterization of her as a criminal. It was not just that she was an alleged impostor. 'Higglers', or peddlars, selling rabbits were reportedly complaining that they were losing money as the market for rabbits had become so deflated: 'they declare they would sue her for Damage'. The evident interest in the progress of the legal case against Toft and Howard that propelled the press coverage suggested a more general sense of the need for retribution. But this was matched by an enduring unease concerning her apparent ability to create monstrosity. Many contemporaries no doubt still believed that Toft had manipulated her foetus with her imagination. In the context of the Enlightenment struggle to decipher the limits of the human, the natural, and the spiritual, monstrosity was endlessly fascinating. Perhaps reason—a leitmotif of the Enlightenment—was not secure. Perhaps the rational mind was in peril of being subsumed by the unthinking, impulsive, and uncontrollable body, here represented by Toft.[18] At this stage in the legal proceedings, with her confessions still not public, a trial not yet underway, and the doctors publishing contradictory accounts, the compulsion to know more about Mary Toft remained strong.

Newspapers had been reporting for weeks, but only after she was imprisoned did the public begin to see pictures of Toft's face. For those who had not been able to see her, such pictures could satisfy their curiosity. And Mary Toft's face was one that could sell. Images of Mary Toft were touted as free gifts to promote other goods to the London public. On the first such occasion, the retailer of an anodyne necklace to prevent fits and convulsions in children promised free accounts of the rabbit affair, 'with the Pictures of the Woman her self Mary Toft, and the RABBITS, and of the Persons who attended her during her pretended Deliveries'.[19] These free images were probably William Hogarth's visual satire on the case, *The Cunicularii, or the Wise Men of Godliman in Consultation* (1726), published in late December. Hogarth presents the hoax as a drama witnessed by a group of elite men (including four of the doctors) and centred on Toft, with a supporting cast of her husband and sister-in-law. The image, as the scholar Dennis Todd has shown, is a parody of the Adoration of the Magi and Mary's delivery of Christ that essentially mocks the doctors for their gullible belief in the idea that the immaterial—the imagination—could hold such sway over the material world.[20] Yet it is Mary Toft that Hogarth puts centre stage.

Fig. 6.1 Detail of Mary Toft's face in William Hogarth, *Cunicularii* (1726) [Wellcome Collection]

If Hogarth's depiction of the men surrounding her had caustic intent, his depiction of Toft is arguably more generous. The art historian Ronald Paulson believed that Hogarth had 'beautified' her face, part of his deist adherence to the notion of 'the principle of natural beauty' and the wider religious satire of the image.[21] We do not know what Toft looked like, so Paulson's interpretation is highly speculative. Yet in the context of the public's desire to know more about Toft, the way her face is depicted—beautiful or not—is important in understanding precisely how contemporaries viewed her during this period.

For William Hogarth himself, the face was 'the index of the mind'. In his own images he self-consciously used a visual language that aligned facial expression with character. In his *The Analysis of Beauty*, published in 1753, he outlined his view that we come to a view of a person's character

Fig. 6.2 Plate I from William Hogarth's *The Analysis of Beauty* (1753) [Wellcome Collection]

through their face, 'before we receive information by any other means'. We sense that people's expressions are legible reflections of their characters, and as a result 'our eyes are riveted to the aspects [the faces] of kings and heroes, murderers and saints'. Reading faces in this way made sense because of the way that the mind and the body worked in consort, the mind imprinting itself onto a person's outward appearance. The passions of the mind, Hogarth explained, moved the muscles of the face. And the habitual movement of the facial muscles gradually fixed a person's expression: traces of the repeated smiles of a good-natured person or the frowns of an angry person were etched into the face for good. And so, Hogarth concluded, 'It is reasonable to believe that aspect to be a true and legible representation of the mind, which gives every one the same idea at first sight; and is afterwards confirm'd in fact: for instance, all concur in the same opinion, at first sight, of a down-right idiot.'[22] More striking than either beauty or idiocy in Hogarth's depiction of Toft's face is her direct gaze upwards. The religious framing of the engraving and its play on the Adoration suggests Mary is gazing towards God. Her upturned face and wide-open mouth might show ecstasy, but they could equally convey astonishment or pain, bespeaking the agony and desperation that emerge from her three statements given earlier that month. Mary Toft's face is difficult to read. Given the interest in her personal motivations and the inner workings of her mind, the inscrutability in Hogarth's depiction is notable.

Fig. 6.3 John Faber, after John Laguerre, *Mary Tofts of Godelman the pretended Rabbit Breeder* (1726 or 1727) [Wellcome Collection]

We can observe a similar inscrutability in the second image of Toft to be produced while she was in the Westminster Bridewell. Drawn by John Laguerre and engraved as a mezzotint by John Faber, this image was likely to have been one of the 'Pictures Engraved of the Pretended Rabbit-Breeder her self Mary Tofts' offered gratis to the public on 21 January 1727, the second time such images had been given away.[23] Laguerre's was the only portrait of Mary Toft ever produced. Faber

was a successful engraver who produced many portraits of the
eighteenth-century elite from paintings by artists as renowned as
Godfrey Kneller and Peter Lely. Unlike some of these images, though,
Toft's face strikes the viewer as plain, even blank. Though not referred to
as an idiot, Mary Toft was described by Nathanael St André as 'sullen
and stupid'.[24] Her expression may reflect this, though it could equally be
read as one of frankness, or openness. The first impression that a
contemporary eighteenth-century viewer might have gathered was perhaps of an honest labouring woman, appropriately dressed in practical
cap and apron with strong and capable forearms suggesting her fitness
for work. Her femininity is marked out by the handkerchief around her
neck and her beaded necklace. Were it not for the presence of the rabbit,
held firmly in Toft's grasp, and the title of the print—'Mary Tofts of
Godelman the pretended Rabbit Breeder'—there would be no obvious
indication that the sitter was a dissembler in a notorious hoax. Art
historian Marcia Pointon has noted that the seated three-quarter-length
composition imposes calm and order on Toft's body. The soft impression given by mezzotint, a technique often used for fashionable sub-
jects, presented Toft as a conventional young woman in a society
portrait.[25] There were many images at this time that differentiated the
faces of the mass of society, expressing difference, categorizing social
groups, and thus creating a vision of order. But this image presented not
a figure of fear or caricature but instead a rather ordinary woman, one
even worthy of the viewer's sympathy. Perhaps this image rendered
Mary Toft unthreatening for the British public, domesticating her as an
honest woman with a genuine liking for rabbits.

Yet on closer examination this apparently innocuous portrait of Toft
presented a distinctly more frightening—even monstrous—vision.
Unlike more conventional portraits of women, the impression Toft
makes on the viewer is not that of a beautiful woman, certainly not
according to eighteenth-century ideals of beauty. According to Hogarth,
the natural principles of beauty meant that a symmetrical face should
always be depicted slightly in profile: 'when the head of a fine woman is
turn'd a little to one side', he wrote, 'which takes off from the exact
similarity of the two halves of the face, and somewhat reclining, so
varying still more from the straight and parallel lines of a formal front
face: it is always look'd upon as most pleasing.' Faces which best exemplified two of Hogarth's other principles—simplicity and variety—were

those which were oval. The oval was particularly pleasing, 'singled out [...] of all variety, to bound the features of a beautiful face'.[26]

Fig. 6.4 William Hoare, *Girl With a Rabbit* (c.1730s) [The Huntington Library]

Such principles were applied in two other portraits of young women holding a rabbit. William Hoare's pastel from the 1730s of 'Girl With a Rabbit' uses soft blues and pinks to epitomize seductive yet modest femininity: the girl is pale but blushing on her cheeks and also on her shoulder. The direct gaze of the girl (or young woman), not to mention her exposed left breast, belies her innocence, though. Her hold over that slightly startled-looking rabbit—not tight but certainly possessive, oddly intimate in the way her fingertips touch the rabbit's foot— suggests her control. Intimacy between this woman and the animal is also evident in that hugely expectant space between the woman's centrally placed nipple and the rabbit's face. Hoare based his pastel on the work of the renowned Italian pastelist Rosalba Carriera, whose 'Girl with a Rabbit' depicted autumn in a series representing the four seasons. In Carriera's image, the space between the nipple and nose is even smaller; the whiskers lightly brushing the girl's light skin. Perhaps Carriera or Hoare had Laguerre's engraving of Mary Toft in mind. But the women in Carriera's exquisite pastel, together with Hoare's inferior copy, clearly exceed the Laguerre portrait in terms of contemporary ideals of visual beauty. Though Toft's face is turned slightly to the right, Laguerre depicted it more directly straight on and as an almost perfectly round shape. Moreover, Toft's face is relatively dark in colour, lacking the light and fair skin of the beautiful.[27] Mary Toft's face resolutely failed to make a beautiful impression.

Fig. 6.5 Rosalba Carriera, *Girl with a Rabbit* (1720–30) [The Huntington Library]

By the time the Laguerre/Faber image was produced, Toft had been in Westminster Bridewell for around four months. She had been vilified by the press. Viewers of the portrait would have been familiar with the case and aware that her guilt was widely presumed. Yet Toft appears neither demonic nor gleeful, frightened nor defiant. Her face is opaque rather than transparent. She feels nothing and shows nothing. This was surely a chilling reaction to her ordeal and one that suggested a callous and criminal character. Faber and Laguerre give us only one important clue to the inner workings of Toft's mind: the rabbit clutched in her left hand. Placed in her lap, the rabbit draws attention to her pelvis; the rabbit is on (if not in) her uterus. This visual element also references one of Toft's early comments on her miscarriage, reproduced in the press. St André reported her as saying that in April of 1726, she and two women had run after a rabbit whilst working in a field. Later that night, 'she dreamt that she was in a Field with those two Rabbets in the Lap, and awaked with a sick Fit, which lasted till Morning; from that time, for above three Months, she had a constant and strong desire to eat Rabbets, but being very poor and indigent cou'd not procure any'.[28] This portrait imagines that scene from Toft's dream, referencing her dangerous imagination and suggesting that beneath her strangely impassive exterior her busy imagination ranged wildly even while she remained a prisoner within the walls of the Westminster Bridewell.

None of this can be read on Toft's face, though. And this impassiveness on Toft's face is perhaps the point. The juxtaposition of these different elements in Laguerre's portrait—the apparent transparency and normalcy of the sitter and the knowledge that she was involved in an extraordinary set of events—is profoundly unsettling. The body was regarded as a highly legible index of emotions in the eighteenth century. In acting and aesthetics there was a well-developed lexicon of reading the face, as well as gesture and deportment more broadly. Indeed, the strength of reactions against Toft arguably triggered the fear that she was using women's ability to manipulate their passions, and in so doing making maternity into a performance.[29] From first impressions people were expected to be able to read the face and body and take the measure of the person. These certainties about people, their character, and our reliable judgement of them were disrupted by the illegibility of Toft's body and her apparent lack of feeling. This illegibility of Toft's face and body suggested the most frightening possibility of all, that Mary Toft was a monster herself.

Thwarted desires

Laguerre's portrait of Mary Toft was unsettling and contributed to the printed coverage in which writers were increasingly baying for her blood. The attempts to prosecute had started aggressively and now the public waited for the case to begin in earnest. By the 27 March it was clear that proceedings had stalled. Newspapers gave conflicting reports about what was going to happen, suggesting some confusion amongst those prosecuting the case. Finally, newspapers reported that on Saturday 8 April, after exactly four months in jail, Mary Toft had been released without charge.[30] Given the involvement of so many high-ranking individuals and the obvious determination to prosecute, it is somewhat surprising that she was not sentenced. Early-eighteenth-century impostors were successfully prosecuted for various offences, including that of common nuisance. Indeed, the period allegedly saw intense scrutiny of deceptions of all kinds.[31] The conditions were surely ripe for the prosecution of either Toft or Howard, or both. In the end, though, neither the case against Toft or Howard made it to trial.

Frustratingly, the records of both the court of the Westminster Sessions and the King's Bench simply dry up. On 13 April, the *Daily Post* contained the following short notice:

> Mary Toft, the Godalming Rabbit Woman, was last Saturday discharg'd from her Recognizance at the Quarter Sessions, Westminster, there being no Prosecution.

The *British Journal* delivered the same information in more critical terms:

> Mary Toft, the pretended Breeder of Rabits [sic], and base Imposter, was last Saturday discharged from her Recognizance at the Quarter Sessions at Westminster, there being no Prosecution against her.

A few weeks later it was reported that Howard, 'the Famous Surgeon and Man-Midwife of Guildford, concerned in the Affair of the Woman who pretended to have Rabbits bred in her Womb, was, upon a Motion made by his Councel, [sic] discharged without any Prosecution'.[32] In Howard's case, it was his privilege and wealth—and the access this gave him to the defence of counsel—that were instrumental in his discharge.

The reasons for Toft's discharge were different. In the end, it appears that there was simply found to be no charge to answer. As one newspaper reported, "'tis said there's a difficulty in the Case, viz. What Statute she and her Confederates shall be try'd upon'.[33] Mary Toft had been charged with committing a fraud or a cheat and imposture, John Howard with acting as her accomplice. Fraud referred to 'any fraudulent practice against which a man of common prudence could not reasonably defend himself'. Fraud also required a false token, such as a false weights or dice. Toft's fraudulent practice was to impersonate a rabbit-breeding woman and producing the rabbits were the closest she had come to proffering a false token; it now seemed evident that a man of common prudence could reasonably defend himself from both. A cheat had to be shown to have been 'defrauding or endeavouring to defraud another of his known Right by means of some artful Device, contrary to the plain Rules of common Honesty'. Whilst reports on the case include several mentions of potential gains for Toft—including the offer of a pension—the only evidence that money was ever exchanged was a secondhand reference to Toft receiving a guinea from Ahlers.[34] Quite simply, the case did not meet the requirements of the law for fraud, cheat, or imposture and the charges against Mary Toft and John Howard were dropped. Mary Toft had not been let off without punishment. She had, after all, already spent several months in the Westminster Bridewell and at hard labour. But on this occasion the details of the law frustrated the palpable desire of those in power to prosecute.

Historians rightly share an impulse to grant the poor agency, to emphasize their limited capacity for power, to celebrate the occasions where they succeeded in initiating change. The case of Mary Toft allows for little of this optimistic reading of the past. By the time of Toft's release, any agency that Mary Toft and her family may have once possessed had evaporated. Though summary courts, like the Westminster Sessions, were used by a wide range of social groups to further their own interests, the magistracy still used those courts to protect their own property and to control the poor.[35] Attempts to convict Mary Toft and her accomplices were ultimately thwarted. But whilst she was not prosecuted, Mary Toft's experience of summary justice highlights the objectification of the poor female body and a disregard for its sufferings, driven by a deep-seated fear of the poor, of women, and especially of poor women. We should not dismiss the Tofts entirely. They managed to orchestrate a hoax which—for three months—managed to fool men in power. In the final analysis, though, Mary Toft's journey from the bagnio, through the court, and into the Westminster Bridewell bespeak the force of the law when used by the elite, rather than any agency of the poor. No court trial had taken place, but Mary Toft was ruthlessly scrutinized in the press. Though she was never prosecuted for her actions, she was subjected to relentless vilification by the public. Indeed, the extensive coverage of the case reveals that the early-eighteenth-century public sphere bore the hallmarks of a court of public opinion.

PART III

THE PUBLIC

CHAPTER 7

THE PRESS

a 'filthy story at best'

The Enlightenment held the promise to sweep away the limits to knowledge about the natural world.[1] This was a culture built upon the theories of early empiricists such as John Locke, who sought 'to search out the *Bounds* between Opinion and Knowledge; and examine by what measures, in things whereof we have no certain Knowledge, we ought to regulate out Assent'. Knowledge came from experience, the deployment of reasoned probability and—in some cases—revelation. The scientific revolution, a key component of the intellectual Enlightenment, was well established by the early eighteenth century, and though the most important advances of seventeenth-century scientists deployed physics and mathematics to understand the natural world, the field of medicine itself slowly became subject to emerging scientific practices of knowledge. The Toft case occurred during this crucial period in the establishment of medical science. The excitement around this incipient discipline of medical science fuelled contemporaries' hunger for news of the case. Surgeons and physicians, together with the wider public, were gripped by the possibility that the case represented a genuinely groundbreaking medical discovery. Much time was spent in scholarly investigation of Mary Toft, both in print and in person, and the men involved in these discussions were serious and dedicated in their pursuit of new knowledge about the workings of the human body. The case of Mary Toft generated a media sensation, thereby becoming a veritable spectacle that underscored the public nature of women's reproductive health.[2] In this way, the case of Mary Toft can be properly positioned in an early-eighteenth-century public sphere of rational debate and the pursuit of knowledge in the spirit of the Enlightenment, striving for human advancement, and freedom from ignorance. The press coverage of the Toft case laid bare the workings of this public sphere, a vibrant and dynamic space in which cultural elites engaged in vigorous debate.

Yet the case reveals other facets of the early-eighteenth-century public sphere. The seventeenth-century explosion of print and the emergence of new genres of publication had, by the early eighteenth century, created a space where authors experimented with the boundary between 'truth' and 'fiction'.[3] Works by writers such as Daniel Defoe and Jonathan Swift used narrative and genre to toy with the notion of 'fact', and in ways that were echoed across newspapers and periodicals. The Enlightenment project may well have been to seek out knowledge, but the literary context reminded readers how difficult it was to tease apart fact, fiction, and fable. Sure enough, rational, civil, and informed discussion were not the hallmarks of the printed discussions about Toft. Instead, authors revelled in the shock, fear, and hilarity that the case engendered. If the case was true, then a modest veil should be drawn over it to protect those uninitiated in sexual matters (especially young people and women). If the affair was false— and the majority of pamphlets suggested it was—it nevertheless offered a rich seam for satirists and pornographers to exploit. As Mary's health deteriorated in the Westminster Bridewell, for example, the theatre audience at Lincoln's Inn Fields was delighted with a reconstruction of the delivery of rabbits, 'which ran about the Stage, and raised such a Laughter as perhaps has not been heard upon any other Occasion'.[4] The impressions of refined Georgian society gained from fine country houses, the emergence of the novel, elaborate choral music, and rational Enlightened debate belie the pulsing current of impoliteness coursing through eighteenth-century culture. Impoliteness ran through both high and low culture. Coy or explicit, humorous or vicious, the many prints, poems, and pamphlets on the Toft case confuse any easy distinctions we might make between popular and elite culture in early Georgian England. Nor can we entirely separate behaviours of 'politeness' and 'anti-politeness', or a society where respectable men were merely occasionally polite. The serious and rational debates about the case were sometimes hardly distinguishable from the rude and hilarious treatments. The rational and the polite was relentlessly entwined with the vulgar and brutish.[5]

Transforming news

By the 1720s, tens of thousands of newspapers circulated across England. Their readership included men and women, rich and poor, living in both town and country. But for every individual who picked up a paper and read it to themselves, several more heard the paper read out loud, saw it pasted up on a public wall, or engaged in a conversation in which the most recent news was discussed, dissected, and debated. Newspapers were the backbone of a dynamic and diverse early-eighteenth-century public sphere. Mary Toft's rabbit births first entered this virtual public sphere on Saturday 22 October 1726, when the *British Journal* published the first newspaper notice about the case:

> They write from *Guildford*, that the three Women working in a Field, saw a Rabit, which they endeavoured to catch, but they could not, they all being with Child at that Time: One of the Women has since, by the help of a Man Midwife, been delivered of something in the Form of a dissected Rabit, with this Difference, that one of the Legs was like unto a Tabby Cat's, and is now kept by the said Man Midwife at *Guilford.*

Few details were given and there is no explicit attempt to provide an explanation for the odd delivery. Three weeks later, on Monday 4 November 1726, the *Daily Journal* published the latest breaking news on its front page:

> From Guildford comes a strange, but well attested piece of News. That a poor Woman who lives at Godalmin, near that Town, who has an Husband and two Children now living with her; was, about a Month past, delivered by Mr. John Howard, an eminent Surgeon and Man-Midwife living at Guildford, of a Creature resembling a Rabbit.

The opening passage of the thirty-line report was designed to spark the curiosity of the reader and unlike the earlier story this longer article clearly emphasized the veracity of the case: 'strange but well attested'. Girding the credibility of the article, the writer explained that the 'Woman'—left unnamed—was a respectable married mother of two, whilst the surgeon John Howard was 'eminent'. In what followed, the writer carefully itemized the details of Toft's early deliveries, noted that 'the Woman' had made an oath, and referred to both the Royal Society and the Prince of Wales. The precision and stamps of authority served to underscore the truth of the story.[6]

Other reports were beginning to appear in the papers and these early reports were reprinted many times in the subsequent weeks.[7] This recycling of material in the first few weeks of the case was typical of early newspapers, with some regional daily newspapers reproducing notices from London papers, all of it to be subsequently repeated in weekly round-ups. The language of the November article was also characteristic of this early coverage of the case. The phrase 'poor woman' in the description of Toft was used in several accounts of the early stages of the affair. For example, William Pountney, a friend of John Howard and also a doctor, wrote a letter to his father about Mary Toft noting, 'of whom I don't doubt you have read in ye news papers'. Pountney had hoped to see Howard to get a full account but had been busy attending patients with the small pox. Drawing his information from the newspapers himself, Pountney described Mary as 'ye poor woman of Godalmin', adding, 'some judge very hard of ye poor woman'. 'Poor' in this case meant both without wealth and unfortunate. John Howard, in a letter dated 22 November and published in the papers, also described her as 'the poor Woman at Godalmin'. William Whiston, a natural philosopher and theologian whose interest in the case arose from his work on prophecy, later reported that Toft had, 'moved great compassion at first, and was relieved by charitable Persons, because of her Poverty'.[8] Such early coverage was marked by a relatively sympathetic tone towards Toft.

Yet the tone was set to change. Once Toft was moved to Guildford and was then subsequently lodged at Roger Lacy's bagnio in London from the 29 November 1726, newspaper reports were openly sceptical and increasingly judgemental about Toft. Even before the hoax was revealed, *The British Journal* declared, 'A fine Story!' At the exposure of the hoax there was an abrupt change in the tone of reporting. So closely knit was the network of observers and reporters in London that even before Toft was taken into custody, the report of the porter of the bagnio triggered journalists to collectively initiate a *volte-face*. It was at this point that the press churned out its most vitriolic words against Toft. The *Daily Post* of Tuesday 6 December 1726, while not overly critical of Toft, referred to the affair as a 'filthy Story at best'. The writer began, 'No Notice hath hitherto been taken in this Paper of the Woman at Godalmin', thus seeking to secure the untarnished reputation of the newspaper. His scepticism was emphasized by his parentheses: 'it being pretended that she is near her Labour (as they call it) or more Rabbits now jumping in her Belly (as the Phrase is)'. By 17 December *The London Journal* had published a letter filling more than three full columns that denounced the imposture as the doing of 'this wicked Woman'. 'I hope', the author writes to the editor, 'you will not fail to make their Crimes equally publick, who have any way wilfully contributed thus to terrify and abuse the Weak and Credulous.'[9] Toft was quickly demonized as a threat to the very readers who were so voraciously consuming the news reporting.

The multiplication of newspaper articles once the case was exposed suggest the public's fascination with the criminality of Toft, rather than the alleged rabbit births. Yet once Toft was in jail there was very little for newspapers to report. On 17 December *The Weekly Journal* was complaining that it lacked material for the issue, partly because 'The Physicians and Surgeons have monopoliz'd the Imposture of the Rabbit Woman for their own Speculation and Defence.' Having no news on the case itself but wanting to trade on readers' interest, the 7 January issue of *Mist's Weekly Journal* produced a two-column feature on similar stories of strange reproduction that had circulated in other parts of Europe and the wider world. Only later in the spring, from 27 March 1727, was there new fodder for newspapers which were now able to cover the legal obstacles to prosecution and the rapidly approaching end to the case. Soon there would be nothing for the press to report, and several papers made sure at least to note Toft's release. One of the last gasps of press coverage of the hoax itself came in May 1727, when John Howard's release from bail was announced.[10]

'In Justice to the Publick'

Avid readers learned about the progress of the hoax from newspapers. Yet there had always been genuine unease that this story should be discussed so publicly. There were concerns that more sensitive readers would be endangered by accounts of the case. An early newspaper account (from before the case was revealed to be a hoax) reported two opinions on the case: 'some looking upon them as great Curiosities fit to be presented to the Royal Society, &c. others are angry at the

Account, and say, that if it be a Fact, a Veil should be drawn over it, as an Imperfection in humane Nature'. A major concern of those commenting on the case was the threat to the public imagination. On the day Toft delivered her second confession (and thus once the case had been exposed) one London letter-writer (John Wainwright) reported to his friend, 'to tell what talk there has been at Tea tables would Stain my Paper all the phrases of Anatomy that are seldom us'd but in cases of necessity have been frequent in the fairest & most modest mouths'. Women were at risk, according to Wainwright, but he was also concerned about the dangers posed to the credulous poor. Wainwright reported the immodest conversations that the case provoked amongst women, but he was most disappointed with 'The Town' because, 'Some of the lower forms have been down in to expose themselves by their credulity & attention to this Imposture.'[11] The case had originated from a poor family and it was 'lower forms' who were revealing their folly in attending to it. Both women and the lower ranks were threatened if indulged in this way.

The threat was potentially far greater, affecting not only women and the poor, though. As suggested by Wainwright, those talking about Toft included a far broader cross-section of London's population than merely the elite men named in the pamphlets. The case was being discussed and debated across town. One newspaper reported that, having exchanged words about a satirical ballad on the case, 'two Persons of Distinction' had set out to fight about the case, only to be arrested before they could do so.[12] This must have worried those who were concerned for public morals and angered those who wished to bring the whole affair to a swift close with a criminal prosecution.

It also frustrated those who wanted to preserve the standard of public debate in the press. By early February, one letter-writer going by the name of 'CATO' bemoaned how the 'incredible Paragraphs' recently appearing in the paper had necessitated all readers to 'shut our Ears, and shew in our Eyes a Disbelief'. This writer went further, using the Toft case to reflect on the wider role of newspapers and the threat they posed to a more general public. The influence the paper had on its readers was like the power of the maternal imagination on the unborn, he wrote. Both showed 'how strongly the Passion of imposing on one another, and the World, actuates on Mankind; and therefore leaving unnatural Births, Monsters, and other Fictions, to the Belief, and Exploration of

Fools'. Cato then offered his ironic round-up of recent news—his 'Labours' with which the paper could either 'entertain' or 'convert' its readers. The list included the obvious and the pointless, from news that Sir Little Finecoat had attended St James's coffee house in a new suit, to reports that 'grub street' writers were living comfortably off the stories of 'the Rabbit Woman'. Cato's exasperation at the press's continued fascination with the case was only barely veiled. Cato had neatly exploited the irony that a case that hinged on the possibility that a woman's maternal imagination would cause her to give birth to rabbits, should give rise to wider concerns about the potential damage to other people's imaginations.[13] Reports of Mary Toft's hoax exemplified the kind of shallow newspaper reporting that abused the powerful influence of the press over their readers' minds. Yet Cato's criticism was ultimately tethered to a faith in the press and its potential in a rational public sphere.

A commitment to the press as a public good was ostensibly what drove much of the coverage of the case, in fact. The initial interest was in the possibility of the rabbit births, though writers would soon turn their attention to the unveiling of the hoax and the progress of the punishment of Toft. Yet throughout the seven months of the most intensive newspaper coverage, from October 1726 to April 1727, newspapers underscored their reports by claiming to fulfil a duty to inform and protect the reading public. One writer characterized his request to *The London Journal* to publish his lengthy letter on the Toft case as, 'a Request for the publick Service'. Pamphlet writers gave the same justification, St André ending his pamphlet with a call to Ahlers to give his own account of what he saw, 'in Justice to the Publick'. Ahlers responded in like manner: 'being call'd upon in so publick a manner, I could not, in justice to my own Reputation, deny that Gentleman as publick a Satisfaction'. Such was the common currency of this claim to protect the public by furnishing appropriate accountability that it was even adopted by the satirists, notably 'Lemuel Gulliver', who reassured readers that he would 'be ready to guard the public' against any future printed outputs by Nathanael St André.[14]

The 'public' was a group to serve or to protect. The 'public' was also a virtual space in which a process of debate would arrive at truthful knowledge. The printed discussions of Toft were shaped through this dynamism of the early-eighteenth-century public sphere. The literary form of the dialogue, used in several texts about the case, was itself a clear expression of the centrality of conversation and debate to this public sphere. But words were not always reliable. It was surely in Mary Toft's words—not that observations of the doctors—where the truth would be found, but at the same time even her words were acknowledged to be indeterminate and untrustworthy.[15] In this public sphere of print, it seemed that almost everyone's words were up for grabs. Here was another understanding of the 'public': a group that exercised judgement on Toft, her associates, and the other groups involved in the case, not least the doctors and the journalists themselves. By the accession of George I, print was a principal tool in the public's role as 'umpire' in social, cultural, and political terms. It was in this context that many of the doctors entered into print, for the sake of both knowledge and reputation, and the professional profit they might accrue. As the reporter for Mist's Weekly Journal remarked, 'the learned Gentlemen, who find themselves mistaken at last in their Judgments of that Affair, are healing their Reputations as well as they can by writing of Pamphlets'.[16]

The accounts by the doctors St André, Ahlers, and Manningham thus reflect not just a medical debate about the veracity of the theory of the maternal imagination but also the attempts by the doctors to establish the truth of their own accounts and secure their professional credit. The papers of these three men do not survive, though we can well imagine the pile of notes, drafts, and printed works of others that they amassed during their research and writing on the case. Some of Richard Manningham's work on the case may have been included in the 'Little Study of Books', as well as many copies of his unsold pamphlets and books, that he possessed at the time of his death in 1759.[17] We do have the papers of James Douglas, the doctor who also visited Toft and scribbled down her hurried confessions as she was questioned by Thomas Clarges and Nicholas Paxton in early December, and these show the considerable efforts of these doctors in attending to the case, recording information and weighing the evidence. In addition to the rough notes of Mary Toft's three confessions, the Douglas papers include letters, drafts of notices, and the pamphlet he would finish on 16 December 1726 and then have printed, amongst other items. Douglas copied an advertisement for a book on the case from the Whitehall Evening Post of 29 December 1726, as well as articles on the prosecution of Toft and

Howard from the *Daily Journal* and *Daily Post* from 9 January 1727. He sketched out a list of rabbit parts, presumably those allegedly removed from Toft's body, on the back of a letter, suggesting he was using whatever he had to hand. And he acquired a single-sheet print of Hogarth's *Cunicularii*, noting 'published about the 20th Decr 1726'.[18] Douglas was recording the events and reading the press coverage while he himself was involved in the case, all in preparation for his own foray into print on the case.

Roast beef, rabbits, and rabbets

This was a serious matter for the doctors, then, as it was for the lone writer who saw in the monstrous births genuine religious portent. William Whiston had been giving his interpretation of the Toft case in amongst lectures on topics ranging from magnetism to sacred temples since autumn 1726, only committing it to print only in 1753. He argued that the evidence showed that Toft's monstrous births were real: her testimony, the involvement of the doctor John Howard, the evidence published by Samuel Molyneux, the Prince of Wales' secretary, and Nathanial St André, and the fact that it was 'believed by King *George* to be real', all pointed to this fact. Along with two other monstrous births, Whiston stated that the rabbit births signalled the completion of the prophecy of Esdras: that as the end of the world approached, women would bring forth monsters. Regardless of his concern for God's judgements, Whiston was acutely aware of the humour that the case had triggered. In his publication of 1753 he acknowledged that the case had 'been so long laughed out of Countenance' and reasoned that the doctors had changed their minds to deny the monstrous births only once they were 'unjustly made Sport of by the Scepticks of the Town'.[19] Whiston was live to such treatment no doubt because he himself was ridiculed for his views as soon as he began uttering them in 1726. The author of *A Philosophical Enquiry into the Wonderful CONEY-WARREN* (1726) thought Whiston may as well argue that Toft had enjoyed 'a Criminal Conversation with a Buck-Rabbit', had been bewitched by a witch or was in fact herself a rabbit in disguise. How can we trust Whiston, this author teased, when he was also curious about a purported story that a woman had birthed a side of roast beef?[20]

The motives in covering Toft's case were often less than noble. The press claimed to satisfy genuine enquiries about the processes of human reproduction and the procedures of law and justice; yet the coverage was also designed to sell copy. Not all the coverage of Toft sought to intervene in public debate about the status of medical professionals, the veracity of the theory of the maternal imagination, or the wider state of the public sphere. As suggested by the responses to the serious-minded Whiston, humourists of different kinds saw in the case a cache of rich source material. Mary Toft provided opportunities for nifty quips and clever satire. It is striking that the extent of this comedic coverage produced a culture of self-referential jokes around the case. *Pudding and Dumpling Burnt to Pot* (1727) replied to the earlier work, *The Dissertation on Dumpling*, teasing 'our most eminent Physicians, Surgeons, Anatomists and Men Midwives' (as well as the 'great Wits') for their lack of consistency in their spelling of rabbit: was it with an 'e' or an 'i'? Humourists ridiculed the doctors more commonly than each other, though. One produced a cheap, three-pence three-page poem relentlessly teasing James Douglas for his excitement about the rabbit births. A more extensive joke was played by the author of the pamphlet *The Anatomist Dissected*, purporting to be Lemuel Gulliver, the protagonist of Jonathan Swift's recent novel, *Gulliver's Travels*, which appeared in October 1726. He combined biting satire with an informed critical engagement with St André's understanding of anatomy. It was, he said, more likely that a woman would have birthed five cucumbers or one hundred letters, than given birth to rabbits, given that animals of one species do not reproduce animals of another. 'Here a wise Man would have smelt a Rat instead of a Rabbit', Gulliver added.[21]

Georgian humour, whether for men or women, rich or poor, combined the bawdy and the refined. This was also a culture in which popular and polite genres alike traded in jokes about the poor and deformed, and about rape and violence. Cruelty and laughter went hand in hand. One of the important drivers of this humour was misogyny. This rendered much of the satire on the Toft case relentlessly brutal but nonetheless very funny for early-eighteenth-century readers. It also fed the prurient interest in Mary Toft's body that traded on the dangerous frisson of making jokes about sex, reproduction, and birth under the veil of medical interest. One commentator joked that 'obscene and indecent Images' about the case had 'fill'd the Minds; and furnish'd out/the Conversation of People of all Ranks, Ages and Conditions'. He wondered, 'whether Ideas of this Nature are fit to be put into the Heads of rude Boys, Boarding-school Girls, and Old Maids', leaving it to 'every discreet and prudent matron to judge'. This writer's evident delight at the frisson of teenage boys and girls, inexperienced widows, and earnest women being excited by the stories of Mary Toft's intimate parts shows the titillation engendered by the case. The idea of women immodestly talking about Toft was clearly a shared fantasy. In one example, women's loquacity was so powerful as to materialize words into ceramic objects to satisfy their desiring nature:

> The Women, fie on 'em, do talk without Shame,
> Nor scruple, in *Latin*, to mention that same;
> And shortly intend to get Figures in *China*
> Of the *Diaboli Morsus*, and eke the *Vagina*.[22]

The *Morsus Diaboli* is a plant, known in the eighteenth century as 'the Devil's bit'. Plants were common metaphors for male genitalia, and this is clearly implied in this poem. *Morsus Diaboli* also referred to the fringed ends of the fallopian tubes. This author thus traded in the contemporary idea that botany itself was an erotic pursuit and a danger to the modesty of its female adherents, not least because of its use of Latin to thinly veil descriptions of sex and body parts.[23]

For all these imaginative reconstructions of women's opinions, the press were not interested in Toft as a person or character. This is in stark contrast to the way in which they described the men involved in the case. It is only in the more literary sources that Toft's character is explored in any depth, usually through humour. The most explicit publication on the case was made all the more obscene by being passed off as having been written by Mary Toft herself. Written in 'her own Stile and Spelling', Merry Tuft's *Much ado about Nothing: or, a Plain Refutation of All that has been Written or Said concerning the Rabbit-Woman of Godalming* (1727) complains that she had been 'mad a sad Cretur of by a parcel of surjohns'. In a particularly vicious passage, the author imagined Toft's adulterous promiscuity and fellatio by drawing analogies between eating rabbits and inserting them in her body as part of the hoax. Unsatisfied with her husband's rabbit, Toft had sampled a neighbour's rabbit, but the neighbour grew 'wary' and brought a group of surgeons: 'but nun of these Rawbitts went doun like his, nor spent hafe so well: and as for takin them at the mouth, I cood not; for evar sense I had tastid his Rawbitt, I tuk them all tuther way'.[24] This crude text questions the motives and the authority of the doctors, but the theme of Toft's insatiable sexual desire lays equally bare its plainly misogynist aspects, common amongst the harsher reactions to Toft.

Other women were similarly ventriloquized in comic works, these imaginary characters speaking lines by the male authors. Toft's mother-in-law appeared in one pamphlet, A Letter from a Male Physician in the Country, to the Author of the Female Physician (1726). This was an extended swipe at John Maubray's The Female Physician, containing all the Diseases incident to that Sex, in Virgins, Wives and Widows (1724), in which Maubray admitted the power of the imaginative faculty to mould the bodies of humans and animals, including the powerful 'Forming Faculty' of pregnant women over the foetus. The most brutal criticisms of Maubray are spoken by the two female characters in the twenty-page 'A Dialogue between the Lady Sne—er, Mrs. Toft Of Godalmin, Midwife, and her Deputy'. The protagonist, Ann Toft, admits that the hoax was her idea, 'a silly, senseless Whim of mine, that came into my Head, after reading the Sooterkin Story, &c. in the Female Physician'. Ann Toft allegedly owns this book and the women read out passages and subject them to lively debate. One woman reads out Maubray's passage comparing unskilled midwives and the 'ingenious Operations of the more judicious Andro-Bœthogynists', another woman fires: 'The what? This is like Shakespear, in his Romeo and Juliet'. Ann Toft agrees: 'it is the same to me as if it were all Greek; I cannot guess at the Meaning of one Word.' And she underlines the fact that for all the 'fine language' used by Maubray, the book is in fact 'Only his fine way of telling us how a Child comes into the World.'[25] The book dramatizes the battle for authority over childbirth between men and women, using the voices of women to lampoon men and underline women's practical and useful knowledge of the process.

The bawdy Enlightenment

There is no doubt that the case of Mary Toft triggered fears about an unrestrained imagination and the ascendance of the corporeal body over the thinking mind. And this tapped into a widespread unease about the blurred boundary between feeling and the imagination on the one hand, and reason and rationality on the other. Arguably, the case itself was a prompt to draw the distinctions ever more clearly.[26] But if the case firmed up the lines of debate in professional circles, it did nothing to end bawdy discussions of Toft or reproduction more broadly. Indeed, one of the ironies of the public discussions of the case is that these stoked the impolite and the bawdy elements of Enlightenment discourse. They gave voice to these enduring impulses of eighteenth-century culture.

Though the different treatments of Toft might sit in different genres, and to some extent their readership may have been distinct, the discussions of Toft in the newspapers, pamphlets, and humorous satires overlapped. The serious and professional discussions of Toft were not entirely distinct from the comedic and lay treatments. Information and entertainment were hard to separate in this culture, and one of the features of the press that this case highlights are the many connections between different forms of print. The newspaper reports were entwined with the medical pamphlets, for example. *The Several Depositions* taken down by Onslow were published on 10 December 1726 and Manningham's *Exact Diary* on 12 December.[27] The 17 December issue of *The London Journal* wove extended extracts from both books into its two-page report on 'this gross Fraud'.[28] The day before, the Exeter paper, *Brice's Weekly Journal*, had remarked that 'for want of better News' the paper would summarize the depositions, giving a short account of the statement of Coston, Stedman, Sweetapple, and Peytoe, followed by a brief precis of Manningham's pamphlet report on Toft's first confession.[29]

Whilst some of the satires were cheaper works, it is not accurate to say they were written for a 'popular', as opposed to an 'elite' audience. The books and pamphlets on Toft found their way into a great many libraries of the eminent and wealthy. Nearly forty book catalogues published in the second half of the eighteenth century included pamphlets on Toft, and they demonstrate how these libraries accommodated a range of works on Toft alongside the full gamut of eighteenth-century books. John Hutton, whose extensive library was sold in 1764, owned no less than fifty-two publications relating to Mary Toft, ranging from the books of the doctors to tracts that came with ballads and 'humorous Designs'. These were listed alongside a number of ecclesiastical works, books on tea, fishing, medicine, and mathematics, and an extensive collection of works on magic, sorcery, and 'other Marvellous Histories'. John Darker, a Midlands businessman who became MP for Leicester in 1766, owned a number of tracts on the case, listed between a book that unveiled the mysteries of opium and a treatise on ruptures. The Earl of Mornington at Dengan (or Dangan) Castle in County Meath, Ireland, possessed a bound volume that included the pamphlets by Manningham, Douglas, Ahlers, and Braithwaite, along with the *Several Depositions* and two of the longest satires on the case, *Much a-do About Nothing: Or, a Plain Refutation of All that has been Written or Said Concerning the Rabbit-Woman of Godalming* and *The Discovery; or, the Squire turn'd Ferret* (both published in 1727). These would have sat on his shelves alongside the novels, memoirs, and philosophy also found in his library.[30] The same men consumed learned treatises and bawdy satires, as these catalogues show. We have few ways to access the views of the poor about the Toft case, yet we can be assured that a cultural elite was steeped in both the serious and the comic.

Humour served serious purposes, of course. It was another tool in a public sphere in which practitioners would be held accountable by the press. The close textual engagement of humorous writers with longer learned texts shows a public sphere where professional or expert writers (in this case doctors) were subjected to sustained and precise critique through humour. Humour might be a check on the growing cultural power of such emerging professionals. In *A Letter from a Male Physician in the Country, to the Author of the Female Physician* (1726), *Pudding and Dumpling Burnt to Pot* (1727), and Thomas Braithwaite's *Remarks on a Short Narrative of an Extraordinary Delivery of Rabbet* (1726), portions of an original text were reproduced, only to be subjected to a sustained forensic—and very funny—virtual cross-examination.

And the doctors could give as good as they got. Their works on the case could also be delivered in this register of biting satire. Even Thomas Braithwaite's forensic critique of St André's account of the case—scrutinizing St André's claims on the moisture of the rabbit head, the size of the lungs, the state of the stomach, faeces, and bladder—launches with a scathing dedication to 'Dr. Meagre' worthy of the best satirists of the Augustan age. It mocks St André as 'a Pedagogue and a Pill-maker', bringing attention to his previous occupation by disingenuously claiming, 'Neither do I think it any more inconsistent for a Doctor to have been an Usher of a School, than for a Dancing-Master to be an

Anatomist.' Braithwaite purposefully bundled the writers of farcical medical treatises and novels together: 'the Gullivers, St Andres and Howards of the Age' peddled stories of tiny men, islands in the sky, and a woman's delivery of seventeen rabbits. These were the true 'monstrous Relations', he pointed out.[31]

While women were a frequent target, the print battle between the doctors and satirists was ferocious. Humorous writers deployed satire as a tool with which to enter the public debate about the state of medical

NATHANIEL S.^T ANDRE,
(Rabbit Doctor)

Fig. 7.1 Line engraving by R. Grave, 'Nathaniel St. Andre. Rabbit Doctor' [Wellcome Collection]

knowledge and the wisdom (or otherwise) of the doctors. The ballad, *St. A-d-è's miscarriage: or, a Full and True account of the Rabbet-Woman* (1727), refers to Toft's duplicity and women's immodesty in speaking about the case, but it is relatively restrained in its handling of these. It reserves the sharpest words for the doctors who were, the author implies, simply after money. The 'Monster of Monsters, beyond Comprehension', he writes, 'Is that they expected a monstrous Pension.' Another short poem targeted James Douglas directly, responding to his lengthy pamphlet which was itself an attack on Manningham. The poem denounced Douglas not on the grounds of his monetary greed but his sexual avarice, portraying him on his knees in preparation to examine Toft's body using a distinctly penis-like instrument, 'With usual Shrug and Pearl at tip of Nose'.[32] The innuendo was barely veiled.

The most well-known and widely reproduced satire in this vein was a poem by Alexander Pope, *The Discovery; or The Squire Turn'd Ferret*, which mocks the men involved for exploiting the hoax for prurient motives. The poem introduces the idea that a weak woman can deceive wise men, before describing how a number of men descended on Toft to explore her body. St André 'Resolv'd this *Secret* to explore, / And search it to the *Bottom*'. One doctor (Howard) roughly inserts a chopped up rabbit into her body, and thus begins a trick that is played on all the men who examine her:

> The Surgeon with a Rabbit came,
> But first in Pieces cut it;
> Then slyly thrust it up that same,
> As far as Man could put it.

The poem pulls on the theme of curiosity as a driver for Enlightened scientists who sought to investigate the natural world with new technology. Pope depicts a second man, Samuel Molyneux, initiating a series of examinations by pointing a telescope directly between Toft's open legs:

> The Instrument himself did make
> He rais'd & levell'd right,
> But all about was so opake,
> It cou'd not aid his sight.[33]

Telescopes were a principal tool of astronomers and thus a key device of the scientific revolution. Isaac Newton had developed his reflecting telescope during the 1660s and Molyneux himself was using a precision reflecting telescope of his own devising during the late 1720s. Pope's satire pokes fun at this scientific investigation as he mocks the men's interest in Toft. Molyneux's telescope becomes a phallus, but its flaws leave him impotent. No wonder the poem ends reflecting on the loss of reputation he suffered.

Pope's poem was published in the *British Journal* on Saturday 7 January 1727, and then subsequently in other newspapers. Pope was clearly intrigued by the Toft case. This was perhaps because he himself had been treated by St André following a travelling accident in early September 1726. His family also happened to be involved in the activities of the 'Blacks': those men believed to be attacking the property of Whigs in organized gangs and whose activities may have been associated with the rabbit-breeding hoax. Pope's brother-in-law, Charles Rackett, married to Pope's half-sister Magdalen, was arrested in 1723 for actions in Windsor Forest, though he was not in the end prosecuted. Other members of Pope's family were involved during the actions in the period 1722–23. Pope's interest was not limited to the political or the literary, though. Once the Toft case was underway, Pope wrote to John Caryll on December 5 1726, asking him whether he believed in 'the miracle at Guildford'. Pope reported that, 'All London is now upon this occasion, as it generally is upon all others divided into factions about it.'[34] It seems that on the eve of the exposure of the hoax, Pope himself was deliberating its truth.

Ten days later, he had published what was likely to have been the first of his two poems on the case. This appeared in the *Flying Post* on 19 December 1726. It was addressed to Dr John Arbuthnot and the chief target was Manningham, rather than St André or Molyneux.[35] The second, longer poem, *The Discovery*, was reproduced in various printed forms and bound with other works in collections on the case. It was also copied and circulated in manuscript form. One extant copy of all twenty-two stanzas survives in a neat and steady hand, showing the care that eighteenth-century men and women took in preserving for posterity in their own personal archives items they had heard or read. The final section of this document shows an informed reader who combined a second poem in his or her manuscript. The author explains that this second poem was a critique of Whiston's claim that Toft's rabbit births were a prophecy and this compiler ended his or her manuscript by reproducing the final stanza of that poem.[36]

Other surviving manuscripts remind us that print culture intersected with a dynamic manuscript culture. The beautifully illustrated manuscript 'An account of the rabbets' is a copy of a tract that was being given free with the anodyne necklace (an amulet still promoted to prevent illness) advertised in Mist's Weekly Journal, 10 November 1726. A letter that John Howard wrote on 9 November 1726 is copied out in full in another surviving manuscript.[37] The practices of such active readers were expressive of the wider Enlightenment, an intellectual movement built on a wide circulation of information through both print and a manuscript 'republic of letters', along with a critical engagement with that information in many settings (such as the home and the coffee house) by a diverse 'public'. The case of Mary Toft reminds us that the ostensibly progressive motives to advance human knowledge did nothing to eradicate a curiosity for the salacious.

By the early summer of 1727 the case was over. Yet writers continued to draw upon Toft as a source of humour. In 1736 several publications carried a surely apocryphal tale that Toft was crossing a warren when 'her Foot slipt into a Rabbit-Burrow, and she broke her Leg in a miserable Manner'. Toft's notoriety retained its value as currency for Grub Street news. When St André married Lady Betty Molyneux, Samuel Molyneux's widow, in 1730, The Grub Street Journal added, 'This famous Surgeon shewed his extraordinary skills at the labours of the Godalmin Rabbit-breeder.' The death of John Howard in 1755 was also covered by the press: he was 'well known to the World about thirty Years since in the Affair of Mary Toft, who so grossly imposed upon the Publick in making them believe she was delivered of live Rabbits'.[38]

Public accounts of the case had always been driven partly by distaste, fear, and anger, as well as curiosity and voyeuristic pleasure. Many of the stories about Toft exploited the very real potential for hilarity—who would not laugh at a woman pretending to give birth to rabbits?—but the humour belied a deep-seated ambivalence. The vicious jokes were testament to the extent to which Mary had offended: offended good taste, public morals or sentiments, and medical expertise. They also reveal a broader concern about women and their unruly passions and their tendency to crime and disorder. Being both poor and female, Toft was a focus for the growing fears about crime and disorder at this time. Stories of crime—and of female criminals in particular—were early Georgian bestsellers. More stories were printed about Toft after the case had been exposed than before. The readers—or at least the journalists and editors—were more interested in the progress of Toft's punishment. We might regard the press interest in her punishment as part of a cathartic process to restore order following the chaos of the hoax. Yet this would be an over-simplification. The hilarity and laughter produced by some of the printed treatments of Toft was part of a brutal culture of comedy. Laughter no doubt operated as a cultural safety valve that released energy and anxiety, leaving the calm order of the rational and the polite undisturbed. Yet this denies the very real and material power that can be exercised through humour. Laughter was also a tool for social control. As literary scholar Simon Dickie contends, laughter at the expense of the poor 'worked to maintain social structures rather than subverting them'.[39] There is no doubt that the press coverage of the case served the patriarchal power of the elite. Politics, religion, and comedy met within this dynamic early-eighteenth-century public sphere. And as the dust began to settle on the case, it was to the political ramifications of the case to which commentators turned.

CHAPTER 8

BODY POLITICS

'the beautiful uniform Order'

The English were well acquainted with monsters by the early eighteenth century.[1] They stalked the printed sheets of popular illustrated broadsides and roamed across the pages of lengthy medical tomes. Religious and political pamphlets of the sixteenth and the seventeenth centuries positively teemed with such creatures. They were deployed tactically to reveal the demonstrable evils of the opposition, whether Catholic, Puritan, Royalist, or Parliamentarian. Prodigy and Providence were running threads in these Reformation and post-Reformation debates. Before Mary Toft, most of the well-known cases of monstrous births were restricted to the printed page, though in some very rare cases were grounded in apparently real incidents. In January 1569, Agnes Bowker gave birth to a cat in Market Harborough, possibly to disguise her delivery of a dead illegitimate baby shortly before. The case that developed around Bowker showed the micro-politics of social rank and gender working through the ecclesiastical court. Monstrous bodies were also put on display. Such was the popularity of unusual bodies in seventeenth-century fairs and taverns that John Spencer complained that they undermined the state, giving 'every pitiful Prodigy-monger ... credit enough with the People'. Ballads and broadsides evidence a buoyant culture of human exhibition well into the eighteenth century.[2] The context for these cases was changing. The popular amusement around the monstrous was matched by a growing learned interest that produced numerous collections of unusual natural forms in proto-museum 'cabinets of curiosities'. Monstrosity and deformity were part of the spectacle of early modern science and served to establish boundaries of the normal within the natural world. By the eighteenth century, printed monstrosities were also situated in a distinctly more secular, often medical, context. God's will, as executed through Providence, may have been waning as the explanation for monstrosity, but the human body remained the product of invisible forces. Eighteenth-century medicine was underpinned by a powerful 'moral biology' in which the form of the body was external evidence of internal human character.[3] In these contexts, bodies continued to be read as signs.

Mary Toft's case exemplified many of these changes taking place in early-eighteenth-century society. There was certainly the potential for her case to be read in a religious context. Eighteenth-century society was not secularized and to a very considerable extent religion not only underpinned people's moral and ethical choices but shaped the infrastructure of their cultural world. This was as true for the body and sexuality as it was for other areas of life.[4] As Mary Toft resided in Westminster Bridewell, for example, William Cowper (the Chairman of the Westminster Quarter Sessions who had presided over her case), gave an address on the threat to the Protestant religion from, 'some powers of Europe (to the destitution of the Religion, Laws, Liberties, and Trade of this Nation)'.[5] Nonetheless, Mary Toft's births were not widely seized upon as a portent or providential sign. Instead, her case was taken up by doctors of medicine and examined according to the emerging standards of empirical and experimental science. The case was still subject to symbolic readings yet the concern was not human sin or redemption, but distinctly more worldly issues. The wider significance of Mary Toft's rabbit births was not Providence, but politics.

Politics in early-Georgian England was thoroughly oligarchic. The Protestant Hanoverian succession of George I in 1714 had brought with it the triumph of the Whig Party, the group comprising the aristocratic elite and landed gentry who had rejected the exiled Catholic Stuarts and presented themselves as championing the constitutional monarchy ushered in by the 'Glorious Revolution' of 1688–89. The other loose political party, the Tories, gained support from country gentry and remained in opposition until 1760. Party politics continued despite the ongoing monopoly of the Whigs, though. It was conducted partly through the press, with politicians and ministers influencing newspapers either through editorial control or post-publication prosecution. The press was one element of a wider vigorous sphere of public politics that blurred the boundaries between high and low politics.[6]

Politicians' control over this sphere was limited, though, and politics as practised on the streets and in coffee houses, as well as in newspapers and periodicals independent of Walpole's government, would become a thorn in the side of the regime. Mary Toft's case was situated in this context. For those opposed to George I or his first minister, Robert Walpole, Toft's rabbit births were a sign that things were rotten at the heart of court politics. For those close to power, Toft's body disrupted principles of virtuous order. Monstrous births had always been thought to disrupt God's 'beautiful uniform Order'.[7] But read allegorically in the Enlightening world of early-eighteenth-century England, Toft's rabbit births meant different sorts of disorder: in government, in social relations, and within the female body.

The rabbit woman and the King

From the moment the case broke in the newspapers, Toft's rabbit births were explicitly linked to the royal family. The press was clear that the King, the Prince of Wales, and Whig courtiers were directly involved. Most of the key players around Toft in November 1726 were associated with the German group surrounding the Royal Household. Cyriacus Ahlers was surgeon to the King's German household and Nathanael St André was surgeon and anatomist to the Royal Household. Samuel Molyneux, who also attended Toft, was secretary to the Prince of Wales, the future George II. Remarkably, his wife, Caroline, Princess of Wales, herself discussed the case in correspondence with her close friend and women of the bedchamber, Charlotte Clayton. In one letter, the Princess confessed to being 'transported' to understand that Clayton's friend—most likely a doctor—'is as much an unbeliever as to the rabbits as I am'. Apparently suffering no damage to his reputation following the case, James Douglas was to become physician to Charlotte once she became Queen.[8] The present King, George I, was himself also directly involved in the case. In his pamphlet, St André included copies of the two letters that Mr Howard sent to Mr Henry Davenant, a courtier of George I. Ahlers' pamphlet reported that on returning to London from seeing Toft at Guildford, he had immediately made a report to the King and showed him part of a rabbit taken from Toft. George I was just one remove from Mary Toft herself. Newspapers were clear that when Toft was brought to London, this was 'by Order of his Majesty'.[9] And just days before the hoax was exposed it was reported that Ahlers and St André, both sent 'by the King's Order' and both 'satisfied in the Truth of the wondrous delivery', 'have made their Report to the King and the Prince'. George I has been characterized as someone who 'took reason as his guide', with 'sensible ideas on medical matters'.[10] His widely known association with the case was permissible before the hoax was revealed, exemplifying a perfectly respectable interest in new science. But once the hoax was revealed, the risk of humiliation was considerable.

Mary Toft's move from Guildford to Leicester-Fields in late November 1726 had not only brought the affair to the very doorstep of the residence of the Prince and Princess of Wales at the north of the square, but also to the borough of Westminster, the heart of the nation's politics.[11] It is perhaps not surprising that her case was deployed in the party-political print battles that characterized the early years of Robert Walpole's government and appeared in several satires on George I's government. The hoax echoed in important ways the recent case of Peter 'the Wild Boy', the teenage boy found in Hanover having apparently grown up without human society but amongst wolves. Peter was another curiosity who, like Toft, attracted the interest of the English royal court, where he was installed in the spring of 1726. The links between Peter—the boy who was barely human—and Mary Toft were apparent for contemporaries. Joseph Mitchell's 1729 poem to Peter declared him 'the World's last Prodigy!', ruminating on whether Nature had slept during the conception and birth of this remarkable figure. Mitchell reflected on the many different readings that had been given of Peter's form: Was he a new species? Born of human and beast? Or conceived naturally but of unnatural parents who had abandoned him to the wolves? The situation was jumped on by political satirists, who deployed Peter in their attacks on the court and the aristocracy. The court was corrupt whilst Peter's feral past represented an unadulterated state of nature.[12]

Mitchell's work is a satirical address to a benevolent and smiling monarch, 'the rightful Wearer of *Britannia's Crown*' at whose feet lay the responsibility for the odd curiosity of Toft. The mock-heroic poem united the real persons of Peter and Mary with the fictional Lemuel Gulliver, the eponymous narrator of Jonathan Swift's novel, which had been published just as the Toft case was breaking in October 1726. Mitchell suggests that one of the reasons Peter had attracted such speculation was because he prefigured Gulliver and Toft. In making this link the poem connected them in a wider culture of anti-government satire. Swift, the Irish Tory propogandist, had been targeting Walpole directly and tensions were revived with new vitriol following a meeting between the men in April 1726. Swift wrote soon after that he now opposed Walpole, who was mercilessly identified as Flimnap, the credulous Treasurer of Lilliput in *Gulliver's Travels*. The novel was read as a political satire on Walpole's regime as soon as it appeared. Direct attacks on the government also drew directly on the Toft hoax. The anti-Walpole newspaper with the broadest readership, *Mist's Weekly Journal*, used the case to make the pointed claim that rabbits would be better governors than the present ministers.[13] Both retrospectively and at the time, Mary Toft's story was thus seamlessly integrated into a patchwork of political satires that targeted both the King and his First Minister.

Allegorical politics

A demystification of the public sphere or a disenchantment of print culture was well in train by the time of the Toft case. Most earlier cases of monstrous births and prodigies in which Providence interacted with politics in direct ways—a monstrous birth in the English Civil Wars, for example—demonstrated God's unhappiness with one or other of the warring factions in the conflict. Later accounts simply lacked that element. The reports of the 'Northumberland Monster' of 1674, for example—a half-horse/half-man delivered by one Jane Paterson—left no room for such a reading.[14] Wonder had been discredited since the second half of the sixteenth century. By the early eighteenth century, providential readings of such events were arguably associated with the lower class and women and defined as superstitious.[15] In some accounts, the accusation of ignorant superstition was used explicitly by those wishing to score political points. In his monthly round-up of political news in *The Political State of Great Britain* for December 1726, Abel Boyer ironically remarked on the Toft case, 'But what a wonder Use PRIEST-CRAFT might have made of this Imposture in a POPISH IGNORANT COUNTRY!' Born in France, Boyer was a committed Protestant who, following a falling out with Jonathan Swift over access to the government's press, had become a resolute Whig supporter.[16] Superstition was a way to isolate one's political opponents. But while some tales of monstrous births tended to situate them off the British shores, connecting such superstitions to the irrationality and primitivism of other cultures, the comparison was not always Protestant reason versus Catholic superstition. The anti-Walpole writer in *Mist's Weekly Journal* gave several column inches to belief in the maternal imagination across Europe, his crowning point being, 'that Stories of this Kind have often obtain'd Belief in other Countries, as well as ours, especially in *Germany*, where the People are, for the most Part, the dullest upon Earth, as well as the most credulous of Witch-craft, and all Kind of Prodigies'.[17] Superstition did not follow confessional lines for this author, who was taking an obvious swipe at the Hanoverian King, George I.

The language used by writers continued to apply a longstanding lexicon of prodigy, nonetheless. This was certainly the case in private letters. Within weeks of the case breaking in the newspapers, the Earl of Peterborough wrote to Jonathan Swift, situating the monstrous births of Toft within a broader state of 'confusion': '[s]trange distempers rage in the nation', he claimed.[18] Letters from within the court traded in the same discourse. Henrietta Howard, the mistress of the Prince of Wales,

Fig. 8.1 William Hogarth, *The Punishment of Lemuel Gulliver* (1726)

woman of the bedchamber to Charlotte, Princess of Wales and resident with the Prince and Princess in Leicester House since their expulsion from St James's Palace in 1717, wrote to Jonathan Swift about the case. She also referred to characters in his *Gulliver's Travels*. She explained that the appearance of 'four perfect black rabbits' gave hope that perhaps 'in time, our female yahoos will produce a race of Houyhnmynms'. Swift responded that the rabbits 'seem to threaten some dark Court Intrigue, and perhaps some change in the Administration'.[19] For these writers close to the centre of power, allegorical politics was the *modus operandi* of discussing the King, the royal family, and political party. Toft's rabbits meant trouble in the nation.

The same dynamics were at work in print. A good illustration of this is the wider context of William Hogarth's first engraving of the case, *Cunicularri*, issued on 24 December. Importantly, Hogarth advertised *Cunicularri* as one of a pair with another engraving, *The Punishment of Lemuel Gulliver*, issuing them just a day apart. *The Punishment of Lemuel Gulliver* illustrated a scene from Swift's novel. Hogarth's depiction of Gulliver being cruelly exploited by a ruthless elite invading his body by administering a clyster worked as a comment on Walpole's circle of ministers. *Cunicularri* mirrored this scene, showing Toft also as a victim of men who invaded her body. The image certainly functioned as a satire about the medical doctors and religious enthusiasm, but the concrete links between some of those doctors and the court, along with the evident parallel with the more overtly political satire of *The Punishment*, opened up this depiction of Toft to a determinedly political interpretation.[20]

Moreover, there were direct links between William Hogarth and critics of Walpole. Hogarth had particularly close ties to Nicholas Amhurst, the editor of the second opposition journal during these early years of the Walpole regime, the Tory-sympathizing *The Craftsman*. The first issue of *The Craftsman* was published on 5 December 1726, just two days after the advertisement for *The Punishment of Lemuel Gulliver*.[21] And the content of *The Craftsman* chimed closely with Hogarth's own work: both used irony, innuendo, and allegory in accounts of medicine and religion, amongst other things, to attack the current political regime. Both Hogarth and Amhurst drew directly upon the Toft case in their shared lexicon of political satire. Nicholas Amhurst wrote about the Toft case on more than one occasion. Following Toft's release from the Westminster house of correction in April 1727, Amhurst's editorial insisted that the longstanding trust that people placed in portents in the public sphere had surely been confirmed by a series of recent amazing cases, of which Mary Toft's was one. Caleb D'Anvers, Amhurst's alter ego in *The Craftsman*, refused to join 'the common cry' that denounced Toft as a fraud, and instead ironically sided with 'men of the greatest Experience, most profound Judgment and unquestionable Integrity' who believed the hoax; her release without prosecution for fraud, he argued, was testament of the truth of the case. Though D'Anvers was sure that 'such an *anomalous Production* can be supposed to prognosticate or point out to us', he deferred interpretation until a later time. Yet he insisted on the value of reading an 'Analogy or Resemblance between two or more extraordinary Events', between 'the *symbol* or Thing *signifying*' and 'the Thing *signified*'. The thing signified for D'Anvers was party and court politics. It was explicitly '*Policy*' 'to which our late *Prodigies* and *Portents* bear so near a Relation'.[22] D'Anvers' assertion of the truth of the Toft case as an instance of monstrous birth allowed Amhurst to discredit Whig court politics as conducted by misguided men unworthy of public trust.

The Craftsman represented a sea change in the relationship between the Walpole administration and the press, being both explicitly critical of the government and completely out of its formal control. In fact, the content of *The Craftsman* led Walpole to adopt a harsher policy towards the papers. It may have also affected the government's attitude to Toft. In the pages of *The Craftsman*, the Toft case served as a vehicle for the paper's political attacks. If the case itself was eradicated, then perhaps these targeted attacks might be stopped. By the same token, perhaps Hogarth's engraving was not just a response to the hoax but itself served to condition responses to Toft and affect her subsequent treatment. The engraving demonstrated how the case might be manipulated and deployed by those critical of the Whig oligarchy. English governments had been able to exercise limited control over the depiction and use of monstrous births in popular print during the sixteenth and seventeenth centuries through pre-publication licensing. Following the lapse of pre-publication licensing in 1695, though, governments uneasy about the potentially destabilizing public discourse around monstrous births were less able to control the production of printed depictions. Their strategy was instead to review printed materials closely for material that might warrant some kind of prosecution, such as libel. It was in fact Nicholas Paxton—the assistant to the Treasury Solicitor who had accompanied Thomas Clarges in his interrogation of Mary Toft—who not only supervised the newspapers under ministerial control but had been employed by Walpole since 1722 to scan the newspapers for material that the regime might wish to pursue, something he himself would then initiate.[23] It is not too far-fetched to imagine Paxton's outrage at the political uses to which Mary Toft's case was put, and his determination to tackle this by using legal weapons to strike at the very heart of the case: Mary Toft herself.

By 1732, enough time had passed for Amhurst to offer a clearer statement about the precise political significance of the Toft case. On 20 May 1732, he used the case to underscore a 'figurative' interpretation of such events. His main interest was a report of a case of vampires in Hungary. A young woman presents this story to a doctor, who is incredulous. She reminds him that not so long again he had tried to make people believe that the rabbit-woman was a fact. The narrator D'Anvers focuses on the central figure of the vampire as a bloodsucker of the state: 'a *ravenous Minister*', 'a *Leech*, or a *Blood sucker*, who preys upon human Gore, and fattens Himself upon the Vitals of his Country'. His targets were ministers who drain the public through taxes, but also private persons such as usurers and stockjobbers. He explicitly addresses the reader to follow a similar allegorical interpretation of the rabbit hoax: 'I think I have said enough to convince you that We are not to understand this Account according to the *Letter*; in which Sense it appears *ridiculous* and *impossible*'; rather, 'in the *other figurative Sense*, which I have put upon it, nothing can be more rational, obvious and intelligible'.[24]

This was not how everyone saw the case. Even critics of Caleb D'Anvers' interpretation nevertheless adopted the same allegorical method. An article in the *Daily Courant* of 27 May 1732 held up D'Anvers' '*penetrating Spectacles*' as the butt of the joke: 'nothing will go down with him but *such wonderful and unnatural Whimsies as Vampyres and Rabbit Women Jugglers*'. D'Anvers' attempts to produce political critique out of the material generated by such curious cases was itself denounced as a form of monstrous birth: he is 'a Male-Monster, [who] can infinitely exceed the *Godalmin* Rabbit Woman in bringing different Species from the same Stock'. Indeed, 'he himself is metamorphos'd into a great

Prodigy than all of Them'. The author imagines another coupling, this time D'Anvers making a match with Mary Toft and from which they both brought forth monsters, '*Caleb*'s proceed from his *Head*, and Madam's from her *Tail*'.[25] Of course, Amhurst no more believed that Mary Toft was breeding rabbits than he did that Walpole was a worthy recipient of his support. But both he and his critics engaged allegory as a tool of witty political discourse.

Allegorical readings that rested on an implicit assumption that the thing seen signified something hidden continued to thrive. This commitment to the belief that things unseen and rationally inexplicable both existed and possessed a social or cultural force might be seen as the persistence of prodigy. The meaning of prodigy had changed from previous centuries, though, and many kinds of phenomena—including natural weather events and demonic action—were now the occasion for political readings in the early eighteenth century.[26] In the same way, for people at the time, Toft's case did or should herald political change. Allegorical and portentous readings of the case were rooted not in a supernatural or a spiritual context but instead in a determinedly earthly world of politics.

Rustic beliefs, Palladian villas, and body politics

The uprooting of beliefs in the supernatural power of portents had marked out boundaries between those who continued to believe and those who did not. Wonders served to demarcate between the informed and educated on the one hand, and those who persisted in holding vulgar beliefs on the other.[27] Beliefs in witchcraft were characterized as rustic, standing in contrast to polite and reasoned scepticism. The category of the vulgar was therefore aesthetic as much as intellectual. It consisted of the unrefined elements that were opposed to the styles associated with the elite. The ruling Whig landowners built their own personal style and public identity, in contrast to what they saw as the chaotic and reprehensible living of the disorderly poor. For these men, order was the anchor of social stability and their own political power. And order was enacted in polite and rational living as well as through the enforcement of laws. Polite manners and learning were thought to set apart the governors—both national politicians and local office-holders—from the governed.[28] Ordered politeness was also enacted in the material world and was most clearly visible in the style of architecture. In the early eighteenth century, the virtues of order, reason, and politeness were embodied in classical architecture. During the 1720s, men at the very apex of the elite eradicated earlier and messier styles from their country seats with the adoption of neo-Palladianism as the dominant style for large houses. Neo-Palladianism was an aesthetics of power, built upon Palladio's five orders of architecture which embodied principles of good order. Elite houses built in this style served as both an expression of a gentleman's status and a tool in its maintenance. The elite values of property and propriety were cemented in architecture.[29] Houses were also utopian. Gentlemen shored up their place in society and articulated how they wished that society to be.

Lord Burlington's singular neo-Palladian house at Chiswick is exemplary of this 1720s style. Burlington's political allegiances are manifest in some of the details, such as the oak leaf festoons which allude to the exiled Stuart king and the roses and thistles that represent the Jacobite cause. Yet regardless of the particular political persuasion of its owner,

Fig. 8.2 Clandon House from John Preston Neale's *Views of the Seats of Noblemen and Gentlemen in England, Wales, Scotland, and Ireland* (London: Sherwood, Jones & Co. 1824) vol. 3, p. 145

all the design elements of the house were united in their expression of good government. 'House and garden were framed as a miniature city state.'[30] And this ideal state left no room for disorder. It is revealing that neo-Palladian style was also adopted by some of the principal gentlemen players in the Toft case. The second Duke of Richmond, present when Mary Toft gave her first statement, happened to be a friend of Burlington who integrated several neo-Palladian elements at his Surrey house, Goodwood. Richmond secured Colen Campbell, author of the guide to neo-Palladian architecture *Vitruvius Britannicus* (1715–25) and architect to the Prince of Wales, to survey the existing house and produce a new design during 1724 and 1725. The house was not built, no doubt because of the cost Richmond would have incurred, though he later secured Burlington to completely rebuild Richmond House in Whitehall.[31]

Nearby in Surrey, Baron Thomas Onslow's property—Clandon House—was another Palladian house built during the 1720s. A full-length painting of Onslow as a middle-aged man alludes to the classical culture of Palladianism, picturing him in long robes in what could be—were it not for the distinctively English trees in the background—a Continental loggia. Using the fortune of his wife, Elizabeth Knight, Onslow rebuilt Clandon as one of the largest and most impressive Palladian houses in England at that time, featuring a remarkable white marble entrance hall. It was perhaps through this hall that Edward Costen, Mary Costen, Elizabeth Mason, Mary Peytoe, Richard Stedman, and John Sweetapple entered the house when they arrived to give their witness statements to Onslow, as he led the local investigation into the Toft case.[32] Large mansions were staffed by armies of servants and visited by many workmen and women who brought provisions and provided services to the house and its inhabitants. Nonetheless, the questioning of these Godalming and Guildford residents—including a framework-knitter, a currier, a weaver and a nurse—in this new Palladian mansion must have been an uncanny encounter for all concerned.

The highly ordered style of neo-Palladianism became the principal new style for political elites during the 1720s, at the point that they were wrought by anxieties about the lower ranks. Pristine in their symmetry, regularity, and refinement, Palladian buildings stood in stark contrast to unsettling visions of unrest and social disorder. They were part of a growing emphasis on order that affected not only buildings and society, but also the human body. In fact, Mary Toft's case sits on the threshold of what some historians regard as a major watershed in 'body politics'. In this society, the same principles of order were thought to shape how both societies and bodies were supposed to work. Since the Renaissance, an essentially Galenic humoral physiology understood the body as governed by the balance of flowing humours; it was a model that prioritized proportion and balance in the humours and the qualities they produced in the body. Real connections were envisaged between the macrocosm of the world, the environment, the body politic and the microcosm of the human body. It was in this context that monstrous births and other phenomena could be seen as portents, because what happened in the body was connected to wider society. By the late eighteenth century, an understanding of bodies was increasingly shaped by an emphasis on solid anatomy, as well as a separation between the body and its environment. The link between the human body and the political body was weakened, and this meant that the body was less invested with meanings of directly allegorical public significance.[33]

It was precisely in this context of a growing cultural emphasis on the ordered and bounded body that Mary Toft's body remained acutely political. In contrast to a body that was seen as closed and disciplined, Toft's body was unstable, unpredictable, and grotesque, a type of body increasingly associated with communal popular culture. It was open to the environment and to internal bodily impulses, it was disordered and chaotic, and was becoming a focus for resistance to official elite culture by the lower orders.[34] Viewing her in the tradition of the grotesque chimes with the possibility that the rabbit hoax was a political protest, drawing on the traditions of inversion and the symbolic power of the apparently chaotic and undisciplined poor body. By the same token, if Mary Toft's body could be controlled, then order might be restored. Whether breeding rabbits, allegorical political critique, or local protest, Mary Toft's body was antithetical to an emerging culture of solidity and order. In this context, her rabbit births expressed a persistent and disruptive presence.

Disenchantment

Mary Toft's hoax existed at the confluence of a number of different currents in the 'disenchantment' of the early modern world.

Disenchantment refers to a decline in the belief in supernatural forces at work in the natural world and the relegation of such beliefs to the category of the superstitious. This process acquired greater force at the time of the hoax because of a particular commitment amongst the Whig elite to radical deism, with its attendant rationalist materialism and a retreat from an emphasis on the role of the spirit in the world. This, combined with natural philosophy, encouraged a belief in the supernatural to fall out of favour amongst those in power. Notably, belief in the ability of witches to harness supernatural powers lost their grip amongst the educated. Such beliefs were presented as the antithesis of the urbane and polite gentleman and increasingly associated with the rustic, the uneducated, and the marginal. In Francis Hutchinson's attack on witchcraft beliefs in *An Historical Essay Concerning Witchcraft* (1718), for example, the touchstones of right thinking were civility, politeness, authority, and order. In contrast, religious non-conformity and belief in the supernatural were lumped together as disorderly.[35]

Witchcraft beliefs did not simply die out, though, but instead changed form. The supernatural retained a cultural force but within the prosaic and material world. Perhaps the best example of this appeared during the year of the Toft case: Daniel Defoe's *The Political History of the Devil*, published in 1726. Defoe presents the Devil as himself enlightened and improved: 'as the World is improv'd every Day', he explained, 'he has bestirr'd himself too, in order to an increase of Knowledge'. Embarking on 'Projects and Inventions' to acquire 'Discoveries and Experiments', he has eradicated the need for witches because he has made men '*Devils* themselves' in the form of Whig politicians. In his next work, *A System of Magic* (1727), Defoe even described the Devil as the 'Head Engineer' of the 'Party Leaders and Politick Scheme-Makers'.[36] Accusations of witchcraft had always followed the contours of religious or political conflict, but by the early eighteenth century such claims were thoroughly entwined with the machinations of party politics, at least for the elite. The last trial for witchcraft heard on the assize home circuit was the 1701 case of Sarah Moredike, accused of bewitching Richard Hathaway. The case was used by members of the beleaguered Whig party to play to popular fears of witches. Similar processes were at work in the trial of Jane Wenham at Hertford in 1712, the last woman in England to be convicted of witchcraft. By this time, though, it was Tory and High Church Anglicans who were using the case to bolster their own support in the face of the recent ascent of the Whigs. The case of Wenham—like that of Toft—was part of a wider story of an early Enlightenment culture in which change was propelled by specific local, familial, and personal issues. Witchcraft beliefs still retained a foothold amongst some of the elite and in learned print; higher standards of proof were demanded, but still in 1712 local clergy and magistrates pursued the case out of a politicized adherence to witchcraft beliefs.[37] Witchcraft beliefs still held force in the public sphere, but instead of being the consequence of supernatural forces they operated within a matrix of prosaic and material power. Historian Ian Bostridge finds that whereas witchcraft had once been a real threat of evil against which everyone could unite, witchcraft became a marker of ideological difference.[38]

The culmination of these changes was an Act of 1736 that finally made a belief in the supernatural a criminal act, defining the crime of witchcraft as one of imposture with the alleged use of spirits. The historian Owen Davies situates the 1736 Witchcraft Act in the context of the Whig protection of property partly through the extension of the capital punishment in the Waltham Act of 1723. With their rejection of the power of the Devil, the Whig governing elite turned to the real threat to their property: the poor. Yet the law did not necessarily reflect the quotidian beliefs of the population. Amongst what Davies identifies as the 'witch-believing majority', an attachment to witchcraft beliefs and thus to the notion of a supernatural evil continued long after the 1736 Act.[39] Whig thinking on the question of witchcraft was way ahead of the wider population, including elite office-holders who worked outside of Parliament. The private discourse of uneven and contested views was quite distinct from the linear picture derived from a public discourse framed by scepticism. Of course, private discourse is by definition difficult for historians to unearth. But though the Act of 1736 may have eradicated witchcraft as a crime of superstition, accusations of witchcraft as a measure of wider beliefs suggest that decline in witchcraft belief was actually most pronounced from the late 1880s.[40]

The sustained religious interest in witchcraft in some quarters, notably amongst Quakers and Methodists, was one context for the links drawn between Toft, witchcraft, and Methodist enthusiasm in some of the satires on the case. Yet there was, in fact, very little discussion at the time that suggested that the case was driven by supernatural forces. A rare reference to Toft as a 'Witch' in the 1730s revealed that her abilities to 'enchant' were actually false and situated her in the context of stories of relatively innocuous old women living in cottages in the woods.[41] If not witchcraft or sorcery, other explanations were required. St André thought the case was within the bounds of the preternatural: an extraordinary occurrence but within the bounds of the human world and without the hand of the divine. Since at least the seventeenth century, such phenomena were no longer viewed as religious portents, though they were still of scientific interest and could operate as signs.[42] More commonly, commentators explored the Toft case as an opportunity to test the idea of a monstrous birth resulting from the maternal imagination; this was about the limits of the scientifically possible and the workings of the natural world. Responses to the case expressed the spread of science against only a partial subscription to the notion of supernatural forces. This was a crucial period in the establishment of medical science, as the field of medicine itself slowly became subject to scientific practices of knowledge that had already taken hold in the case of physics and mathematics. Mary Toft's hoax took shape in an early-eighteenth-century public sphere of rational debate and the pursuit of knowledge in the spirit of the Enlightenment, driven in particular by the new sciences.

Changes in medical knowledge were an important element of disenchantment. When it became irrefutably clear that Mary Toft was not herself breeding rabbits, a very public shaming of several of the doctors ensued. The rabbit births were evidently not the first observed evidence of a monstrous birth, but instead the result of a very man-made hoax. It is perhaps a surprise, then, that the revelation of the pretence did not bring an immediate end to the theory of the maternal imagination. In fact, the very opposite happened. The Toft case triggered a virulent pamphlet battle which served to circulate the idea of the maternal imagination to a much wider audience than before. In 1727, the French physician James Blondel published his pamphlet, *The Strength of Imagination in Pregnant Women Examin'd*. It was, he later explained, published 'upon the Occasion of the Cheat of *Godalming*'.[43] But it was seen by Daniel Turner to be a denunciation of his recent work on skin diseases, the third edition of which had been published in 1726 just prior to the Toft hoax. Turner had discussed the 'almost incredible Power of Imagination, most especially in pregnant Women', and particularly how marks were 'imprest upon the Skin of the *Foetus*, by the Force of the Mother's Fancy'. He had gone much further to reinforce his claim, giving examples of all manner of monstrous births either reproduced from other texts, passed on through hearsay, or simply reported without a source: a woman whose mother had played with a pet ape when she was pregnant, and who resembled such an animal; the woman who was frightened when a lizard jumped onto her bosom and whose child was born with a fleshy lump on its chest; and the woman who held a frog, only to be delivered of a child who looked like a frog.[44]

In response, Blondel denied that skin marks on infants were caused by mothers' imaginations, attempting to consider the wider question of the mother's imagination 'in a regular and Methodical way'. He denounced wholeheartedly the idea of the maternal imagination creating any kind of literal impression on the unborn child as 'a vulgar Error'. Turner then produced a further edition of his book in 1729, as well as a direct attack on Blondel and a defence of Turner's own claims about infant marks, restating his position that the mother's imagination could cause a physical effect on the unborn child. Blondel felt compelled to respond with an expanded version of his own book, in which he reminded readers of the Toft case and bemoaned the fact that still these ideas 'are now generally received'. As in his earlier edition, he vigorously denied the specific claim that 'the strong Attention of the Mother's Mind to a *determined* Object can cause a *determinate*, or a *specifick* Impression upon the Body of the Child, without any Force, or Violence from abroad'.[45] His careful use of evidence showed that the mechanics of the theory could not be sustained: what we know about conception and gestation demonstrates that the foetus is to a large extent an independent body over which the mother's imagination has no influence, and this is confirmed when we acknowledge that the vast majority of infants are born without deformities even though many of their mothers will have experienced frightening or angry thoughts during pregnancy. In this respect, mind and body were distinct. Blondel's carefully argued work did represent a shift in the status of the long-standing discourse of the maternal imagination. The notion that thoughts in women's minds could be directly imprinted on the unborn child was exposed to wider scrutiny within both popular and elite circles. The Toft case had triggered a very public discussion of the theory of the maternal imagination and ultimately what followed was a transformation of what was widely regarded legitimate scientific medical knowledge.

The contours of this account certainly fit neatly with what we might expect about medical knowledge inexorably improving over time. But the detailed picture is more complex. Neither the Toft case nor Blondel's first pamphlet dislodged the theory of the material imagination. As Blondel himself repeatedly reminds us, still in 1729 'Most People' believed in the theory of the maternal imagination; it was, he reported, 'the Current Opinion'. In fact, his work acknowledged that the imagination—meaning the thoughts women had in response to external objects—related to the foetus in six ways: if pregnant women have a strong desire that is either gratified or not; if they experience sudden surprise; if they see something ugly or frightful; if they study something that delights their imagination; if they experience considerable fear; and if their passions—of anger, grief, or joy—are excessive. Blondel was keen to exculpate women from blame, but he was equally clear that women's desires and passions could have an accidental impact on their unborn child. Though Blondel's views were in the ascendant, Turner's book was not entirely discredited by Blondel's pamphlet and continued to be published in several editions later in the eighteenth century. The idea that women could affect their unborn child through their imaginative faculties remained alive in both popular and elite works in the century that followed, and it remained widely accepted for many decades.[46] Medical opinion bifurcated and then transformed, but lay attitudes remained receptive to the idea that women's emotional states would directly impact on the health of their children.

If the case set off a short-lived wave of pamphlets about the possibility of genuine monstrous births, some writers launched a mighty defence of reason, facts, and truth. Toft was denounced as casting 'an almost irreparable Disgrace upon natural Knowledge' by blinding sober and judicious men to the truth, leading them to fall prey to their own 'Imaginations of the Credulous'.[47] The discourse of the 'monstrous' was discredited as a way to explain the deformed or strange. Such cases did persist in attracting attention, though they were framed—perhaps as a foil for voyeurism—with medical authority. Along with others, a boy and girl sharing one body, three arms and three legs, were displayed at the Rummer tavern on Fleet Street in 1736, though they had supposedly been legitimized by Sir Hans Sloane and several other physicians 'to be the greatest curiosity that ever was seen'.[48] The forward march of medical knowledge had certainly been drawn along by Mary Toft's hoax.

Fig. 8.3 William Hogarth, *Credulity, Superstition, and Fanaticism. A Medley* (1762) [Wellcome Collection

Ultimately, the case was widely considered to have proved that the theory that the maternal imagination could work directly on the foetus to produce a monstrous birth was false. The road to this was neither smooth nor direct, though, and the question of precisely how a pregnant woman's mind might affect her unborn child remained unresolved.

Beliefs about the natural world and its possibilities are rarely tethered directly to scientific 'fact'; older 'irrational' ideas are always accommodated within newer rational bodies of knowledge. Years after the Toft case, Voltaire himself, the great Enlightenment philosopher, claimed in the *Encyclopédie* that the maternal imagination could transform the contents of the uterus. The discourse of the maternal imagination continued to proliferate, serving as a trope through which people could debate the relationship between body and mind.[49] Continuing disquiet about the potential transformative effects of the imagination were connected to unease about a form of religious fervour that was taking hold in eighteenth-century Britain: 'Enthusiasm' championed an emotional and embodied worship of God, but critics viewed it as an unthinking and over-zealous brand of Protestantism. For critics, both Enthusiasm and the maternal imagination allowed an embodied and feverish imagination to defy reason. This was why William Hogarth brought them together in his second depiction of Toft, *Credulity, Superstition, and Fanaticism* (1762). This engraving was set in a Methodist chapel and displayed a collection of well-known wonders and impostures, undermining Methodism by association. The congregation has been transported to the giddy heights of lust, ecstasy, fits, and madness by the sermon of the crazed preacher. In the left foreground of the image, Toft is slumped on the floor, resting against the pews which are teeming with a rowdy crowd of worshippers, most of their faces frozen in contorted groans. Her body is awkwardly braced, both arms held apart from her body with fists tightly clenched; her legs are raised and held open, balancing on her heels. Her mouth is wide open, her teeth are exposed, her eyes are rolled back and her expression fixed in a grimace. This face is grotesque, articulating her own pain but also the emotional turmoil engendered by the enthusiastic gullibility satirized by the print. She embodies the disorder of the entire scene. As rabbits spill from between her legs, Toft also reinforces the sexual connotations of the engraving, evident from the swooning couple directly beneath the pulpit, where the man inserts a large stay busk into the front of woman's bodice, while the thermometer to the right is set to measure 'LUST'.

In an earlier version of this engraving, *Enthusiasm Delineated* (1760), Hogarth positioned the same prostrate figure swooning in the lusty heat

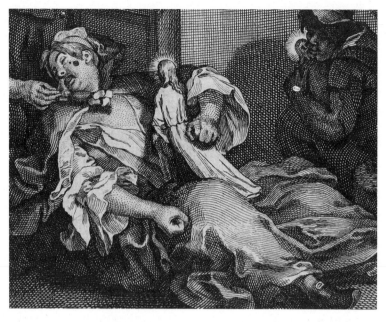

Fig. 8.4 Detail from William Hogarth, *Enthusiasm Delineated* (1760–62) [British Museum: 1858,0417.582]

but with the figure of Christ rising from between her legs. The overriding message of these images is the value of scepticism. And Hogarth drew on a well-established critique of enthusiasm, superstition, and imagination, all long considered threats to order in the way they seduced people to act in potentially subversive unthinking and irrational ways. But at the same time this re-invoking of Toft also served to muddy the Enlightened waters, stirring up memories of the miraculous and the superstitious that clouded over rationality and scepticism.[50]

Renewed interest in the person of Mary Toft may have been sparked by Hogarth's decision to return to the subject in 1760. By 1769, Toft's image was displayed in an exhibition alongside a collection of mostly caricatures and other notorious hoaxes.[51] Newspapers articles about Toft also continued to appear. In 1769, a letter-writer who signed himself 'The Englishman' wrote scathingly of the '[s]uperstitious and weak minds' that invented meaning out of remarkable events. Just as Whiston had done with his prophetic reading of 'the vile story of the *Rabbet Woman*', so people were now doing with the recent comet, he complained. It was not mistaken to use such events to reflect on our lives—this was 'laudable and pious'—but it was wrong to claim that such events happened for any divine purpose. He feared that the comet would take on 'the merit of the prediction and change', were there to be 'a material alteration in politics'. Writers understood that the interpretation of such cases was directly linked to current affairs and government. One claimed that a period of domestic peace would allow 'a Rabbit-Woman, or a Fortuneteiler [*sic*], a Quack, or a Bottle Conjurer' to engross the public. In 1777, another listed 'the Bottle Conjurer, Rabbit Woman, Cock-lane Ghost' as events cooked up by the government to distract the population from their mistakes. There is no doubt that Toft soon came to occupy a place in the pantheon of great eighteenth-century imposters. She was commonly listed alongside the story of the bottle conjuror (the magician who, in 1749, sold tickets to a London performance in which he vowed he would jump into a wine bottle), Elizabeth Canning (a servant who claimed to have been kidnapped in 1753 but was ultimately convicted of perjury), and the Cock-Lane ghost (a fraud that was successfully prosecuted in 1762). People rarely gave these events a specifically religious interpretation, but they were still miraculous to some.[52] In the realm of allegorical politics the emphasis may have been on earthly affairs, but the repeated return to Toft's rabbits on the occasion of these more recent hoaxes shows a thread of persistence in superstition and beliefs in the supernatural, even if the elite had retreated from such things.

In the final analysis, Mary Toft's rabbit births of 1726 did not sound the death knell to beliefs in the power of the maternal imagination, the force of superstition, or other unseen forces. Narratives are seductive, and a story of the spread of medical knowledge and the retreat of superstition is compelling. Yet an account of the Enlightenment that privileges the sort of rational knowledge created by the authoritative few fails to fully account for eighteenth-century culture. The unevenness

in the persistence of beliefs, and thus the existence of fierce denunci-
ations of Toft as a fraud alongside portentous readings of the case,
shows the social nature of knowledge: what was true and what could
be true depended on who was speaking. Formal or 'expert' knowledge
about the natural world—and the ways in which knowledge was
made—was political; it was made from the standpoint of a particular
position, invariably men with property or formal philosophical education. For such men, legitimate beliefs in the superstitious and the
wondrous were banished not by reason, science, or secularization, but
instead by the man-made distinction between genteel and vulgar knowledge and the social practice of excising the latter from their learned
world.[53] Our very categories of 'rational knowledge' and 'superstition'
are themselves labels created to prioritize certain forms of knowing
over others. Superstition was lifted out of elite knowledge and relegated
to a different (for some a socially lower form) of explaining the natural
world.

The case of Mary Toft exposes the faltering steps being taken away
from a discredited supernatural reading of the natural world and
towards an Enlightened materialist application of reason to the creation
of knowledge. This was evident in the fields of both medicine and
religion. Unseen forces were still at work, though. The meaning of the
rabbit births was not self-evident but had to be teased out; this uncer-
tainly itself was potentially chaotic. The allegorical force of the case
therefore lay in its pliability. In the end, though, the spectacle of Mary
Toft triggered anxieties about social disruption as much as curiosity
about the monstrous. Toft's body was the very antithesis of the well-
ordered. Above all, it was politics that were implicated in coverage of
the case. The prosaic concerns of a disaffected and disenfranchised poor
and the endeavours of their anxious governors patterned the case. The
threat was no longer evil spirits. Instead, it was the poor—represented
by Mary Toft, her family and community—who were the real and
tangible threats to the social order. Yet despite the defining effect that
scepticism had on the public sphere, there continued a fascination with
allegorical politics. That lexicon of public debate—in which the observable natural world signalled forces of power at work behind the
scenes—allowed for the possibility that the world could not be wholly
explained by natural laws. The continuing allegorical readings of the

case for hidden meaning, the enduring attachment to witchcraft beliefs and the supernatural amongst those outside the Whig elite, and the reactivation of debates about superstition and hoaxes late in the eighteenth century, show that Toft's case sustained tenacious ideas about the power of things unseen and immaterial.

CHAPTER 9

AFTERLIFE

'The Imposteress Rabbett Breeder'

For all the grim details of her experiences of the rabbit births in the autumn of 1726 and her four-month imprisonment in the Westminster Bridewell, Mary Toft survived her ordeal. She was released because the rabbit-birth hoax was not deemed to have broken any law—it was simply not a crime. Yet her reputation as a hoaxer stuck fast and an interest in her reproductive life endured. Another pregnancy—and the expectation of prurient inquiry into this—was reported in the newspapers in August 1727, just four months after her release from the Westminster Bridewell: 'the Rabbet-Woman, is breeding again; which may be the Subject of curious Speculation to those ingenious Gentlemen who went deep into her former Affair'. Elizabeth was subsequently born in February 1728 and the entry in the registers of Godalming's parish church reveals the notoriety that her mother was fast acquiring: 'Elizabeth Daughter of Joshua Toft and Mary his wife being ye first child after her pretending Rabett breeding'. Joshua and Mary's fourth and final child, John, was born in October 1729, but died within a month.[1] This child was not mentioned in newspapers, though a rather prurient curiosity for Mary Toft continued. The Duke of Richmond reportedly wheeled Toft out as an exhibit for his fellow diners at his Godalming residence some years later.[2] By the time of her death in 1763, her reputation was assured. The remarkable entry for her burial in the parish register of St. Peter's Church at Godalming memorialized her involvement in the extraordinary hoax: 'January 13 Mary Toft (Widow) the Imposteress Rabbett Breeder'.

Toft's death was also reported in several newspapers, where she was immortalized 'for an imposition of breeding rabbits'.[3] Since her death, the case has been told afresh by each new generation. Victorians sought out the modern medical knowledge of some of the doctors. In contrast, mid-twentieth-century pioneers in medical history treated the same doctors as ignorant and ill-informed, implicitly shoring up the reputation of contemporary, modern, twentieth-century medical professionals as more knowledgeable. More recent academic interpretations have reflected broader trends in scholarship, treating the doctors on their own terms and exploring how medical knowledge was made in social and political contexts, rather than measuring early-eighteenth-century doctors' actions against the standards of our own time.[4]

Reflecting on the case of Mary Toft through the lens of our own contemporary context can be instructive, though, for our understanding of both the past and the present. At first glance, the case appears to underline conventional chronologies of a transition from an early modern to a modern Western society. It was surely an exemplar of a period when there were different explanations for events in the natural and the social world, testament to an enduring belief in the supernatural but indicative also of the challenges that world view was facing. We then expect such an extraordinary case to show—above all else—dramatic change over time. A present-centred view of the past is quite rightly one of which we should be highly sceptical. The past can serve as fertile territory in which to reflect on the present, though. The case is a prompt to examine contemporary medical knowledge about foetal development in ways that can challenge simplistic notions of medical progress. The figure of Mary Toft also offers rich material for a consideration of the experiences of women, both now and in the past, and their responses to the sometimes traumatic events of miscarriage and birth. Despite the passage of time since 1726, there remain some important continuities in how we think about women and reproduction.

Imagining Mary Toft

Since her death, Mary Toft has been reimagined in different ways. The consensus in the eighteenth century was that Toft had set out to defraud the medical community. By the nineteenth century, Toft was no longer an exemplar of wider unsettling social ills, but had instead become something of a curiosity. John Laguerre's singular portrait of Toft from 1727 was being reproduced in various versions as part of a small series of images of notorious late-seventeenth- and early-eighteenth-century criminal men and women, which included Thomas Britton (who ran a music concert series in London from the late seventeenth century), Jane Scrimshaw (who reputedly lived to well over a hundred years), and Hannah Snell (the cross-dressing female soldier). Toft's inclusion in this group suggests notoriety rather than criminality. Almost a hundred years since the rabbit began appearing in Godalming, the sting had gone out of the case. With a blush in her cheeks and a lively green dress, the coloured versions by the engraver Maddocks brought a modicum of character to a person who had appeared inscrutable in the original.

Fig. 9.1 Two watercoloured engravings of Mary Toft by William Maddocks (1819), based on the earlier portrait by John Laguerre after John Faber, and published in J. Caulfield's *Portraits, memoirs, and characters, of remarkable persons* (London, 1819) [Wellcome Collection]

More recent interpretations have tried to imagine Toft's motivations, granting her distinctly modern motives. She has been described as 'the Monica Lewinsky of the 1700s'. A review of a London Weekend Television programme referred to Toft, knowingly, as a 'bunny girl'. The writer of a 2011 BBC Radio 4 play called 'Rabbit Tale', granted Toft remarkable drive and determination: 'She was someone who turned round and said, "I'm bored of my life and want to change it".'[5] Art does not need to be faithful to the historical record, yet these portrayals would simply fall apart if subjected to historical scrutiny. Mary Toft was neither a scheming deviant, a feisty example of glamorous early-eighteenth-century 'girl power', and even less a proto-feminist.

A different and more historically sensitive treatment of the case was given by the novelist Hilary Mantel. In her novel, *The Giant O'Brien* (1998), Toft's case serves the purpose of illustrating the modernity of the doctor at the heart of the story. The eponymous character is Charles Byrne (1761–83), who at over eight feet tall was himself a curiosity in life and whose skeleton, which he had expressly requested to be sunk at sea, is now on display at the Royal College of Surgeons in London. It was John Hunter, anatomist and surgeon, who acquired the skeleton. In the novel, John Hunter remembers the 'tomfoolery' around the case of Mary Toft; his dismissal of the rabbit births as 'fairy tales, and rabbit skins and scraps smuggled under the skirts' marks him out as a man who refuses to be fooled by false claims. The novel thus trades in the characterization of Toft—already familiar by the late eighteenth century in which it is set—as a product of a more credulous age. Yet Mantel complicates the story of modernity. John Hunter's praise of Manningham for his threatening treatment of Toft, and his proud refusal to be so naïve as to 'give you threepence for a woman pregnant with rabbits', throws into relief what we have already seen in the novel of his sometimes rough handling of the poor and his desperation to purchase—illegally—rare skeletons for medical examination. His insistence that he would not have got swept up in the Toft affair is followed fast by his stated wish for 'a free savage, the dust of the bush still upon him, his wanton yodel rattling through the clear pipes of his chest, his tribal scars still raw, his cheeks and ribs fresh scored, his parts swinging and unfettered'. In her proposal for this novel, Mantel explained, 'I don't intend that it should be fact-based [...], but I need to do a good bit of reading for background'. Her reading on Enlightenment Europe included works that discussed Mary Toft and the Royal College of Surgeons.[6] Her literary deployment of the case succeeds in underlining both the change that had happened in the period of time between Toft and Hunter, as well as the continuities in the attitudes of elite medical men towards the poor and their bodies.

Quite a different context is given to the case of Mary Toft in Emma Donoghue's carefully researched short story, 'The Last Rabbit' (2002). Donoghue imagines the episode from the perspective of Toft herself, in this account an independent woman with a ferocious sense of humour. The opening scene is a pregnant Toft playing a cruel joke on her husband, Joshua, pretending to give birth to a rabbit one day when he came home for his dinner: 'I thought he might spew up his breakfast', she says. In this story, the rabbit births were a fraud perpetrated for money. Toft is initially egged on by her sister-in-law, for whom the original joke birth is the trigger, but is then manoeuvred into the hoax by her family and John Howard. They are moved by distinctly worldly motivations in their exploitation of Toft. The story closes as it began, with another fictitious sequence that is no less powerful for its lack of support in the historical record. Toft has been ground down: 'for a month I had been nothing but a body. Though I believed that every body had a soul, as my mother taught me, I had no idea where it might reside'. She tries to escape from the bagnio but cannot find her way out and is trapped. As she desperately looks for an exit, she spies a young woman and an old man having sex, a commercial transaction, she assumes. 'It came to me then that it is the way of the world for a woman's legs to be open, whether for begetting or bearing or the finding out of secrets.'[7] This is a disenchanted vision of the early eighteenth century in which Donoghue makes plain the selfishness and the cruelty of the people around Toft. Donoghue's vision is a compelling study of Toft as a figure of sympathy who is manipulated by those around her.

Not all modern literary treatments of the case raise questions about historical time and the past's relationship to the present. Some modern writers largely dispense with an historical context and instead engage the emotional aspects of the case. John Whale's poem, 'Mary Toft', imagines Mary's own emotional state following her miscarriage. The poem opens with Toft's description of the miscarriage, 'My child pulled itself away from me', and sets in train the key trope of the loss of a discernible and known infant. Whale makes the miscarriage and its emotional effects all the more palpable in giving the lost child a sex—he was a son. Chasing the rabbit (also a 'him') is a direct response to this loss. The many parts that soon appear are part of her lost boy; the lung that once breathed is his: 'my boy had once sucked vital air'. Whale subtly interweaves historical detail into the poem and the shape of Toft's monologue echoes the narrative of her accounts from the early eighteenth century. Mary dreams of a rabbit, before Manningham and St André come to watch her deliver a series of animal parts. The tender poem moves to a chilling penultimate image, in which Toft's womb suffocates her own child: 'he could not breathe inside my womb', she says, and she is left to 'think of him now alive on the down / where the wild thyme scents the turf'. It is not clear what she believes, but Toft seems to imagine things impossible: that she was carrying a child who miscarried, that there were rabbit births, and perhaps also that the child and the rabbit were one. The opacity on the part of Toft the narrator is a product of her state of mind.[8]

Reaching back through time to imagine a woman's innermost thoughts deploys the skills of the poet or novelist. Historians are much less well equipped for this kind of leap, but the past can certainly speak to our present. Toft's was an astonishing case. It seems to belong firmly to a very different, pre-Enlightenment society, and from our distance the temptation may be to despatch with the hoax as belonging to a more superstitious and less knowledgeable time. Nonetheless, the case is relevant to us for two important reasons. First, Mary Toft embodied—literally—economic and social injustice. Her case exposes how a range of complex power relations could operate around the reproducing female body. Second, Toft's case exposes the long and complex history of how ideas, beliefs, myths, and fears about human reproduction were entangled. In these ways, Toft's case is closer to us than we might at first imagine.

Medical knowledge past and present

In the early twenty-first century, our comprehension of the processes of conception and gestation is considerable, giving us the ability to control and manipulate them to an extraordinary degree. Whether this is best described as 'progress' is, of course, a moot point. On matters of contraception, artificial insemination, and genetic modification of embryos, debates between passionate advocates and ardent opponents are fierce. On the question of medical knowledge, it would be easy to dismiss the theory of the maternal imagination as a direct result of a distinct lack of understanding of foetal development. If we consider the modern history of reproductive science, though, our own understandings of reproduction appear to resemble in some principal ways those from three hundred years ago.

Modern medical knowledge of pregnancy and foetal development is dominated by research on genomic and environmental imprinting within foetal programming: in other words, the influence of parental behaviour on animal and human offspring by creating changes to the DNA. Since the thalidomide case of the late 1950s and early 1960s, medics have been acutely aware that the placenta does not protect the developing foetus from substances ingested by the mother. The DNA sequence of an infant can therefore be affected by its experiences within the uterus. Our DNA, located in the genome, is largely locked and fixed. Yet we know that a number of factors can affect how the DNA sequence 'works' or is expressed, even though it will remain unchanged. The processes involved are complex and arouse considerable debate. For many, the processes should be understood using the notions of the genome and the 'epigenome'. If the genetic information provides the 'blueprint' of the organism, the epigenetic information provides 'additional instructions on how, where and when' that blueprint will be used.[9] There is vociferous debate about how epigenomic mechanisms operate, yet there is a consensus that several forms of epigenomic modifications are determined by a dynamic combination of inheritance and other factors. In other words, it is the epigenome that mediates between the DNA sequence and the observable characteristics of the offspring, and which can reflect environmental and physiological changes. What interests me here is less what we think we know and more how we might characterize this reproductive research.

A landmark in scientists' understanding of epigenetic modifications *in utero* was the 'fetal origins hypothesis' developed by epidemiologist David Barker in the 1970s. Barker examined the impact of nutritional deprivation amongst mothers during the Dutch famine of 1944–45 on their infants. Babies had been affected by the poor diet of their mothers and this could cause delayed physical effects later in the child's life, although good nutrition following the period of poor nutrition allowed children to 'catch up' developmentally. The 'fetal origins hypothesis' has been widely taken up in examinations of *in utero* health in order to assess the aggregate impact on life chances. It underpins the prominent discourse on good diet for expectant mothers, as well as proscriptions on substances such as alcohol and tobacco. Medical research has gone on to examine in more detail the effect of maternal nutrition, health, and illness on placental function. Current research on environmental effects on genomic imprinting explores precisely the impact of mothers' physical health of the unborn. Studies suggest that exercise before and during pregnancy can stimulate molecules in the placenta that then compensate for placental or vascular dysfunction in some pregnancies (especially those of hypertension or preeclampsia). Relatively minor environmental experiences of mothers can affect not just the epigenome of the foetus but also the female foetus' eggs; thus, effects felt in one generation affect the next two, or the grandmother affects the grandchildren. This is the case with obesity and diabetes, for example, as well as for other diseases. The role of the placenta is crucial: as an interface between the foetus and mother, it allows the passage of matter in two ways. A key study of thirty women in 1969 detected all those women who went on to have boys by the male cells found in their blood taken during pregnancy. Since then, the presence of foetal cells in the mother's blood has been widely accepted.[10]

The epigenome is not only affected by the mother. The behaviour of both parents can impact the epigenome of offspring in the perinatal period, when they are very young. Research on three-spined sticklebacks, a fish in which fathers are the sole provider of offspring care, shows that quality care provided by fathers reduces offspring anxiety through epigenetic mechanisms. But perhaps more strikingly, fathers can cause physiological effects in offspring through the cells in their sperm. It has become clear in recent years that a paternal influence can be observed in both animal and human offspring, though this influence is expected to interact with many others in complex but as yet unknown ways. A small 2017 study showed that the sperm of men in couples receiving IVF treatment carried traces of environmental effects that affected the 'quality' of the couples' embryos.[11] In other words, male health would seem to be a factor in embryo development.

Interest in the impact of environmental factors *in utero* focuses not just on physical health and nutrition, but also the area of stress. This has been shown to have ramifications for the incidence of mental health disorders later in life. A large body of work on rats shows that stressful or adverse environments experienced by the mother affects the cognitive, emotional, and endocrinal responses to stress on the part of the offspring, essentially rendering them more sensitive to stress and with an increased risk of chronic illness. But for both animals and humans, links have been identified between antenatal stress and the subsequent behaviour and health of offspring. One study of rats found a link between serotonin inhibitor drugs administered to the pregnant rat and increased display of anxiety-associated behaviour in the offspring.[12] We know that the placental production of serotonin (obtained through the maternal diet) affects normal foetal brain development. Disruptions in serotonin production in the placenta correlate with an increased risk of some mental health conditions or behavioural difficulties, even into adulthood. Emotional experiences, as well as parents' physical health, can also have impacts upon the child. A study of almost 3 million births in Sweden between 1973 and 2006 showed that women experiencing bereavement during pregnancy were at higher risk of stillbirth. Prenatal stress—caused by factors such as shock, noise, or physical restraint—has been found to affect offspring's behaviour in areas such as language and attention, essentially by affecting brain development in the foetus.[13] Medical researchers resist claims that they are showing the impact of women's 'emotions' on their offspring, insisting that they are observing measurable factors, such as hormonal change.

It is important to state that such studies do not show inevitable effects but statistical correlations. They should not be read as predictions. We also still have much to learn about the mechanism through which these effects are generated. But an echo of the classical and early modern theory of the maternal imagination—the theory which made the Toft case possible—is audible here. This work shows an enduring interest in how our children are affected by experiences prior to birth. Indeed, reproductive medicine researchers and obstetricians with whom I have discussed the Toft case themselves draw connections between the theory of the maternal imagination and the role that forms of social stress might play in birth abnormalities.[14] This is a revealing response that counsels us not to simply dismiss as absurd the credulity of early-eighteenth-century people. An interest in the complex ways in which both parents affect their children even before they meet them persists; what may have changed—though even this is debatable—is the recategorizing in modern medicine as physiological those triggers once conceptualized as imaginative or emotional.

This modern research has redrawn the map of human understanding of how reproduction operates, but we should dispel the idea that our own experts know all, while early-eighteenth-century people were simply ignorant. A wealth of reproductive medicine research has generated new knowledge, but it has not eradicated ignorance. One running thread in much of this biomedical research is the acknowledgement that our understanding in this area is severely limited. We know that smoking harms babies but not about the effects of nicotine patches and e-cigarettes; we know that placental serotonin from maternal diet is important for foetal brain development, but not how babies are affected by serotonin reuptake inhibitors found in the drugs that might be prescribed to pregnant women suffering from severe depression. As two authors have recently noted, 'to a surprising degree pregnancy remains a "black box"'.[15] We undoubtedly understand better the process of reproduction now than in the early eighteenth century. Yet there remain gaps, debates, and disagreements. An historical perspective cannot settle these, of course. What the historical approach does allow, though, is a consideration of contemporary medical professionals using the same analytical and interpretive skills that we bring to the theories of early modern medics, and the ability to situate current debates in a longer tradition. For all the ease with which we might reckon Toft and her contemporaries held back by ill-informed naivety, it is striking that current reproductive medical researchers continue to examine the way that mothers and fathers influence their unborn offspring, searching out the mechanisms through which these unseen influences take effect.

Contemporary responses to the case

Our fascination with how new life is shaped endures. Our curiosity about Mary Toft arises from this, but it also stems from a desire to connect through time with her experiences. Experiences of pregnancy and childbirth are not universal to all women, but in the course of the research for this book, I have spoken to many women about the case and have been struck by an impulse to understand her and her reproductive experiences. We can build on this to explore what the case might tell us about women's responses to reproductive events, traumatic and otherwise, and the broader context of ideas that we all harbour about the ways that our bodies work. Many have expressed sympathy for Toft, perhaps even an affinity in being a woman and of experiencing some kind of reproductive event or trauma—rather than historical distance. Several women have wanted to explore with me the agency Toft may have had over her own body. And some women have also seen in the case a mirror for their understanding of how the pregnant body works. One women, herself a midwife, told me, 'When I was pregnant with [my] third child. I could imagine how she looked and that is how she looked but I couldn't choose what she would look like. A maternal instinct? Have no idea. I wasn't influencing the way she looked. I don't have the powers.' Another woman remembered, 'I had this thing about a blue-eyed girl and I got that!' Women feel that an older form of female knowledge about their bodies has been displaced by new technology. 'You don't have chance to test out your instincts', one woman commented, because of high-quality ultrasound scans that show us the inside of the uterus. As one midwife eloquently put it, 'It's not that women are less intuitive in their bodies but that they have less faith in their bodies.'[16] In these conversations with women, an interest in both the physical and emotional experiences of Mary Toft came to the fore. Within these reflections we might see echoes of older ideas of an imaginative connection between the mother's mind and her unborn child.

As in the past, though, a conviction that there are potent unseen forces jostles with a commitment to empirical truth. At the same time that women acknowledge their belief in a particular kind of sensory knowledge about their unborn child, midwives are adamant that the theory of the maternal imagination deployed by Toft and others as an explanation for the rabbit births belongs to an earlier world of super-stition. One woman commented, 'Science wasn't as developed as today. They were more prone to believe something like this might happen.' Midwives themselves are aware of the suspicion their practice has sometimes aroused in the past; they distance themselves from this partly with knowledge that has since been revised or replaced by an improved understanding of the body. The midwives I have spoken to about the case (all women, as it happened) were interested in identifying a physiological cause and a medical explanation for what Toft had described. They were interested in the truth or otherwise of the histor-ical evidence. Assessing whether Toft's descriptions were to some extent truthful, they drew upon their expert knowledge as midwives to assess the veracity of Mary Toft's reported miscarriage. Indeed, Toft's report was convincing to these midwives as a description of a late (though not an early) miscarriage. Her descriptions of the parts that emerged during her miscarriage appeared to resemble either a malformed foetus or a teratoma, a growth that might contain flesh, bones, hair, and teeth and that can occur anywhere in the body. These are now rarely seen because we have been able to identify them with ultrasound since the 1970s, but before this technology they could be left undetected for some time until they came away from the woman's body.[17] The occupational training and experience of these expert midwives leads to an interpretation of the evidence of Toft's experiences not as bizarre fictions (which is how some historians have characterized them) but instead as sources for the reproductive experiences of a poor early-eighteenth-century woman.

Putting Toft at the centre of her own story brings our focus to her mental state. We might acknowledge that Toft was ill-informed, a liar, or exploited by others, but at the same time we are able to recognize her suffering in the context of reproductive trauma. When I have spoken to women about this case they often ask about Toft's emotional well-being and state of mind. On several occasions, women have discussed how heightened emotional states and distress are often a consequence of a prolonged miscarriage. It has even been suggested to me that the creation of the rabbit-birth hoax was a direct reaction to the miscarriage, a process somehow intended to keep the idea of the lost baby alive and an expression of her attachment to it. Constrained by the patchy documents we have about the case, these areas are difficult for an historian to explore. Yet we can nevertheless recognize the truth of what one woman described to me as the 'irrational voice' that might stir when a woman experiences such a trauma, a voice that perhaps persists across time. Though miscarriage was not always hidden and both women and men could be involved in the process, there has never been a widely shared ritual that marks the experience of miscarriage. Distress has long been one response to the loss of a pregnancy. The Miscarriage Association now advises women on what they might do to mark their loss, in effect creating their own ritual—in the absence of one that is shared and public—that acknowledges this event.[18] The lack of a public discourse about this still relatively private experience is one reason why the process can be so traumatic.

Women have often met childbirth with trepidation, though a phobia of childbirth—tokophobia—is extremely rare. It is difficult to assess the extent of fear, but worries about death, pain, and loss of the child could all cause unease or downright terror. It is no accident that the dominant discourse concerning the demeanour of eighteenth-century women in pregnancy and childbirth was fortitude.[19] Today, at least in the Western world, women share some of the same unease as women in the past. Fuelled by dramatic scenes of childbirth in television documentaries and dramas, expectant mothers worry about what might go wrong in the birthing room. Sometimes these concerns relate to their own health and safety, as well as that of their infants. The widely reported rise in caesarean sections results partly from a fear of the physical damage that a vaginal delivery might cause; a medicalized and thus apparently more controlled option, mothers are willing to replace the risks of one form of delivery with the risks of another, surgical, one. Cognizant of the risks of mortality, as well as complaints and legal action, medics— like mothers—are also becoming more risk averse. The medicalization of childbirth, displayed through near-universal hospital birth and increased proportions of caesarean sections, goes hand in hand with a discourse of risk. The increase in caesarean sections may also be caused by women's anxiety about how they might behave during a vaginal delivery. The shame of losing control and acting like an animal, showing their bodies in immodest or unattractive ways, or simply not perform- ing in an appropriate way during labour are concerns that women have shared with medical professionals. Underpinning these concerns sometimes lurk deep-seated feelings of disgust about the female body and childbirth.[20] Such feelings can exist alongside the feelings of joy, elation, and wonder that might also be felt during pregnancy and birth.

Mary Toft's deliveries were marked by the consistent involvement of women, as was typical for her period. Such encounters could be positive social occasions for the women involved, yet were often characterized by tense relations between women. Mary Toft, for one, felt she was being controlled by women whose greater claim to authority arose from social status, occupation, or age. Her fear of these more authori- tative women, as expressed in her confessions, must have been shared by other birthing women. The women-only lying-in ritual has all but disintegrated in our Western society, yet the negotiations between those present at a birth can still be fraught. Usually unaccompanied by their own mothers or female friends during labour, women today often derive comfort from the midwives who assist them. An historical perspective cautions us not to assume that a group of women will automatically provide support, though. Women in labour can express anger towards their midwives. And midwives themselves are a varied group. Sometimes pronounced generational differences can affect their practice, as does the route through which they arrive in the birthing room (via nursing or directly through midwifery). For some birthing women, midwives can appear intimidating, overly assertive, or controlling. Midwives themselves feel under threat, overworked, and increasingly unable to provide what they regard as an appropriate level of care, especially for those delivering at home. In my conversations with midwives, the 'danger' that the profession faces was a recurring theme, one that is prominent in many recent news stories on childbirth care, at least in the United Kingdom. For these women, the control that elite men assumed over Mary Toft elevates the case as a *cause célèbre* for their beleaguered profession. In this, as in other ways, Toft's case remains relevant.

* * *

On 13 January 1763 the record of Toft's burial preserved forever her notoriety as 'the Imposteress Rabbett Breeder'. Historians and literary scholars have also understood the case through its peculiarities, and these are of course undeniable. The case was certainly exceptional. Yet this book has situated the case in the broader social and cultural world of early-eighteenth-century Britain: in the context of women's working and reproductive lives; of changing communities and social relations; of political interests and public concerns. In understanding what the case meant to contemporaries, particularly those who investigated the criminal case, the possibility of monstrous births was perhaps initially important but quickly became relatively insignificant. The affair was triggered in amongst relations between women situated within a local community unsettled by social unrest. Its progress was propelled by those committed to furthering medical knowledge and others dedicated to the defence of the law and the preservation of order. Its meaning was imprinted with all the fear, anxiety, and hilarity that a poor woman's delivery of rabbits might well be imagined to generate. Toft's rabbit births were not ordinary. By the same token, situating this case in the context of modern biomedical knowledge about foetal development, and of women's personal and midwives' professional experience of reproduction, suggests that Toft's case was not just—if at all—a remarkable historical curiosity. Mary Toft's delivery of rabbits in 1726 was extraordinary. But in this case we can also see traces of the experiences of many other women, then and now.

NOTES

Chapter 1

1. Ralph Nevill, 'The Corporation of Godalming', *Surrey Archaeological Collections*, Vol. 19 (London, 1906), p. 106; H. E. Malden, 'Answers made to the visitation articles of Dr. Willis, The Bishop of Winchester. From the parishes of Surrey, excluding the peculiars of Canterbury, 1724–25', *Surrey Archaeological Collections*, Vol. 39 (London, 1931), p. 92; P. J. Corfield, *The Impact of English Towns, 1700–1800* (Oxford: Oxford Paperbacks, 1982), pp. 8–9; Peter Borsay, *The English Urban Renaissance. Culture and Society in The Provincial Town 1660–1770* (Oxford: Clarendon Press, 1989), pp. 4–5.

2. See, for example, J. A. Sharpe, *Crime in Early Modern England 1550–1750* (London: Longman, 1984), p. 75; Shani D'Cruze, 'The middling sort in eighteenth-century Colchester: independence, social relations and the community broker', in Jonathan Barry and Christopher Brooks (eds), *The Middling Sort of People: Culture, Society and Politics in England, 1550–1800* (Basingstoke and London: Macmillan and St Martin's Press, 1994), pp. 181–207; Naomi Tadmor, 'Where was Mrs Turner? Governance and gender in an eighteenth-century village', in Steve Hindle, Alexandra Shepard, and John Walter (eds), *Remaking English Society: Social Relations and Social Change in Early Modern England* (Woodbridge: Boydell and Brewer, 2013), pp. 89–111.

3. See 'Hearth Tax Online' [http://www.hearthtax.org.uk/communities/surrey/]. Calculation based on the data provided in http://www.hearthtax.org.uk/communities/surrey/surrey_1664L_tables.pdf (accessed 17/10/14) and based on C. A. F. Meekings, 'Surrey hearth tax 1664', *Surrey Record Society*, Vol. 17 (1940). Of the seventy-four households deemed exempt, twenty-nine had one and forty had two hearths. Surrey History Centre (SHC): LM/616/2 [c.1689 x 1719] A List of the names of the severall poor people [in Godalming] to whom the charity of £5 is to be given.

4. H. E. Malden, *A History of the County of Surrey: Volume 3* (Victoria County History, 1911). Via British History Online (accessed 4/12/2013).

5. Bills and vouchers of the 2nd Duke and Duchess of Richmond paid between July 1723 and Michaelmas 1732. 1723–1732, West Sussex County Archive (WSCA): Goodwood MSS: 88, 82; Glasgow University Special Collections (GUSC): MS Hunter D324 (confession 1), 7 December 1726, f2.

6. Will of Robert Byde (X) of Godalming, woolen weaver, sick and weak 20 Sep 1718. Proved 22 May 1719. [DW/PC/5/1719/3], in Cliff Webb, 'Commissary Court of Surrey. Surrey Will Abstracts Unregistered Wills, 1697–1728' (Vol. 27); Will of John Chitty of Godalming, frameworkknitter, snr. 3 Aug 1721. Proved 23 Jun 1722 [DW/PA/7/19 ff. 13–14; DW/PA/5/1722/25], in Cliff Webb, 'Surrey Will Abstracts Archdeaconry Court of Surrey, Registered and Unregistered Wills, 1722–1725' (Vol. 30).

7. WSCA: GWD99: ff. 48–52 Inventory of his Grace the Duke of Richmond's Goods at Godalming taken Novr 1733'; Goodwood MS 118, ff. 11–13.

8. SHC: LM/1397/35A Rentals for Godalming, ff. 1–3.

9. SHC: LM/S/9 Volume recording references in eighteenth and nineteenth-century Godalming manor court records to freehold and leasehold property, f.31, 150. Abraham Toft pays rent on various properties in the same area of the town, including a tenement and lands called 'Coles' (6d) and two other tenements in a building called 'Bridgers' (2s each). SHC: LM/1397/35A Rentals for Godalming, ff. 4–5. Will of Abraham Toft of Godalming, clothier 31 Jan 1727/8. Proved 1 Jun 1728 [DW/PC/5/1728/25], in Webb, 'Commissary Court of Surrey…Unregistered Wills, 1697–1728'. 'Toft' or 'Tofts' is an extremely common name in this part of Surrey. The nineteenth-century antiquarian, Percy Woods, reconstructed the several branches of Tofts and placed Joshua and Mary apart from all the other (often interconnected) branches. See GM: Woods MS Collection Vol. 50, f122. Abraham Toft the clothier, his wife Charity Toft and his grandchildren Charity and Mary Toft were no relation to Mary and Joshua Toft.

10. Stanley C. Dedman (ed.) *Godalming and its Neighbourhood. Notes by Charles Softley, 1829–1916* (1966), p. 23.

11. Rosemary Sweet, *The English Town, 1680–1840: Government, Society and Culture* (Harlow: Longman, 1999), p. 201; Robert Shoemaker and Tim Hitchcock, *London Lives. Poverty, Crime and the Making of a Modern City, 1690–1800* (Cambridge; Cambridge University Press, 2015), pp. 27–69.

12. SHC: 2253/3/1 Minute book of Godalming Corporation, ff. 74, 186.

13. Quoted from Tittler, *Architecture and Power*, in Christopher R. Friedrichs, *The Early Modern City, 1450–1750* (London and New York: Longman, 1995), p. 247.

14. Malden, *History of the County of Surrey*, Vol. 2, 1–2; Brodie Waddell, 'Governing England through the Manor Courts, 1550–1850', *The Historical Journal*, Vol. 55, No. 02 (June 2012), pp. 279–315.

15. SHC: G70/68/1 'Godalming Court Book', 1710–52, includes the records of courts of the Hundred and the Manor.

16. SHC: Deed 1942/3/6(2).

17. SHC: QS2/6 Sessions Papers, Easter 1724 (84), Petition of the inhabitants of Godalming, against Stephen Boxall of Godalming; SHC: QS2/6 Sessions Papers, Easter 1724 (4) a list of subscribers to the market place repairs in 1729; SHC: LM/615/1 'A List of the inhabitants of Godalming or town

tithing', early eighteenth century; and SHC: LM/615/3 'A List of Inhabitants of the town of Godalming of all under ye years of sixty and above ye years of sixteen', 3 October 1733.

18. Eighty-one wills have been considered: twenty-five the Prerogative Court of Canterbury, primarily for the wealthy who had property in more than one diocese in the southern province and selected for Godalming for the period 1700–1740, held at The National Archives; thirty-five from the Archdeaconry Court, and twenty-one from the Commissary Court selected for the period 1697–1733, held at the London Metropolitan Archive (LMA). The excellent series of indexes to these LMA wills produced by Cliff Webb have been used; these give summaries of the details of the wills.

19. For a list of wardens of Godalming see Nevill, 'Corporation of Godalming', pp. 136–8.

20. Will of Joan Freeman, Widow of Godalming, Surrey, 7 November 1719, PROB 11/571/87, TNA.

21. Will of Joan Barton (X) of Godalming, widow 20 May 1713. Proved 20 Feb 1724/5 [DW/PA/7/19 ff. 377–8; DW/PA/5/1725/7], LMA. See Cliff Webb, 'Surrey Will Abstracts Archdeaconry Court of Surrey, Registered and Unregistered Wills, 1722–1725' (Vol. 30). Barton is sister to Margaret Edsal and Elizabeth Tofte. She left a guinea in gold and £1 1s 6d in silver to each. For Thomas Edsal/Edsall see G70/68/1 'Godalming Court Book', for 1721. For Abraham Toft see petition against Boxall, QS2/6 Sessions Papers, Easter 1724 (84).

22. George Chitty (X) of Godalming, mason, weak 30 Mar 1728. Proved 13 May 1728 [DW/PC/5/1728/7], LMA: leaves to his son John Chitty a field and houses in Ockford Lane. His son-in-law is John Shrubb. See Cliff Webb, 'Commissary Court of Surrey. Surrey Will Abstracts Unregistered Wills, 1697–1728' (Vol. 27).

23. Will of Mary Warton, Widow of Godalming, Surrey, 22 December 1719, PROB 11/571/484, TNA.

24. SHC: Parish Registers for Godalming (St Peter and St Paul). See also GM: *The Parish Registers of Godalming: Indexes.*

25. Carpenters' Company Minute Book, 3 January 1721–3 October 1727, 2 February 1725. Accessed via Tim Hitchcock, Robert Shoemaker, Sharon Howard, and Jamie McLaughlin et al., *London Lives, 1690–1800* (www. londonlives.org, version 1.1, 24 April 2012) (accessed 26/10/14), LL refs. GLCCMC251040219 and GLCCMC251050088, Guildhall Library, MS. 4329/14. At this point John took the room of Thomas Denyer. He chose to move into another room, of a deceased man, on 7 June 1726: GLCCMC251040287. His room became available when he died on 2 June 1730: See Carpenters' Company Minute Book, LL ref. GLCCMC251050250. *The Parish Registers of Godalming: Indexes* do not clarify if this is Mary Toft's brother, as they show burials of John Denyers in 1727, 1730, and 1731.

26. Carpenters' Company Minute Books, 5 March 1734. LL ref: GLCCMC251050358.
27. Dennis Todd, *Imagining Monsters: Miscreations of the Self in Eighteenth-Century England* (Chicago: University of Chicago Press, 1995), n.7, pp. 270–1. See Steve Hindle, *On the Parish? The Micro-Politics of Poor Relief in Rural England, c.1550–1750* (Oxford: Clarendon Press, 2004), on the processes of negotiation involved in acquiring formal, semi-formal, and informal relief, from parish authorities, family, kin, and neighbours.
28. SHC: QS2/5/1726, Surrey Quarter Sessions Roll, No. 23. See also SHC: QS2/2/4 Surrey Quarter Sessions Minute Book, 12 July 1726, No. 23, where it is recorded that Joshua Toft agrees to keep the peace.
29. John Craig, 'Co-operation and Initiatives: Elizabethan Churchwardens and the Parish Accounts of Mildenhall', *Social History*, Vol. 18, No. 3 (1993), pp. 357–80. This study is earlier in focus but also notes that in one clothing parish, fourteen of the twenty-seven men who served as churchwarden were clothiers or weavers. See p. 363.
30. Painter and Stedman are listed in LM/615/1: 'A List of the inhabitants of Godalming or town tithing', early eighteenth century. Grover, Painter, and Pincot are listed in LM/615/3: A List of Inhabitants of the town of Godalming (16–60) 3 Oct 1733. In the parish records, I have been able to find no parish records of a Timothy Grover or William Pincot, and only one record each of a Jonathan Painter and Richard Stedman. Jonathan Painter: *bap.* 20 Nov 1709; Richard Stedman: *bap.* [no day] Feb 1677. There is only one birth of a Thomas Underwood in Godalming during this period, and two boys baptized as Caleb Tickner. All parish records accessed via *Anglican Parish Registers*, Woking, Surrey: Surrey History Centre. www.Ancestry.com. *Surrey, England, Baptisms, Marriages and Burials, 1538–1812* [database online]. Provo, UT, USA: Ancestry.com Operations, Inc., 2013 (accessed 10/14) Hereafter, GOD/1/4, www.Ancestry.com.
31. For relevant wills see: Will of George Constable, carpenter, 26 Jun 1716 [DW/PA/5/1716/38]. See Cliff Webb, 'Surrey Will Abstracts Archdeaconry Court of Surrey Unregistered Wills, 1716–1721' (Vol. 29); Will of Margaret Shrubb of Godalming, sp., 30 Apr 1711. Proved 7 Apr 1714 [DW/PA/5/1714/91]: Cliff Webb, 'Surrey Will Abstracts. Archdeaconry Court of Surrey Unregistered Wills, 1709–1715' (Vol. 28); Will of Elizabeth Hart (X) of Godalming widow of George Hart 4 Sep 1717. Proved 9 Jul 1719 [DW/PC/5/1719/13]. See Cliff Webb, 'Commissary Court of Surrey. Surrey Will Abstracts Unregistered Wills, 1697–1728' (Vol. 27). For the George Chitty births are recorded in Godalming during this period: 27 Dec 1700 son of William and Jeane, and 21 Dec 1707 son of Thomas and Frances, both GOD/1/4, www.Ancestry.com. See Will of George Chitty (X) of Godalming, mason, weak 30 Mar 1728. Proved 13 May 1728 [DW/PC/5/1728/7]. See Webb, 'Commissary Court of Surrey…1697–1728' (Vol. 27).
32. Will of James Finch on Godalming, dyer 9 Nov 1730. DW/PA/7/21; DW/PA/5/1731/42. See Cliff Webb, 'Surrey Will Abstracts Archdeaconry Court of

Surrey, Registered Wills, 1726–1733'. There are no Timothy Grovers in the parish records for Godalming.

33. Will of Abraham Toft of Godalming, clothier 31 Jan 1727/8. Proved 1 Jun 1728 [DW/PC/5/1728/25]. See Webb, 'Commissary Court of Surrey... Unregistered Wills, 1697–1728'. Parish registers for the period show two James Tofts and one Thomas Pinkett born in Godalming. James Toft: 26 Dec 1681, son of Joshua Toft and Anne [Bridger] and 5 May 1699. Son of Abraham Tofte and Elizabeth his wife. Thomas Pinkett: baptized 3 Nov 1700 at Godalming. Father Thomas Pinkatt and mother Mary: GOD/1/4, www.Ancestry.com.

34. Will of carpenter, John Costen, in 1709. Proved 11 Sep 1723 [DW/PA/7/19 ff/169–71; DW/PA/5/1723/32]. See Cliff Webb, 'Surrey Will Abstracts Archdeaconry Court of Surrey, Registered and Unregistered Wills, 1722–1725' (Vol. 30). This is likely to be the Caleb Tickner in the recognizance as there is only one noted in the parish records for Godalming: Caleb Tickner: Caleb son of Richard Tickner 14 Jan 1666; Caleb Ticknar, son of Thomas Ticknar and Darling [Darling May], 5 Dec 1700: GOD/1/4, www.Ancestry.com.

35. Will of Edward Bonner (X) of Godalming, labourer 26 Mar 1701. Proved 5 Jul 1708. [DW/PC/5/1708/5]. See Webb, 'Commissary Court of Surrey... Unregistered Wills, 1697–1728'.

36. Though note that Stedman is able to sign his deposition in 1726. See *The Several Depositions of Edward Costen, Richard Stedman, John Sweetapple, Mary Peytoe, Elizaneth Mason, and Mary Costen; relating to the Affair of Mary Toft* (London, 1727), p. 8. Those who do not sign—all the women—are noted as leaving their mark. This is likely to be the same Stedman, however, given that the parish registers show only one in these decades: Richard son of John Stedman and Elizabeth born in Godalming Feb 1677, Anglican Parish Registers, Woking, www.Ancestry.com.

37. Will of William Ray of Godalming, cooper, snr. 7 May 1720. Proved 5 May 1720 [DW/PC/5/1720/10], LMA. See Webb, 'Commissary Court of Surrey. Surrey Will Abstracts Unregistered Wills, 1697–1728'. He leaves to his daughter his half of five houses in the occupation of four people including '(widow) Toft'. Elizabeth, wife of Abraham, had died in 1723 but Charity Toft, widow of Abraham, is still living at this time. See Toft family tree, GM: Woods MS Collection Vol. 50, f122.

38. Mary Costen may have been the widow of the carpenter John Costen, who left his wife the rents of his two houses, though it is impossible to be sure. See Will of John Costen, carpenter, in 1709. Proved 11 Sep 1723 [DW/PA/7/19 ff/169–71; DW/PA/5/1723/32]. See Webb, 'Surrey Will Abstracts Archdeaconry Court of Surrey, Registered and Unregistered Wills, 1722–1725'. There are no parish records for a Mary Costen in Godalming.

39. *Several Depositions*, p. 9.

NOTES TO PAGES 14–15

40. Library of the Religious Society of Friends, London (LRSF): Benjamin Sweetapple's paper of Acknowledgement on marrying by a Priest, 1728, in TEMP MSS 30/1/12, Papers & Certificates relating to marriages, 1673–1780. Benjamin Sweetapple later left for London. See LRSF: TEMP MSS 30/1/4 Certificates of removal, letters of Settlement 1707–1780, 'Concernig Benj. Sweetapple & Wife's Settlement, also Rebecka Russell's', 17 August 1729.

41. Will of Henry Woods of Godalming, malster, snr., sick and weak, exec. 8 June 1714, proved 9 Feb 1726/7 [DW/PA/7/20; DW/PA/5/1727/116]. See Webb, 'Surrey Will Abstracts Archdeaconry Court of Surrey, Registered Wills, 1726–1733'.

42. Malden, *A History of the County of Surrey*, Vol. 2, pp. 39–40; Malden, 'Answers made to the visitation articles of Dr. Willis', p. 82; Bill Stevenson, 'The status of post-Restoration dissenters, 1660–1725', in Margaret Spufford (ed.), *World of Rural Dissenters*, (Cambridge: Cambridge University Press, 1995), p. 354; Bill Stevenson, 'The social integration of post-Restoration dissenters', in Spufford (ed.), *World of Rural Dissenters*, pp. 382–3.

43. Margaret Spufford, 'The importance of religion in the sixteenth and seventeenth centuries', in Spufford (ed.), *The World of Rural Dissenters*, pp. 40–7.

44. The will of the shopkeeper Caleb Hart, lists George Hart, butcher (signatory to the petition against Boxall) and Richard Balchin, husbandman (a member of the town tithing). See will of Caleb Hart of Godalming, shopkeeper, 13 Jan 1719/20. Proved 5 Feb 1719/20. [DW/PA/5/1720/48]. See Cliff Webb, 'Surrey Will Abstracts Archdeaconry Court of Surrey Unregistered Wills, 1716–1721' (Vol. 29).

45. Will of James Shrubb, Clothier of Godalming, Surrey, 26 January 1725, PROB 11/601/185, TNA. A codicil to the will of James' sister, Margaret Shrubb of Godalming, sp., 30 Apr 1711, proved 7 Apr 1714 [DW/PA/5/1714/91], LMA, showed that she left £40 to the poor of Godalming. See Cliff Webb, 'Surrey Will Abstracts. Archdeaconry Court of Surrey Unregistered Wills, 1709–1715' (Vol. 28).

46. SHC: LM/616/2 [c.1689 x 1719] A List of the names of the severall poor people [in Godalming] to whom the charity of £5is to be given; SHC: QS2/5/1726, Surrey Quarter Sessions Roll, No. 23.

47. 2253/3/1 Minute book of Godalming Corporation, f. 73; 'The jury for the town of Godalming 1726': LM/267/23, 1–250 1724–1726, f. 248; A list of subscribers to the market place repairs in 1729, SHC: G70/68/1 Godalming Court Book, f.77v. On parish communities see K. D. M Snell, *Parish and Belonging: Community, Identity and Welfare in England and Wales, 1700–1950* (Cambridge: Cambridge University Press, 2006). On middling-sort precarity see K. Tawny Paul, *The Poverty of Disaster: Debt and Insecurity in Eighteenth-Century Britain* (Cambridge: Cambridge University Press, 2019).

48. Jurors for the Godalming Frank Pledge Court 1726, G70/68/1 Godalming Court Book, f. 56.

49. 2253/3/1 Minute book of Godalming Corporation, ff. 74, 78.
50. SHC: LM/S/9: Volume recording references in eighteenth and nineteenth-century Godalming manor court records to freehold and leasehold property, f150; quote from LM/267/231–250 1724–1726, f. 249.
51. 2253/3/1 Minute book of Godalming Corporation, f. 78.
52. SHC: QS2/6/1725/Mid/Midsummer 1725, number 38 and f. 8, A list of names of high constables Godalming. Richard Firknell and Caleb Firknar respectively; SHC: QS2/6/1725/Mic/Michaelmas 1725, Number 45. The accounts for the Warden include a payment of 6s to Keen for four days' work. See SHC: 2253/3/1 Minute book of Godalming Corporation, f36.
53. Bills and vouchers of the 2nd Duke and Duchess of Richmond paid between July 1723 and Michaelmas 1732. 1723–1732, West Sussex County Archive: Goodwood MSS 120, f.61.
54. Paul Langford, *Public Life and the Properties Englishman, 1689–1798* (Oxford: Clarendon Press, 1991), esp. pp. 1–70; P. B. Munsche, *Gentlemen and Poachers: The English Game Laws 1671–1831* (Cambridge: Cambridge University Press, 1981), pp. 4–5.
55. Eric Hobsbawm, 'Distinctions between Socio-Political and Other Forms of Crime', *Bulletin of the Society for the Study of Labour History*, Vol. 25 (1972); John Rule, 'Social Crime in the Rural South in the Eighteenth and Nineteenth Centuries', *Southern History*, Vol. 1 (1979), pp. 135–53.
56. See Carl J. Griffin, *Protest, Politics and Work in Rural England, 1700–1850* (Basingstoke: Palgrave Macmillan, 2014), pp. 49–54, 62; Lane, 'Work on the Margins', p. 95.
57. John Broad, 'Whigs and deer-stealers in other guises: a return to the origins of the Black Act', *Past & Present*, No. 119 (1988), pp. 56–72, quote at p. 71.
58. E. P. Thompson, *Whigs and Hunters: The Origins of the Black Act (1975)* (Harmondsworth: Penguin, 1977). Important revisions include Broad, 'Whigs and deer-stealers in other guises' and Eveline Cruickshanks and Howard Erskine-Hill, 'The Waltham Black Act and Jacobitism', *Journal of British Studies*, Vol. 24, No. 3 (July 1985), p. 365. Of offences in Windsor Forest between 1722 and 1724, for example, 14.9 per cent were for fishponds and 58.8 per cent for deer-hunting. See Thompson, *Whigs and Hunters*, p. 83.
59. David Lemmings, 'The dark side of the Enlightenment: *The London Journal*, moral panics, and the law in the eighteenth century', in David Lemmings and Claire Walker (eds), *Moral Panics, the Media and the Law in Early Modern England* (Basingstoke: Palgrave Macmillan, 2009), p. 153.
60. Perry Gauci, 'Surrey: 1690–1715', http://www.historyofparliamentonline.org/volume/1690–1715/constituencies/surrey (accessed 2/2/16); Romney R. Sedgwick, 'Surrey: 1715–45', http://www.historyofparliamentonline.org/volume/1715–1754/constituencies/surrey (accessed 2/2/16); *The History of Parliament: the House of Commons 1715–1754*, ed. R. Sedgwick, 1970. Accessed via http://www.historyofparliamentonline.org/research (accessed 11/9/15).

61. *The London Journal*, Saturday, 7 September 1723. All newspapers have been accessed via the seventeenth–eighteenth-century Burney Collection of Newspapers.
62. Thompson, *Whigs and Hunters*, pp. 205–10.
63. Quoted in Thompson, *Whigs and Hunters*, p. 209.
64. The wrapper of the recognizance lists only some of the thirty-eight listed as bound over to appear. See SHC: QS2/5/1726, 23. Joshua Toft is listed on the recognizance and not on the wrapper. Nevertheless, at the Sessions, Joshua Toft agreed to keep the peace QS2/2/4 Sessions Minute book, 12 July 1726, No. 23.
65. One of these, William Musgrove, is listed as receiving charity in another document. See SHC: LM/616/2 [c.1689 x 1719] A List of the names of the severall poor people [in Godalming] to whom the charity of £5 is to be given, f. 1r.
66. See SHC: LM/620/1–21, 620/A. Letter from John Netley to Thomas Molyneux, dated 15 April 1710; QS2/6/1725/Xmas CHRISTMAS 1727, 43 examination of John Balchin of Godalming—robbing Mr Walters's fishponds; QS2/6/1725/Xmas CHRISTMAS 1727, 44 examination of John Charriott.
67. Mark Bailey, 'The Rabbit and the Medieval East Anglian Economy', *The Agricultural History Review*, Vol. 36, No. 1 (1988), p. 18; John Sheail, 'Rabbits and Agriculture in Post-medieval England', *Journal of Historical Geography*, Vol. 4, No. 4, (1978), p. 353.
68. Douglas Hay, 'Poaching the game laws on Cannock Chase', in Douglas Hay, Peter Linebaugh, John G. Rule, E. P. Thompson, and Cal Winslow, *Albion's Fatal Tree: Crime and Society in Eighteenth-Century England* (Harmondsworth: Penguin, 1975), pp. 189–253. Deer were dropped from the list of game The Game Act of 1605 in 1671 and rabbits in 1692. See P. B. Munsche, *Gentlemen and Poachers: The English Game Laws 1671–1831* (Cambridge: Cambridge University Press, 1981), pp. 4–5.
69. *London Gazette*, 20 July 1725–24 July 1725.
70. Sheail, 'Rabbits and Agriculture', p. 348.
71. Thirsk, *Alternative Agriculture A History: From the Black Death to the Present Day* (Oxford: Oxford University Press, 1997), pp. 53–4. See attested copy of marriage settlement between Thomas Onslow and Elizabeth Knight, 8 November 1708, SHC: 1427/8/2 for Onslow's acquiring of rabbit warrens as part of his marriage. On Godalming soil see Malcolm Thick, 'Market gardening in England and Wales', in J. Thirsk (ed.), *The Agrarian History of England and Wales, Vol. 5: 1640–1750. II. Agrarian Change* General Editor, Joan Thirsk (Cambridge: Cambridge University Press, 1985), p. 511.
72. Nathanael St André, *A Short Narrative of an Extraordinary Delivery of Rabbets* (London, 1727), p. 24.
73. St André, *A Short Narrative*, p. 24. The coverage of Toft in *Mist's Weekly Journal* on 10 December 1726 is immediately followed by one about deer in

Windsor escaping. The main story in this paper on the front page is about employing the poor.

74. Mary Fissell and Roger Cooter, 'Exploring natural knowledge: science and the popular', in Roy Porter, David C. Lindberg, and Ronald Numbers (eds), *The Cambridge History of Science: Vol. 4: Eighteenth-Century Science* (Cambridge: Cambridge University Press, 2003), p. 151.

75. Cyriacus Ahlers, *Some Observations concerning the Woman of Godlyman* (London, 1726), p. 21.

76. James C. Scott, *Domination and the Arts of Resistance: Hidden Transcripts* (New Haven: Yale University Press, 1990), p. 137.

77. David Rollinson, 'Property, Ideology and Popular Culture in a Gloucester-shire Village, 1660–1740', *Past & Present*, No. 93 (Nov. 1981), pp. 70–97; Jane Humphries, 'Enclosures, Common Rights and Women. The Proletarianiza-tion of Families in the Late Eighteenth and Early Nineteenth Centuries', *Journal of Economic History*, Vol. 50, No. 1 (1990), p. 38.

Chapter 2

1. Nathanael St André, *A Short Narrative of an Extraordinary Delivery of Rabbets* (London, 1727), p. 23. The quote in the chapter title is from Mary Toft's first confession, 7 December 1726, MS Hunter D324, f2. All confessions are stored at Glasgow University Special Collections (GUSC).

2. Philip K. Wilson, 'Toft, Mary (*bap.* 1703, *d.* 1763)', *Oxford Dictionary of National Biography*, (Oxford: Oxford University Press, 2004).

3. St André reports that Mary and Joshua had had three children by the time of the hoax. See St André, *A Short Narrative*, p. 23. Parish records only record two children born to Joshua and Mary by 1726, however. For baptisms and burials, see SHC: Parish Registers for Godalming (St Peter and St Paul). See also Godalming Museum: *The Parish Registers of Godalming: Indexes*.

4. Mary Toft's first confession, MS Hunter D324, f5.

5. *British Journal*, Saturday 22 October 1726; *Daily Journal*, Monday 14 November 1726.

6. St André, *A Short Narrative*, pp. 23, 25.

7. Mary Toft's first confession, 7 December 1726, MS Hunter D324, f1, f2.

8. Michael Roberts, 'Sickles and Scythes: Women's Work and Men's Work at Harvest Time', *History Workshop Journal*, Vol. 7, No. 1 (1979), pp. 3–28; Pamela Sharpe, 'The Female Labour Market in English Agriculture during the Industrial Revolution: Expansion or Contraction?', *The Agricultural History Review*, Vol. 47, No. 2 (1999), pp. 168, 171, 176; Deborah Valenze, *The First Industrial Woman* (Oxford: Oxford University Press, 1995), pp. 13–28.

9. Olwen Hufton, *The Poor of Eighteenth-Century France* (Oxford: Clarendon Press, 1974), p. 16; Olwen Hufton, 'Women and the Family Economy in Eighteenth-Century France', *French Historical Studies*, Vol. 9 (1975), pp. 1–22;

Steven King and Alannah Tomkins (eds), *The Poor in England, 1700–1850: An Economy of Makeshifts* (Manchester: Manchester University Press, 2003), p. 13.

10. Jane Humphries and Jacob Weisdorf, 'The Wages of Women in England, 1260–1850', *Journal of Economic History*, Vol. 75, No. 3 (2015), p. 410; Peter King, 'Customary Rights and Women's Earnings: The Importance of Gleaning to the Rural Labouring Poor, 1750–1850', *Economic History Review*, Vol. 44, No. 3 (1991), pp. 461–76.

11. Jane Humphries, 'Enclosures, Common Rights and Women. The Proletarianization of Families in the Late Eighteenth and Early Nineteenth Centuries', *Journal of Economic History*, Vol. 50 (1990), p. 38; J. L. Hammond and Barbara Hammond, *The Village Labourer* (1911; London: Longmans, 1966), pp. 89–90; E. J. Hobsbawm and George Rudé, *Captain Swing* (1969; London: Penguin, 1973), pp. 202–3, 208–9.

12. Peter Earle, 'The Female Labour Market in London in the Late Seventeenth and Early Eighteenth Centuries', *Economic History Review*, Vol. 42 (1989), pp. 328–53; Mark Hailwood and Jane Whittle, 'Women's Work in Rural England, 1500–1700: A New Methodological Approach', *Local Population Studies*, Vol. 96, No. 1 (Spring 2016), p. 71 and *passim*.

13. Penelope Lane 'Work on the Margins: Poor Women and the Informal Economy of Eighteenth and Early Nineteenth-Century Leicestershire', *Midland History*, Vol. 22, No. 1 (1997), pp. 90–1.

14. Naomi Tadmor, 'Where was Mrs Turner? Governance and gender in an eighteenth-century village', in Steve Hindle, Alexandra Shepard, and John Walter (eds), *Remaking English Society: Social Relations and Social Change in Early Modern England* (Woodbridge: Boydell and Brewer, 2013), pp. 89–111; See Robert Shoemaker and Tim Hitchcock, *London Lives. Poverty, Crime and the Making of a Modern City, 1690–1800* (Cambridge: Cambridge University Press, 2015); Lane, 'Work on the Margins', pp. 93, 94.

15. Calendar of prisoners for Guildford House of Correction, QS2/6/1727/Easter, f31: Surrey History Centre.

16. St André, *Short Narrative*, p. 25; K. D. M. Snell, *Annals of the Labouring Poor. Social Change and Agrarian England, 1660–1900* (Cambridge: Cambridge University Press, 1985), pp. 152–3.

17. Mary Toft's first confession, 7 December 1726, MS Hunter D324, f2.

18. Humphries and Weisdorf, 'Wages of Women in England', pp. 406, 417; Pamela Sharpe, 'The Female Labour Market in English Agriculture during the Industrial Revolution: Expansion or Contraction?', *The Agricultural History Review*, Vol. 47, No. 2 (1999), pp. 172–3.

19. See Craig Muldrew and Stephen King, 'Cash, wages and the economy of makeshifts in England, 1650–1800', in Peter Scholliers and Leonard Schwarz (eds), *Experiencing Wages: Social and Cultural Aspects of Wage Forms in Europe since 1500* (New York: Berghahn, 2003), pp. 155–80.

20. Mary Toft's first confession, 7 December 1726, MS Hunter D324, f2; [no. 394] Will of Mary Hart (X) of Godalming, 29 Dec 1731, proved 4 Mar 1731/2 [DW/ PA/7/21; DW/PA/5/1732/37]. See Cliff Webb, 'Surrey Will Abstracts Archdeaconry Court of Surrey, Registered Wills, 1726–1733' (Vol. 26).

21. Nicola Phillips, *Women in Business, 1700–1800* (Woodbridge: Boydell Press, 2006), pp. 101–3.

22. Humphries and Weisdorf, 'Wages of Women in England', pp. 37, 40–1, 405–47.

23. Bernard Capp, *When Gossips Meet: Women, Family, and Neighbourhood in Early Modern England* (Oxford: Oxford University Press, 2003), pp. 365–73; Amanda E. Herbert, *Female Alliances: Gender, Identity, and Friendship in Early Modern Britain* (New Haven: Yale University Press, 2014), p. 13; William Gouge, *Of Domesticall Duties* (London, 1622), p. 251.

24. St André, *A Short Narrative*, p. 7; *Several Depositions*, pp. 17–18.

25. St André, *A Short Narrative*, p. 8.

26. St André, *A Short Narrative*, pp. 8, 38; Ahlers, *Some Observations concerning the Woman of Godlyman*, pp. 3–4; Richard Manningham, *An Exact Diary of What was Observ'd during a Close Attendance upon Mary Toft* (London, 1726), pp. 7, 11, 26.

27. Roy Porter, 'A touch of danger: the man-midwife as sexual predator', in G. S. Rousseau and Roy Porter (eds), *Sexual Underworlds of the Enlightenment* (Manchester: Manchester University Press, 1987), pp. 206–32.

28. Mary Toft's first confession, 7 December 1726, MS Hunter D324, ff 1, 2, 3.

29. Keith Wrightson, *English Society, 1580–1680* (1982; London: Routledge, 2003), pp 59–69; Tim Reinke-Williams, *Women, Work and Sociability in Early Modern London* (Basingstoke: Palgrave Macmillan, 2004), pp. 127–35. Quote at p. 155.

30. Samantha Williams, 'The Experience of Pregnancy and Childbirth for Unmarried Mothers in London, 1760–1866', *Women's History Review*, Vol. 20, No. 1 (2011), p. 75; Laura Gowing, *Common Bodies: Women, Touch and Power in Seventeenth-Century England* (New Haven: Yale University Press, 2003), p. 156.

31. Laura Gowing, 'Secret Births and Infanticide in Seventeenth-Century England', *Past & Present*, No. 156 (1997), pp. 87–115; Lisa Forman Cody, *Birthing the Nation: Sex, Science, and the Conception of Eighteenth-Century Britons* (Oxford: Oxford University Press, 2005), pp. 269–92; Rachel Weil, 'The politics of legitimacy: women and the warming-pan scandal', in Lois G. Schwoerer (ed.), *The Revolution of 1688–1689: Changing Perspectives* (Cambridge: Cambridge University Press, 1992), pp. 65–82.

32. Jennifer Evans and Sara Read, '"before midnight she had miscarried": Women, Men, and Miscarriage in Early Modern England', *Journal of Family History*, Vol. 40, No. 1 (2015), pp. 3–23. Lisa Smith and special subject articles.

33. Mary E. Fissell, *Vernacular Bodies: The Politics of Reproduction in Early Modern England* (Oxford: Oxford University Press, O2004), pp. 30–1, 148–53; Doreen Evenden, *The Midwives of Seventeenth-Century London* (Cambridge: Cambridge

University Press, 1999); David Harley, 'Provincial midwives in Lancashire and Cheshire, 1660–1760', in Hilary Marland (ed.), *The Art of Midwifery. Early Modern Midwives in Europe* (London: Routledge, 1993), pp. 28–31; Gowing, *Common Bodies*, pp. 159–63.

34. Williams, 'Experience of Pregnancy and Childbirth', p. 70. Gowing, *Common Bodies*, pp. 149–76. See also Linda A. Pollock, 'Childbearing and Female Bonding in Early Modern England', *Social History*, Vol. 22 (1997), pp. 286–306; Adrian Wilson, 'Participant or patient: seventeenth-century childbirth from the mother's point of view', in Roy Porter (ed.), *Patients and Practitioners: Lay Perceptions of Medicine in Pre-industrial Society* (Cambridge: Cambridge University Press, 1985), pp. 129–44; Adrian Wilson, 'The ceremony of childbirth and its interpretation', in V. Fildes (ed.), *Women as Mothers in Pre-industrial England: Essays in Memory of Dorothy Maclaren* (London: Routledge, 1990), pp. 68–107; Sarah Fox, 'Reconceptualizing the Birth Process in Eighteenth-Century England' (unpublished PhD, Manchester, 2017), chapter 4.

35. Capp, *When Gossips Meet*, p. 365–73.

36. Mary Toft's first confession, 7 December 1726, MS Hunter D324, f2; St André, *Short Narrative*, p. 25; *The Parish Registers of Godalming: Indexes*. See burials for Widow Smith December 1728, Mrs Tickner April 1737, and Mary Edsell September 1762. Neither the Archdeaconry of Surrey Muniment book for April 1708—December 1720 (DW/OB/2) or February 1720/1–January 1730/1 (DW/OB/3), held at the London Metropolitan Archives list Ann Toft.

37. Ann Giadina Hess, 'Midwifery practice amongst the Quakers in southern rural England in the late seventeenth century', in Hilary Marland (ed.), *The Art of Midwifery. Early Modern Midwives in Europe* (London: Routledge, 1993), p. 50.

38. Mary Toft's first confession, 7 December 1726, MS Hunter D324, f3.

39. Mary Toft's third confession, 12 December 1726, MS Hunter D328, 1r, f2v; Mary Toft's second confession, 8 December 1726, MS Hunter D327, f9.

40. Keith Wrightson, 'The "Decline of Neighbourliness" revisited', in Norman L. Jones and Daniel Woolf (eds), *Local Identities in Late Medieval and Early Modern England* (Basingstoke: Palgrave Macmillan, 2007), pp. 37–8.

Chapter 3

1. The quote in the chapter title is taken from St André, *A Short Narrative*, p. 7.

2. Will of John Howard, dated 1751, proved 1755, National Archives (TNA): prob11/814/290.

3. Letter from John Howard, surgeon, to Surrey Quarter Sessions, 4 October 1726: Surrey History Centre (SHC): QS2/6/88 Michaelmas 1726.

4. Nathanael St André, *A Short Narrative*, pp. 7, 4–5, 8, 11, 14.

5. Ahlers, *Some Observations concerning the Woman of Godlyman*, pp. 5, 10–11, 8–9, 7, 15.

6. Manningham, *An Exact Diary*, pp. 12, 14, 20–21.

7. Tobias B. Hug, *Impostures in Early Modern England: Representations and Perceptions of Fraudulent Identities* (Manchester: Manchester University Press, 2009), pp. 3, 11.

8. Samantha Williams, 'Experience of Pregnancy and Childbirth', pp. 72–3; Harvey, *Reading Sex*, pp. 102–123.

9. Mary Fissell and Roger Cooter, 'Exploring natural knowledge: science and the popular', in Roy Porter, David C. Lindberg, and Ronald Numbers (eds), *The Cambridge History of Science: Vol. 4: Eighteenth-Century Science* (Cambridge: Cambridge University Press, 2003), p. 150. See also Angus McLaren, 'The pleasures of procreation: traditional and bio-medical theories of conception', in W. F. Bynum and Roy Porter (eds), *William Hunter and the Eighteenth-Century Medical World* (Cambridge: Cambridge University Press, 1985), pp. 323–42.

10. Marie-Hélène Huet, *Monstrous Imagination* (Cambridge, MA: Harvard University Press, 1993); Olivia Weisser, 'Grieved and Disordered: Gender and Emotion in Early Modern Patient Narratives', *Journal of Medieval and Early Modern Studies*, Vol. 43, No. 2 (Spring 2013), pp. 247–73.

11. Daniel Turner, *De Morbis Cutaneis. A Treatise of Diseases Incident to the Skin* (London, 1714), pp. 102–7, 120; John Maubray, *The Female Physician, containing all the Diseases incident to that Sex, in Virgins, Wives and Widows* (London, 1724), p. 59.

12. Todd, *Imagining Monsters*, pp. 106–39.

13. Tim Hitchcock, 'Cultural representations: rogue literature and the reality of the begging body', in Carole Reeves (eds), *A Cultural History of the Human Body in the Enlightenment* (London: Bloomsbury, 2012), p. 183.

14. Letter from William Pountney, no date: GUSC: MS Hunter D321/1; St André, *A Short Narrative*, p. 7.

15. Mary Toft's first confession, 7 December 1726, MS Hunter D324, f3; St André, *A Short Narrative*, pp. 5–6; Mary Toft's second confession, 8 December 1726, MS Hunter D327, f8r.

16. St André, *A Short Narrative*, pp. 7, 20, 28, 31, 33; Ahlers, *Some Observations concerning the Woman of Godlyman*, pp. 1–2; Manningham, *An Exact Diary*, pp. 6, 7.

17. St André, *A Short Narrative*, p. 32; *Evening Post*, December 1–December 3, 1726; Manningham, *An Exact Diary*, p. 38; 'Postscript' to the Preface dated 8 December, Ahlers, *Some Observations concerning the Woman of Godlyman*, no page number.

18. Nathanael St André, *A Short Narrative of an Extraordinary Delivery of Rabbets* (1727), pp. 3–4; Ahlers, *Some Observations concerning the Woman of Godlyman*, preface, no page number.

19. St André, *A Short Narrative*, pp. 13, 10, 20, 5–6, 7, 32–40. See *The History and Description of Guildford; the Country Town of Surrey*, Guildford, 1801, p. 235, on Joseph Burtt (mayor in 1726) and James Cliffton mayor in 1720 and 1730.
20. St André, *A Short Narrative*, pp. 8, 12, 9.
21. Ahlers, *Some Observations concerning the Woman of Godlyman*, pp. 5, 24, 28.
22. Manningham, *An Exact Diary*, pp. 8–9, 11, 14, 19.
23. Manningham, *An Exact Diary*, p. 17; Lisa Forman Cody, '"The doctor's in labour; or, a new whim wham from Guildford"', Gender & History, Vol. 4 (1992), pp. 179–82.
24. St André, *A Short Narrative*, pp. 9, 20, 23–24.
25. Manningham, *An Exact Diary*, p. 36.
26. Mary Toft's second confession, 8 December 1726, MS Hunter D327, f11.
27. Thomas Braithwaite, *Remarks on a Short Narrative of an Extraordinary Delivery of Rabbet, perform'd by Mr. John Howard, Surgeon at Guildford* (London, 1726), p. 32; *Evening Post*, 6 December 1726–8 December 1726.
28. J. Douglas, M. D., *An Advertisement Occasion'd by Some Passages in Sir. R. Manningham's Diary Lately Publish'd* (London, 1727), p. 29; Mary Toft's first confession, 7 December 1726, MS Hunter D324, f9, v10; St André, *A Short Narrative*, pp. 28–9.

Chapter 4

1. The quote in the chapter title is taken from Richard Manningham's description of the people in the bagnio in *An Exact Diary of what was observ'd during a close attendance of Mary Toft* (1726), p. 21.
2. *British Journal*, Saturday 3 December, 1726.
3. *Survey of London*, General Editor F. H. W. Sheppard (London: Athlone Press, University of London, 1966), Vol. II, p. 68. See http://www.hrionline.ac.uk/strype/index.jsp
4. Westminster Archives (WA): Lease for Leicester Square, St Martin-in-the-Fields, 12 March 1723, WA: 0067/035; *Survey of London Volume XXXIV*, p. 429.
5. *Survey of London Volume XXXIV*, pp. 492; 500. See also WA: New Street Ward, Scavenger's Rate Ledger (1726), volume F5606, f1-2; and Lease for Leicester Square, St Martin-in-the-Field, 8 June 1726, WA: 0067/047. The property also had the joint fourth highest rateable value in that stretch of Leicester Field properties lying in the parish of St Martin's in the Fields. WA: New Street Ward, Scavenger's Rate Ledger (1726), volume F5606, f1-2.
6. Lacy v Underwood, complaint of Lacy, 5 December 1726, National Archives (TNA): C 11/1462/24(1); Answer of William Wilcocks and Catherine Roos, 1727. TNA: C 11/1823/9.
7. *Daily Post*, 8 March 1726.
8. Lacy v Underwood, complaint of Lacy, 5 December 1726, TNA: C 11/1462/24(1).

9. Douglas, *An Advertisement Occasion'd by Some Passages in Sir R. Manningham's Diary*, p. 7.
10. St André, *A Short Narrative*, p. 27; Lord Hervey to Henry Fox, 3 December 1726. Lord Hervey to Henry Fox, 3 December 1726; Hervey MS.941/47/4, pp. 29–32. Suffolk Record Office, Bury St Edmunds. Quoted in Todd, p. 29.
11. *Daily Journal*, Friday, 2 December 1726.
12. Arthur MacGregor, 'Sloane, Sir Hans, baronet (1660–1753)', physician and collector, *Oxford Dictionary of National Biography* (Oxford: Oxford University Press, 2004). http://www.oxforddnb.com/view/10.1093/ref:odnb/9780198614128.001.0001/odnb-9780198614128-e-25730 (accessed 22/11/18).
13. Manningham, *An Exact Diary*, p. 19; Nathanael St André, Anatomist to George I: Letter to Sir H. Sloane, British Library (BL): Sloane MS 4060, f. 233 (1726).
14. Letter from St André to James Douglas, 29 Nov. 1726. Glasgow University Special Collections (GUSC): MS Hunter D322; Douglas, *An Advertisement Occasion'd by Some Passages in Sir R. Manningham's Diary*, p. 6.
15. Douglas, *An Advertisement Occasion'd by Some Passages in Sir R. Manningham's Diary*, p. 8; Letter from William Pountney, no date: GUSC: MS Hunter D321/1; BL Add Ms 70400 Letters to the 2nd Lord Oxford 1723–39: John Wainwright to Edward Harley, 8 December 1726.
16. Philip Rhodes, 'Manningham, Sir Richard (*bap.* 1685, *d.* 1759)', man-midwife. *Oxford Dictionary of National Biography* (Oxford: Oxford University Press, 2004). http://www.oxforddnb.com/view/10.1093/ref:odnb/9780198614128.001.0001/odnb-9780198614128-e-17982 (accessed 19/12/17); Will of Richard Manningham, 12 April 1759: The National Archives, PROB 11/84/352.
17. Helen Brock, 'Douglas, James (*bap.* 1675, *d.* 1742)', anatomist and man-midwife. *Oxford Dictionary of National Biography* (Oxford: Oxford University Press, 2004). http://www.oxforddnb.com/view/10.1093/ref:odnb/9780198614128.001.0001/odnb-9780198614128-e-7899 (accessed 19/12/17); Manningham, *Exact Diary*, p. 24; Dennis Todd, 'St André, Nathanael (1679/80–1776)', anatomist and surgeon. *Oxford Dictionary of National Biography* (Oxford: Oxford University Press, 2004). http://www.oxforddnb.com/view/10.1093/ref:odnb/9780198614128.001.0001/odnb-9780198614128-e-24478 (accessed 19/12/17).
18. Letter from St André (1680–1776) to James Douglas, 3 December 1726, trying to persuade him to continue his interest in the case. MS Hunter D323; Manningham, *Exact Diary*, pp. 19–20.
19. Douglas, *An Advertisement Occasion'd by Some Passages in Sir R. Manningham's Diary*, p. 10.
20. Peter Dear, *Revolutionizing the Sciences: European Knowledge and its Ambitions, 1500–1700* (Princeton: Princeton University Press, 2009), pp. 99–126.
21. See BL: Sloane MS 4058/f54 and 4058/f260.
22. Thomas Brathwaite, *Remarks on a Short Narrative of an Extraordinary Delivery of Rabbets* (London, 1726), p. 21.

23. Manningham, *Exact Diary*, p. 19; Douglas, *An Advertisement Occasion'd by Some Passages in Sir R. Manningham's Diary*, pp. 11–12.

24. Manningham, *Exact Diary*, pp. 24, 25.

25. *Daily Journal*, Friday 2 December, 1726.

26. Manningham, *Exact Diary*, p. 24; John Maubray, *The Female Physician, containing all the Diseases incident to that Sex, in Virgins, Wives and Widows* (London, 1724), p. 62. For references to 'cunny', see *Round about our coal-fire: or Christmas entertainments. Containing, Christmas gambols, tropes, figures* (London, [1730]), p. 24. Hogarth himself was to later live in Leicester Square at no. 33. See *Survey of London Volume XXXIV: The Parish of St Anne Soho*, General Editor F. H. W. Sheppard (London: Athlone Press, University of London, 1966), p. 501.

27. St André, *A Short Narrative*, pp. 39, 30.

28. Cody, *Birthing the Nation*.

29. St André, *A Short Narrative*, p. 38.

30. Dana Y. Rabin, 'Searching for the Self in Eighteenth-Century English Criminal Trials, 1730–1800', *Eighteenth-Century Life*, Vol. 27 (2003), p. 86.

31. *Several Depositions*, p. 19.

32. GUSC: Statement in unknown hand, MS Hunter D331. On the dating of the depiction in the image, see Dennis Todd, 'Three Characters in Hogarth's *Cunicularii* and Some Implications', *Eighteenth-Century Studies*, Vol. 16, No. 1 (1982), p. 37.

33. *Daily Journal*, Wed 11 January 1727; *British Journal*, Saturday 10 December, 1726; Manningham, *Exact Diary*, p. 25.

34. *British Journal*, Saturday 10 December, 1726.

35. Indenture of Lease for Leicester Square, 1723, LMA: HMD/X/145. The deed is for 1723 between John, Earl of Leicester and Constance Susannah D'Agar. Like several of the leases for the other side of the square (above) Sir Arthur Onslow from Clandon is also mentioned (alongside many parties). Onslow was the cousin of the Thomas Onslow, 2nd Baron, who investigated the case in Surrey. But Arthur had lost his parents young and had been taken in by Thomas' father, Richard.

36. *Several Depositions*, pp. 7, 10.

37. Arthur Onslow, 'An Account of the Onslow Family', in *The Manuscripts of the Earl of Buckinghamshire, the Earl of Lindsey, the Earl of Onslow, Lord Emly, Theodore J. Hare Esq., and James Round, Esq., M.P, Historical Manuscripts Commission 14th Rep. Appendix, ix*, (London, 1895), p. 495. Thanks to Mary Clayton for this reference.

38. Thomas Onslow, 2nd Baron Onslow to Sir H. Sloane, BL: Sloane MS 4048/f227.

39. These three men were all mentioned in Manningham, *Exact Diary*, p. 20.

40. Bills and vouchers of the 2nd Duke and Duchess of Richmond paid between July 1723 and Michaelmas 1732. 1723–1732, WSCA: Goodwood MSS 120, f61;

WSCA: Goodwood/56 1726–1748; Timothy J. McCann, 'Lennox, Charles, second duke of Richmond, second duke of Lennox, and duke of Aubigny in the French nobility (1701–1750)', *Oxford Dictionary of National Biography* (Oxford: Oxford University Press, 2004). http://www.oxforddnb.com/view/article/16450 (accessed 14/5/13)

41. West Sussex County Archive (WSCA): Goodwood papers, GWD112, 289; Goodwood MSS 123: Ledger, kept by Peter Labbe. July 1726–July 1732, ff3, 8, 11, 16, 17; Goodwood MSS 120: Bills and vouchers of the 2nd Duke and Duchess of Richmond paid between July 1723 and Michaelmas 1732. 1723–1732, ff. 79, 92, 97, 143.

42. Manningham, *Exact Diary*, p. 32.

43. Todd, *Imagining Monsters*, p. 32; 'Report for the Lords Comm^r of Trade for his Ma^{ys} Approbation of Mr Calvert to be Governor of Maryland', Privy Council, Colonial Papers, PC 1/48/22, TNA. Accessed via www.AALT.law.uh.edu (accessed 3/9/15). On Baltimore see *The History of Parliament: the House of Commons 1715–1754*, ed. R. Sedgwick, 1970. Accessed via http://www.historyofparliamentonline.org/research (accessed 3/9/15); Troy O. Bickham, 'Calvert, Charles, fifth Baron Baltimore (1699–1751)', *Oxford Dictionary of National Biography* (Oxford: Oxford University Press, 2004). http://www.oxforddnb.com/view/article/75619 (accessed 3/9/15).

44. He paid £32 12s to John Booth for 'Law Charges' on 7 December 1726. See Northampton County Record Office (NCRO): Montagu Cash Book (Household Accounts) 1726–1746; For the candles see Montagu Housekeeper's Journal 1726–1746, f27 Dec 5 and F28–Dec 13. For other household items for Blackheath see Montagu Steward's Accounts 1726–1728, First No. 74–1 Jan 1725/6–1 Jan 1726/7, f52. On Montagu see Edward Charles Metzger, 'Montagu, John, second duke of Montagu (1690–1749)', *Oxford Dictionary of National Biography* (Oxford: Oxford University Press, 2004). http://www.oxforddnb.com/view/article/19025 (accessed 14/5/13).

45. NCRO: Montagu to the Duchess of Montagu, Montagu Volume 5—letters of the Montagu Family (Vol. III), 1673–1758, f23; Montagu Volume 7—Letters to the Montagu family 1536–1747, f209, f210–11, f215.

46. Letter to the Duke from R. Jones congratulating him on the birth of a son. Dated 14 Nov. 1725. NCRO: Montagu Volume 7—Letters to the Montagu family 1536–1747, F157. For the nursing payment see NCRO: Montagu Steward's Accounts 1726–1728, No. 74 Mr Marchant's Account from 1 January 1725/6 to Michmas 1727, F18, 26 May 1727 'Paid Ann Wall for Nursing' £3 3s.

47. Montagu to the Lady Mary Churchill, Duchess of Montagu, no date, NCRO: Montagu Volume 5—Letters of the Montagu Family (Vol. III), 1673–1758, f23; John Montagu, 2nd Duke of Montagu: Letter to Lord Macclesfield, 27 June 1726, BL: Stowe MS 750, f. 420.

48. Manningham, *Exact Diary*, p. 32.

49. Papers relating to the Royal Household, Privy-purse expenditure, and establishments for members of the Royal Family, principally in the rein of George II., BL Add MS 33045: f. 19 George I of England: Expenses of the royal household: circ. 1726.

50. Thomas Onslow, 2nd Baron Onslow: Warrant to, as Teller of the Exchequer: 8 August 1727. (III. ff. 371). 1727. BL Add MS 36127: Sir Robert Walpole, 1st Earl of Orford; Prime Minister: Warrants signed by, as Chancellor of the Exchequer: 1721–1733, f. 45.

51. See for example Richmond's request for Montagu's support in lobbying the Bishop of London in 1723: Charles Lennox, 2nd Duke of Richmond to Montagu, 4 June 1723, NCRO: Montagu Volume 2 Original letters (Vol. II) 1681–1765, f76.

52. Thompson, *Whigs and Hunters*, pp. 151, 212–13.

53. *London Gazette*, 20 July 1725–24 July 1725; *Daily Journal*, Thursday 10 March, 1726. Clarges was a Tory, though favoured by the Whigs. He was made a gentleman of the privy chamber under George II (in Nov. 1728), having already served in the Middlesex lieutenancy since 1716. Source: http://www.historyofparliamentonline.org/volume/1690–1715/member/clarges-sir-thomas–1688–1759. See also Norma Landau, *The Justices of the Peace, 1679–1760* (Berkeley: University of California Press, 1984); Sharpe, *Crime in Early Modern England*, pp. 28–9. On summary justice see Faramerz Dabhoiwala, 'Summary Justice in Early Modern London', *The English Historical Review*, Vol. 121, No. 492 (2006), pp. 796–822; Lee Davison and Tim Keirn, 'The Reactive State: English Governance and Society, 1689–1750', in Lee Davison, Tim Hitchcock, Tim Keirn, and Robert B. Shocmaker (eds), *Stilling the Grumbling Hive: The Response to Social and Economic Problems in England, 1689–1750* (New York: St. Martin's Press, 1992), pp. xxxv–xxxvi.

54. See *Daily Post*, Tuesday 6 December, 1726; *Parker's Penny Post*, Wednesday 7 December, 1726; *The London Journal*, Saturday 17 December 1726; Manningham, *Exact Diary*, pp. 31, 32.

55. *British Journal*, Saturday 10 December, 1726.

56. *Daily Post*, Thursday 18 May 1727; *Daily Post*, Saturday 20 May 1727; Court of Common Please Affidavits, CP 3/5, 1726–1727 (and CP 3/6, 1728–1729).

Chapter 5

1. The quote in the chapter title is taken from Mary Toft's third confession, 12 December 1726, MS Hunter D328, 2r.

2. Manningham, *Exact Diary*, p. 25.

3. *Daily Post*, Tuesday 6 December 1726; Manningham, *Exact Diary*, p. 31.

4. Manningham, *Exact Diary*, pp. 33–5; *The London Journal*, Saturday 17 December 1726.

5. Statement of why James Douglas cannot publish an account of Mary Toft's confession. MS Hunter D329, recto: GUSC.
6. *British Journal*, Saturday 22 October 1726; *Daily Journal*, Monday 14 November 1726; St André, *A Short Narrative*, p. 36.
7. *The London Journal*, Saturday 17 December 1726.
8. Mary Toft's first confession, 7 December 1726, MS Hunter D324, f1.
9. Mary Toft's first confession, 7 December 1726, MS Hunter D324, f14.
10. Mary Toft's first confession, 7 December 1726, MS Hunter D324, f14.
11. On the difficulties in using such collaborative documents, see Frances E. Dolan, *True Relations: Reading, Literature, and Evidence in Seventeenth-Century England* (Philadelphia: University of Pennsylvania Press, 2013), pp. 56–86, 112–17.
12. Mary Toft's first confession, 7 December 1726, MS Hunter D324, f13.
13. MS Hunter D327 (confession 2), 8 December 1726, f6.
14. Fair copy of Mary Toft's confession, MS Hunter 325: GUSC, f3.
15. Fair copy of Mary Toft's confession, MS Hunter 325, f4–f4v.
16. Mary Toft's first confession, 7 December 1726, MS Hunter D324, f8.
17. An account of Mary Toft's first confession, GUSC: MS Hunter D326, f1v.
18. Mary Toft's first confession, 7 December 1726, f1, 5–5v, 6.
19. Mary Toft's first confession, 7 December 1726, f14.
20. Mary Toft's second confession, 8 December 1726, MS Hunter D327, f8v.
21. *Daily Journal*, Saturday 10 December, 1726.
22. Mary Toft's third confession, 12 December 1726, MS Hunter D328, f3v.
23. Mary Toft's third confession, 12 December 1726, MS Hunter D328, f1.
24. GSC: MS Hunter D327 (confession 2), 8 December 1726, 6r.
25. On assessing truth in statements see Aldert Vrij, *Detecting Lies and Deceit: Pitfalls and Opportunities*, 2nd edn (Chichester: Wiley-Blackwell, 2008), pp. 204–18. Mary Toft's confessions meet at least fourteen of Vrij's nineteen criteria for identifying a statement of truth.
26. Diane Purkiss, 'Losing babies, losing stories: attending to women's confessions in Scottish witch-trials', in Margaret Mikesell and Adele F. Seeff (eds), *Culture and Change: Attending to Early Modern Women* (Newark, DE: University of Delaware Press, 2003), p. 147.
27. Jennifer Evans and Sara Read, '"before midnight she had miscarried": Women, Men, and Miscarriage in Early Modern England', *Journal of Family History*, Vol. 40, No. 1 (2015), pp. 3–23.
28. Mary Toft's first confession, 7 December 1726, MS Hunter D324, 1r; Mary Toft's second confession, 8 December 1726, MS Hunter D327, 1r.
29. St André, *A Short Narrative*, p. 24; Mary Toft's first confession, 7 December 1726, MS Hunter D324, 1r, f2.
30. St André, *A Short Narrative*, pp. 25–6.
31. Thanks to Lizzie Eger for this reference. See also Joanne Begiato, '"Breeding" a "little stranger": managing uncertainty in pregnancy in later Georgian

England', in Ciara Meehan and Jennifer Evans (eds), *Perceptions of Pregnancy from the Seventeenth to the Twentieth Century* (Basingstoke: Palgrave Macmillan, 2016), pp. 13–33; and Elizabeth Raisanen, 'Pregnancy Poems in the Romantic Period: Re-Writing the Mother's Legacy', *Women's Studies*, Vol. 45, No. 2 (2016), pp. 101–21.

32. E. Kamgobe, A. Massinde, D. Matovelo, E. Ndaboine, P. Rambau, and T. Chaula, 'Uterine Myometrial Mature Teratoma Presenting as a Uterine Mass: A Review of Literature', *BMC Clinical Pathology*, Vol 16, No. 5 (2016): doi:10.1186/s12907-016-0026-8.

33. Williams, 'Experience of Pregnancy and Childbirth', p. 81.

34. Thomas Howard, surgeon of Guildford, described that Ahlers had taken animal parts from Toft's uterus. See St André, *A Short Narrative*, pp. 39–40. Ahlers categorically denied this in his Preface.

35. St André, *A Short Narrative*, pp. 8, 19.

36. Mary Toft's first confession, 7 December 1726, MS Hunter D324, 2r, 4r; Mary Toft's second confession, 8 December 1726, MS Hunter D327, 3r; Mary Toft's third confession, 12 December 1726, MS Hunter D328, 1r.

37. See Jennifer Corns, 'The Inadequacy of Unitary Characterizations of Pain', *Philosophical Studies: An International Journal for Philosophy in the Analytic Tradition* (2014), pp. 169, 355–78; G. R. Gillett, 'The Neurophilosophy of Pain', *Philosophy*, Vol. 66 (1991), pp. 191–206; Ronald Melzack and Patrick D. Wall, *The Challenge of Pain* (1982; Harmondsworth: Penguin, 1996), pp. 15–33; Elaine Scarry, *The Body in Pain* (Oxford: Oxford University Press, 1985); Jan Frans van Dijkhuizen and Karl A. E. Enenkel, 'Introduction: constructions of physical pain in early modern culture', in Jan Frans van Dijkhuizen and Karl A. E. Enenkel (eds), *The Sense of Suffering: Constructions of Physical Pain in Early Modern Culture* (Leiden: Brill, 2008).

38. Mary Toft's second confession, 8 December 1726, MS Hunter D327, 1r; Mary Toft's first confession, 7 December 1726, MS Hunter D324, 11r. See also St André, *A Short Narrative*, p. 29 for an earlier reference to the metaphor of tearing paper. On pain in childbirth in this period, see Sharon Howard, 'Imagining the Pain and Peril of Seventeenth-century Childbirth: Travail and Deliverance in the Making of an Early Modern World', *The Society for the Social History of Medicine*, Vol. 16 (2003), pp. 367–82.

39. Didier Fassin and Richard Rechtman, *The Empire of Trauma: An Inquiry into the Condition of Victimhood*, trans. Rachel Gomme (2007; Princeton: Princeton University Press, 2009); Louise DeSalvo, *Writing as a Way of Healing: How Telling Our Stories Transforms Our Lives* (London: Beacon Press, 1999), pp. 181–7.

40. Mary Toft's second confession, 8 December 1726, MS Hunter D327, f9; Mary Toft's third confession, 12 December 1726, MS Hunter D328, 3r.

41. Mary Toft's third confession, 12 December 1726, MS Hunter D328, f2v.

42. Mary Toft's first confession, 7 December 1726, 5–5v, 6, 6r.

43. Mary Toft's second confession, 8 December 1726, MS Hunter D327, f9.

44. Mary Toft's second confession, 8 December 1726, MS Hunter D327, f8.
45. Mary Toft's third confession, 12 December 1726, MS Hunter D328, f1, f2, f3.
46. Mary Toft's third confession, 12 December 1726, MS Hunter D328, 2r.
47. Mary Toft's third confession, 12 December 1726, MS Hunter D328, 2v.
48. Pollock, 'Childbearing and female bonding', pp. 290–1; Linda Pollock, 'Embarking on a rough passage: the experience of pregnancy in early modern society', in V. Fildes (ed.), *Women as Mothers in Pre-industrial England: Essays in Memory of Dorothy Maclaren* (London: Routledge, 1990), pp. 47–9; Herman Roodenburg, 'The Maternal Imagination: The Fears of Pregnant Women in Seventeenth-Century Holland', *Journal of Social History*, Vol. 21 (1988), pp. 701–16.
49. Purkiss, 'Losing babies, losing stories', pp. 143–60. Jonathan B. Durrant, *Witchcraft, Gender and Society in Early Modern Germany* (Leiden: Brill, 2007). Lyndal Roper, '"Evil Imaginings and Fantasies": Child-Witches and the End of the Witch Craze', *Past & Present*, No. 167 (2000), pp. 107–39; Louise Jackson, 'Witches, Wives and Mothers: Witchcraft Persecution and Women's Confessions in Seventeenth-Century England', *Women's History Review*, Vol. 4 (1995), p. 74 and *passim*; Lyndal Roper, *Oedipus and the Devil: Witchcraft, Sexuality and Religion in Early Modern Europe* (London: Routledge, 1994), pp. 199–225.
50. St André, *A Short Narrative*, p. 23.
51. St André, *A Short Narrative*, pp. 23–4.
52. Amanda Jane Whiting, *Women and Petitioning in the Seventeenth-Century English Revolution* (Turnhout, Belgium: Brepols, 2015); Paula McDowell, *The Women of Grub Street: Press, Politics and Gender in the London Literary Marketplace, 1678–1730* (Oxford: Clarendon, 1998). See also James Daybell (ed.), *Women and Politics in Early Modern England, 1450–1700* (Aldershot: Ashgate, 2004); Kathryn Gleadle and Sarah Richardson (eds), *Women in British Politics, 1760–1860: The Power of the Petticoat* (Basingstoke: Macmillan, 2000); Karen Green, *A History of Women's Political Thought in Europe, 1700–1800* (Cambridge: Cambridge University Press, 2014); Barbara J. Harris, 'Women and Politics in Early Tudor England', *Historical Journal*, Vol. 33 (1990), pp. 259–8; Elaine Chalus, '"My Minerva at My Elbow": the political roles of women in eighteenth-century England', in Stephen Taylor, Richard Connors, and Clyve Jones (eds), *Hanoverian Britain and Empire: Essays in Memory of Philip Lawson* (Woodbridge: Boydell, 1998), pp. 210–28; Elaine Chalus, *Elite Women in English Political Life, c.1754–1790* (Oxford: Oxford University Press, 2005); Ingrid Tague, *Women of Quality: Accepting and Contesting Ideals of Femininity in England, 1690–1760* (Woodbridge: Boydell, 2002); Elaine Chalus, '"Ladies Are Often Very Good Scaffoldings": Women and Politics in the Age of Anne', *Parliamentary History*, p. 158; Caitlin Blackwell, '"The Feather'd Fair in a Fright": The Emblem of the Feather in Graphic Satire of 1776', *Journal for Eighteenth-Century Studies*, Vol. 36, No. 3 (2013), pp. 353–76; Peter Stallybrass

and Rosalind Jones, 'The needle and the pen: needlework and the appro-priation of printed texts', in *Renaissance Clothing and the Materials of Memory* (Cambridge: Cambridge University Press, 2000), pp. 134–71.

53. Laura Gowing, 'Ordering the body: illegitimacy and female authority in seventeenth-century England', in Michael J. Braddick and John Walter (eds), *Negotiating Power in Early Modern Society: Order, Hierarchy and Subordination in Britain and Ireland* (Cambridge: Cambridge University Press, 2001), pp. 43–62.

54. J. A. Sharpe, 'Witchcraft and Women in Seventeenth-Century England', *Continuity and Change*, Vol. 6 (1991), pp. 179–99; Jonathan Barry, *Witchcraft and Demonology in South-West England, 1640–1789* (Basingstoke: Palgrave Macmillan, 2012), p. 204. See also Garthine Walker, *Crime, Gender and Social Order in Early Modern England* (Cambridge: Cambridge University Press, 2003), where Walker points out that 'Women's violence was a manifest-ation of contests for feminine superiority' (p. 98).

55. Lisa Forman Cody, '"The doctor's in labour, or, A new whim wham from Guildford"', *Gender and History*, Vol. 4 (1992), p. 182.

56. *Daily Journal*, Saturday 10 December, 1726; *Brice's Weekly Journal*, Friday 16 December, 1726.

Chapter 6

1. As suggested by the description of her crime in the title of this chapter, taken from the 'Calendar of yᵉ names together with a Copy of yᵉ Causes of Committals' for the house of correction, 5 January 1726/7.

2. Nicholas Rogers, 'Popular Protest in Early Hanoverian London', *Past & Present*, No. 79 (May 1978); David Lemmings, 'The dark side of the Enlight-enment: *The London Journal*, moral panics, and the law in the eighteenth century', in David Lemmings and Claire Walker (eds), *Moral Panics, the Media and the Law in Early Modern England* (Basingstoke: Palgrave Macmillan, 2009); J. M. Beattie, *Crime and the Courts in England, 1660–1800* (Oxford: Oxford University Press, 1986), p. 517; Thompson, *Whigs and Hunters*, pp. 196–7. On women in particular see, Robert B. Shoemaker, 'Print and the Female Voice: Representations of Women's Crime in London, 1690–1735', *Gender & History*, Vol. 22, No. 1, April 2012, p. 75; J. M. Beattie, *Policing and Punishment in London 1660–1750: Urban Crime and the Limits of Terror* (Oxford: Oxford University Press, 2001), p. 65; Robert B. Shoemaker, *Prosecution and Punishment: Petty Crime and the Law in London and Rural Middlesex* (Cambridge: Cambridge University Press, 1991), pp. 185–6; John Beattie, '"Hard-pressed to make ends meet": women and crime in Augustan London', in Valerie Frith (ed.), *Women and History: Voices of Early Modern England* (Toronto: Coach House Press, 1995), p. 105.

3. Four recognizances survive (three for witnesses to give evidence and one for John Howard to appear before the court to 'Answer what shall be objected

against him on Suspicion of/Conspiring with one Mary Toft'. See LMA: MJ/ SR/2475 January 1727, 37, 160, 161, and 162. No recognizance can be found for Mary Toft herself. On early modern policing within communities, see Paul Griffiths, *Lost Londons: Change, Crime, and Control in the Capital City, 1550–1660* (Cambridge: Cambridge University Press, 2008).

4. 'Calendar of ye names together with a Copy of ye Causes of Committals' for the house of correction, 5 January 1726/7, LMA: MJ/SR/2475 January 1727, number 160, 161, and 162; *Mist's Weekly Journal*, Saturday 14 January, 1727. For the reference to Elizabeth Williams appearing at King's Bench, see LMA: MJ/ SB/B/0084, 847/27.

5. On the move to King's Bench see *The London Journal*, Saturday 14 January 1727; Index to Plea Roll, 13 Geo. I, fo. 557: TNA, KB 29/386; Draft Rule Book, 13 Geo. I, fo. 1: TNA, KB 36/42. Howard's bail was reported in LMA: MJ/SB/B/0084, 847/46 and *Daily Journal*, Wednesday 11 January 1727. On King's Bench see Ruth Paley, 'The King's Bench (Crown Side) in the long eighteenth century', in Christopher Dyer et al. (eds), *New Directions in Local History since Hoskins* (Hatfield, 2011), 232. Defendants could remove convictions to King's Bench from lower courts so as to quash them: see Douglas Hay (ed.), *Criminal Cases on the Crown Side of King's Bench: Staffordshire, 1740–1800, Collections for a History of Staffordshire*, fourth series, Vol. 24 (Staffordshire Record Society, 2010), pp. 6–9. The Toft case was being handled by the sessions in the vacation between the Michaelmas and Hilary terms 1726–27.

6. *Daily Journal*, 20 December 1726. There is no record of any actions relating to this case in the records of the Privy Council. The Attorney General or Solicitor General could bring an information 'ex officio' for a criminal prosecution in King's Bench, though these were supposed to be used for serious misdemeanours. See Hay (ed.), *Criminal Cases on the Crown Side of King's Bench*, p. 277. On Howard's voting see poll book for Guildford Borough election, SHC: 1251/8, pp. 1, 8.

7. Statement of why James Douglas could not publish an account of Mary Toft's confession, GSC: MS Hunter D329. On Paxton see Beattie, *Policing and Punishment*, pp. 388–9, and pp. 370–423 for the increasing involvement of the government in criminal prosecution.

8. Cody, *Birthing the Nation*, pp. 130–2; Todd, *Imagining Monsters*, p. 275, n. 28.

9. St André, *A Short Narrative*, pp. 4–5; Ahlers, *Some Observations*, pp. ii, v; *Daily Journal*, Friday 2 December, 1726

10. For example, the Westminster Bridewell Kalendar Sept Sessions 1727, LMA: MJ/CP/P/35, lists the fifty-eight prisoners, thirty-eight of whom are women.

11. General Order book, LMA: WJ/OC/001, 20 April 1720–26 April 1728, ff92, 109.

12. *Brice's Weekly Journal*, Friday 16 December 1726; *Mist's Weekly Journal*, Saturday 14 January 1727; *British Journal*, Saturday 14 January 1727.

13. Andrea McKenzie, 'The Real Macheath: Social Satire, Appropriation, and Eighteenth-Century Criminal Biography', *Huntington Library Quarterly*, Vol. 69, No. 4 (December 2006), pp. 581–605.

14. 'Calendar of ye names together with a Copy of ye Causes of Committals', Number 160; *Daily Journal*, Tuesday 20 December 1726. Republished in *British Journal*, Saturday 24 December 1726.

15. Mary Smith, Margaret Davies, trial for grand larceny, 13 January 1727, Old Bailey Proceedings Online: t17270113-38. On the growing publicity of birth see Lisa Forman Cody, 'The Politics of Reproduction: From Midwives' Alternative Public Sphere to the Public Spectacle of Man-Midwifery', *Eighteenth-Century Studies*, Vol. 32, No. 4 (1999), pp. 477–95.

16. Eleven were published after the hoax was revealed and four before. This is only for those published in 1726. Another seventeen were published in the spring of 1727.

17. *Mist's Weekly Journal*, Saturday 4 February 1727; *Daily Journal*, 9 January 1727; *Mist's Weekly Journal*, Saturday 14 January 1727.

18. *Daily Journal*, Tuesday 20 December 1726; *Mist's Weekly Journal*, Saturday 24 December 1726. On monsters in the Enlightenment see Jack Lynch, *Deception and Detection in Eighteenth-Century Britain* (Aldershot: Ashgate, 2008), pp. 97, 142–4; Julia V. Douthwaite, *The Wild Girl, Natural Man, and the Monster: Dangerous Experiments in the Age of Enlightenment* (Chicago: University of Chicago Press, 2002); and Marie-Hélène Huet, *Monstrous Imagination* (Cambridge, MA: Harvard University Press, 1993). See especially Todd, *Imagining Monsters*, p. 126, on Toft in this context.

19. *Mist's Weekly Journal*, Saturday 31 December 1726.

20. Todd, 'Three Characters in Hogarth's Cunicularii', pp. 26–46.

21. Ronald Paulson, 'Putting out the Fire in Her Imperial Majesty's Apartment: Opposition Politics, Anticlericalism, and Aesthetics', *ELH*, Vol. 63, No. 1 (Spring, 1996), p. 99.

22. William Hogarth, *The Analysis of Beauty. Written with a view of fixing the fluctuating Ideas of Taste* (London, 1753), p. 125.

23. *Mist's Weekly Journal*, 21 January 1727. See Paulson, 'Putting out the Fire', p. 107, n. 55.

24. St André, *A Short Narrative*, p. 23.

25. Marcia Pointon, *Hanging the Head: Portraiture and Social Formation in Eighteenth-Century England* (New Haven: Yale University Press for Paul Mellon Centre for Studies in British Art, 1993), pp. 87–9. Pointon also notes that the image may have served as the inspiration for Hogarth's image of the convicted murderess Sarah Malcolm (p. 87).

26. Hogarth, *Analysis of Beauty*, pp. 19, 23.

27. Shearer West, 'Secrets and Desires: Pastel Collecting in the Early Eighteenth-Century Dresden Court', *Oxford Art Journal*, Vol. 38, No. 2 (2015), pp. 209–23. On beauty and whiteness see Kimberly Poitevin, 'Inventing Whiteness:

Cosmetics, Race, and Women in Early Modern England', *The Journal for Early Modern Cultural Studies*, Vol. 11, No. 1 (2011), pp. 59–89. Pointon comments on a possible connection between the images of Toft and Carriera in *Hanging the Head*, p. 87.

28. St André, *A Short Narrative*, pp. 23–4.

29. Juliet McMaster, *Reading the Body in the Eighteenth-Century Novel* (Basingstoke: Palgrave Macmillan, 2004); Kathryn Woods, '"Facing" Identity in a "Faceless" Society: Physiognomy, Facial Appearance and Identity Perception in Eighteenth-Century London', *Cultural and Social History*, Vol. 14, No. 2 (2017), pp. 137–53. On Toft as performer see Jenifer Buckley, *Gender, Pregnancy and Power in Eighteenth-Century Literature: The Maternal Imagination* (Basingstoke: Palgrave Macmillan, 2017), pp. 39–71.

30. *Daily Post*, 27 March 1727; *Evening Post*, 11 April 1727; *Parker's Penny Post*, Friday 14 April 1727.

31. See Jennine Hurl-Eamon, 'The Westminster Impostors: Impersonating Law Enforcement in Early Eighteenth-Century London', *Eighteenth-Century Studies*, Vol. 38, No. 3 (Spring 2005), pp. 461–83; and Lynch, *Detection and Deception*.

32. *Daily Post*, 13 April 1727; *British Journal*, 15 April 1727; *British Journal*, 20 May 1727.

33. *Daily Post*, Monday 27 March 1727.

34. Tom Hadden, 'The Origin and Development of Conspiracy to Defraud', *The American Journal of Legal History*, Vol. 11, No. 1 (January 1967), p. 26; William Hawkins, *A treatise of the pleas of the Crown: or a system of the principal matters relating to that subject, digested under their proper heads*, 2nd. edn, Vol. 1 (London, 1724), p. 187.

35. Peter King, 'The Summary Courts and Social Relations in Eighteenth-Century England', *Past & Present*, No. 183 (2004), p. 156.

Chapter 7

1. The quote in the chapter title is taken from *Daily Post*, Tuesday 6 December 1726.

2. John Locke, *An Essay Concerning Humane Understanding in four books* (London, 1690), p. 1; Roy Porter, 'Medical science and human science in the Enlightenment', in Christopher Fox, Roy Porter, and Robert Wokler (eds), *Inventing Human Science: Eighteenth-Century Domains* (Berkeley: University of California Press, 1995), pp. 53–87. On the publicity of reproduction see Lisa Forman Cody, 'The Politics of Reproduction: From Midwives' Alternative Public Sphere to the Public Spectacle of Man-Midwifery', *Eighteenth-Century Studies*, Vol. 32, No. 4, (1999), pp. 477–95.

3. Dolan, *True Relations*; Lisa Zunshine, 'Eighteenth-Century Print Culture and the "Truth" of Fictional Narrative', *Philosophy and Literature*, Vol. 25, No. 2 (2001), pp. 215–32.

4. *Brice's Weekly Journal*, Friday 16 December 1726.

5. Karen Harvey, *Reading Sex in the Eighteenth Century: Bodies and Gender in English Erotic Culture* (Cambridge: Cambridge University Press, 2004), pp. 68–77; Vic Gatrell, *City of Laughter: Sex and Satire in Eighteenth-Century London* (London: Atlantic Books, 2006). On anti- and occasional politeness see Helen Berry, 'Rethinking Politeness in Eighteenth-Century England: Moll King's Coffee House and the Significance of Flash Talk', *Transactions of the Royal Historical Society* 6th series, XI (2001), pp 65–81. Kate Davison, 'Occasional Politeness and Gentlemen's Laughter in Eighteenth-Century England', *The Historical Journal*, Vol. 52, No. 4 (2014), pp. 921–45.

6. *British Journal*, Saturday 22 October 1726; *Daily Journal*, Monday 14 November 1726.

7. Another brief report had also appeared on Monday 14 November in *Parker's Penny Post*. The *British Journal* article from 22 October was reprinted in the *Evening Post* dated Tuesday 18 October to Thursday 20 October, though covering stories from as late as 26 October. The article published in the *Daily Journal* on 14 November was reprinted in the *Weekly Journal or British Gazeteer* on Saturday 19 November 1726 and *Farley's Exeter Journal*, Wednesday 23 November 1726. On newspapers and their circulation see Uriel Heyd, *Reading Newspapers: Press and Public in eighteenth-century Britain and America* (Oxford: Voltaire Foundation, 2012), p. 16.

8. Letter from William Pountney, no date, GUSC: MS Hunter D321/1; *Parker's Penny Post*, Monday 28 November 1726; William Whiston, *Memoirs of the life and writings of Mr. William Whiston. Containing, memoirs of several of his friends also. Written by himself.* (London, 1753), p. 110.

9. *British Journal*, Saturday 3 December, 1726; *Daily Post*, Tuesday 6 December 1726; *The London Journal*, Saturday 17 December 1726.

10. *Weekly Journal or British Gazetteer*, Saturday 17 December 1726; *Mist's Weekly Journal*, Saturday 7 January 1727; *British Journal*, 20 May 1727.

11. *Mist's Weekly Journal*, Saturday 19 November 1726; Letter from John Wainwright to Edward Harley, 8 December 1726, BL: BL Add MS 70400.

12. *The London Journal*, Saturday 24 December 1726.

13. *Mist's Weekly Journal*, 4 February 1727.

14. *The London Journal*, Saturday 17 December 1726; Nathanael St André, *A Short Narrative*, pp. 31–2; Cyriacus Ahlers, *Some Observations concerning the Woman of Godlyman in Surrey. Made at Guilford [sic] on Sunday, Nov. 20. 1726. Tending to prove her extraordinary Deliveries to be a Cheat and Imposture* (London, 1726), p. ii; Lemuel Gulliver, *The Anatomist Dissected: or the Man-Midwife finely brought to Bed. Being an Examination of the Conduct of Mr. St André. Touching the late pretended Rabbit-bearer; as it appears from his own Narrative. By Lemuel Gulliver, Surgeon and Anatomist to the Kings of Lilliput and Blefuscu, and Fellow of the Academy of Sciences in Balnibarbi. 3rd edition* (London, 1727), p. 24. Nicolson and Rousseau suggest strongly that Arbuthnot, a Scriblerian, was the

author of *The Anatomist Dissected*. Its level of detail and medical knowledge implies a doctor wrote it. See Marjorie Hope Nicolson and George Sebastian Rousseau, *'This Long Disease, My Life': Alexander Pope and the Sciences* (Princeton: Princeton University Press, 1968), p. 115.

15. Cody, '"The Doctor's in Labour"'.

16. Mark Knights, *Representation and Misrepresentation in Later Stuart Britain: Partisanship and Political Culture* (Oxford: Oxford University Press, 2005), pp. 5–6; *Mist's Weekly Journal*, Saturday 17 December, 1726.

17. Will of Sir Richard Manningham, 12 April 1759, TNA: PROB 11/845/352.

18. Transcribed extract regarding Mary Toft from *Whitehall Evening Post*, 29 December 1726. GSC: MS Hunter D332; Transcribed extract from *Daily Journal* and from *Daily Post*, 9 January 1727, on prosecution of Mary Toft and Mr Howard. GSC: MS Hunter D333; Letter to James Douglas from W. Kinleside, ND. Verso—A list of parts of rabbit, presumably those removed from Mary Toft. GSC: MS Hunter D335; Annotated copy of William Hogarth, *Cunicularii, or the wise men of Godliman in consultation*. GSC: MS Hunter D321/2.

19. Whiston, *Memoirs of the life*, pp. 110, 118–19, 116.

20. *Philosophical Enquiry into the Wonderful CONEY-WARREN* (1726), p. 2. Whiston was criticized in less brutal terms in 'The Rabbit-Man-Midwife', in *A New Miscellany* (London, 1730), p. 33.

21. *Pudding and Dumpling Burnt to Pot; or a Compleat Key to the Dissertation on Dumpling* (1727), p. 14; Flamingo, *A Shorter and Truer Advertisement By way of Supplement, To what was published the 7 Instant: or, Dr. D—g—l—s in an Extasy, Lacey's Bagnio, December the 4th, 1726* (London, 1727); Gulliver [pseud.], *The Anatomist Dissected*, pp. 9–10.

22. Gulliver [pseud.], *The Anatomist Dissected*, pp. 33–4; Anonymous, *St A-d-è's miscarriage: or, a Full and True account of the Rabbet-Woman* (London, 1727), p. 6. On cruelty and humour in this period see Simon Dickie, *Cruelty and Laughter: Forgotten Comic Literature and the Unsentimental Eighteenth Century* (Chicago: University of Chicago Press, 2011).

23. See Richard Bradley, *Dictionarium botanicum: or, a botanical dictionary for the use of the curious in husbandry and gardening* (London, 1728), no page number, and Mr. [Pierre] Dionis, *A general treatise of midwifery* (London, 1719), p. 29. On plants and erotic writing see Harvey, *Reading Sex*, pp. 22–3, 57.

24. *Much a-do About Nothing: Or, a Plain Refutation of All that has been Written or Said Concerning the Rabbit-Woman of Godalming. Being A Full and Impartial Confession from her Own Mouth, and under her Own Hand, of the whole Affair, from the Beginning to the End. Now made publick for the General Satisfaction*, (London, 1727), pp. 11–12, 13–14.

25. John Maubray, *The Female Physician, containing all the Diseases incident to that Sex, in Virgins, Wives and Widows* (London, 1724), p. 63; 'A Dialogue between the Lady Sne—er, Mrs. Toft Of Godalmin, Midwife, and her Deputy', in *A*

Letter from a Male Physician in the Country, to the Author of the female Physician in London (London, 1726), pp. 38, 245, 46, 49.

26. Lisa Forman Cody, *Birthing the Nation: Sex, Science, and the Conception of Eighteenth-Century Britons* (Oxford: Oxford University Press, 2005), p. 122.

27. *Daily Post*, Saturday 10 December 1726. The *Daily Courant*, Wednesday 14 December 1726, gives the date of Manningham's pamphlet as 14 December.

28. *The London Journal*, Saturday, 17 December 1726.

29. *Brice's Weekly Journal*, Friday 16 December 1726.

30. Sam Paterson and W. Bristow, *A catalogue of the large and curious English library of Mr. John Hutton, Late of St Paul's Church-Yard, London, Deceased.* (London, 1764) pp. 96, 104, 100; Thomas and John Egerton, *A catalogue of the genuine library of John Darker, Esq; deceased, late treasurer of St Bartholomew's Hospital* (London, 1785) p. 11. Darker was born in 1722 so must have acquired the tracts some time after the case. See Darker, John (?1722–84), of Clerkenwell, London, and Gayton, Northants. Published in *The History of Parliament: the House of Commons 1754–1790*, ed. L. Namier, J. Brooke, 1964. http://www.historyofparliamentonline.org/volume/1754–1790/member/darker-john–1722-84 (accessed 25/1/18); R. E. Mercier and Co, *Dengan sale. Part the first; containing the books. A catalogue of the extensive and valuable library, prints, paintings, Statues, Music, Mathematical Instruments And Superb Furniture Of At The Chapel which belonged to the late Right Hon. Earl of Mornington, at Dengan Castle* (Dublin, 1795), p. 10.

31. Thomas Braithwaite, *Remarks on a Short Narrative of an Extraordinary Delivery of Rabbet, perform'd by Mr. John Howard, Surgeon at Guildford* (London, 1726), pp. iii–iv; v, vi.

32. Anonymous, *St A-d-è's miscarriage*, p. 5; Flamingo, *A shorter and truer advertisement by way of supplement, to what was published the 7 instant: or, Dr. D—g—l—s in an extasy, at Lacey's Bagnio* (London, 1727), p. 4. James Douglas' original pamphlet was *An Advertisement Occasion'd by Some Passages in Sir. R. Manningham's Diary Lately Publish'd* (London, 1727).

33. [Alexander Pope], *The Discovery; or, the Squire turn'd Ferret. An Excellent New Ballad* (London, 1727), pp. 5, 6.

34. Pope's *Correspondance*, II. 418–19, quoted in Nicolson and Rousseau, 'This Long Disease, My Life', p. 110. On Pope and St André see Nicolson and Rousseau, 'This Long Disease, My Life', pp. 30, 110. For background on Pope's family see Pat Rogers, 'The Waltham Blacks and the Black Act', *Historical Journal*, Vol. 17, No. 3 (1972), p. 472; Pat Rogers, *The Symbolic Design of Windsor-Forest: Iconography, Pageant, and Prophecy in Pope's Early Work* (Delaware: University of Delaware Press, 2004), pp. 156–7.

35. Nicolson and Rousseau, 'This Long Disease, My Life', p. 112.

36. Poem on the Godalming Rabbits (c.1726), Leeds Brotherton Library: MSS Lt116.

37. 'An Account of the Rabbets &c', Wellcome Collection: T.347.1; 'John Howard's letter, 9 November 1726', Wellcome Collection: T.347.a1.
38. *British Gazeteer*, 31 July 1736 (see also *The Grub Street Journal*, 5 August 1736); *The Grub Street Journal*, 28 May 1730; *Whitehall Evening Post or London Intelligencer*, 4–6 March 1755.
39. Simon Dickie, *Cruelty and Laughter: Forgotten Comic Literature and the Unsentimental Eighteenth Century* (Chicago: University of Chicago Press, 2011), p. 130.

Chapter 8

1. The quote in the chapter title is taken from 'A Dissertation upon Generation', in *A Letter from a Male Physician in the Country, to the Author of the female Physician in London* (London, 1726), p. 77.
2. John Spencer, *A Discourse Concerning Prodigies*, 2nd edn (London, 1665), preface, sig. a3r. Quoted in Stephen Pender, 'In the bodyshop: human exhibition in early modern England', in Helen Deutsch and Felicity Nussbaum (eds), *'Defects': Engendering the Modern Body* (Ann Arbor: University of Michigan Press, 2000), p. 101; Anita Guerrini, 'Advertising monstrosity: broadsides and human exhibition in early eighteenth-century London', in Patricia Fumerton and Anita Guerrini (eds), with the assistance of Kris McAbee, *Ballads and Broadsides in Britain, 1500–1800* (Farnham: Ashgate, 2010), pp. 109–26. See also David Cressy, 'Agnes Bowker's cat: childbirth, seduction, bestiality, and lies', in *Agnes Bowker's Cat: Travesties and Trangressions in Tudor and Stuart England* (Oxford: Oxford University Press, 2000), pp. 9–28 and David Cressy, 'Lamentable, strange, and wonderful: Headless monsters in the English Revolution', in Laura Knoppers and Joan Landes (ed.), *Monstrous Bodies/Political Monstrosities in Early Modern Europe* (Ithaca, NY: Cornell University Press, 2004), pp. 40–63.
3. On change see Pender, 'In the bodyshop', p. 114 and Katharine Park and Lorraine Daston, 'Unnatural Conceptions: The Study of Monsters in Sixteenth- and Seventeenth-Century France and England', *Past & Present*, No. 92 (1981), pp. 20–54. On body and morality see Juliet McMaster, 'The Body Inside the Skin: The Medical Model of Character in the Eighteenth-Century Novel', *Eighteenth-Century Fiction* Vol. 4, No. 4 (July 1992), pp. 277–300 and Kevin Siena, 'Pliable bodies: the moral biology of health and disease', in Carole Reeves (ed.), *A Cultural History of the Human Body in the Enlightenment* (Oxford: Berg, 2010), pp. 34–52.
4. See David Nash, 'Reconnecting Religion with Social and Cultural History: Secularization's Failure as a Master Narrative', *Social and Cultural History*, Vol. 1 (2004), pp. 302–25; William Gibson and Joanne Begiato, *Sex and the Church in the Long Eighteenth Century* (London: I. B.Taurus, 2017).

5. Address given on 16 February 1726 [1727], London Metropolitan Archive: General Orders of the Court Book, WS/0C/002, October 1724–April 1731, ff. v59, 60.

6. Steve Pincus, *1688: The First Modern Revolution* (New Haven: Yale University Press, 2009), pp. 14–21; Brian Cowan, 'Geoffrey Holmes and the Public Sphere: Augustan Historiography from Post-Namierite to the Post-Habermasian', *Parliamentary History*, Vol. 28 (2009), pp. 166–78; Michael Harris, *London Newspapers in the Age of Walpole: A Study of the Origins of the Modern English Press* (Toronto: Fairleigh Dickinson University Press, 1987), pp. 113–54.

7. 'A Dissertation upon Generation', in *A Letter from a Male Physician in the Country, to the Author of the female Physician in London* (London, 1726), p. 77.

8. Letter from Charlotte, Princess of Wales, to Mrs. Clayton, Clayton Papers, Royal Archives: GEO/ADD/28/010. The main subject of the letter is the medical advice being given for the poorly young Princess Amelia. Charlotte may have been referring to Dr John Friend, who she later appointed one of her physicians. See Anita Guerrini, 'Friend, John (1675–1728), physician', *Oxford Dictionary of National Biography* (Oxford: Oxford University Press, 2004). http://www.oxforddnb.com/view/10.1093/ref:odnb/9780198614128. 001.0001/odnb-9780198614128-e-10153 (accessed 31/5/18); Helen Brock, 'Douglas, James (*bap.* 1675, *d.* 1742), anatomist and man-midwife', *Oxford Dictionary of National Biography* (Oxford: Oxford University Press, 2004). http://www.oxforddnb.com/view/10.1093/ref:odnb/9780198614128.001.0001/ odnb-9780198614128-e-7899 (accessed 31/5/18).

9. Nathanael St André, *A Short Narrative of an Extraordinary Delivery of Rabbets* (1727), p. 5; Cyriacus Ahlers, *Some Observations concerning the Woman of God-lyman* (London, 1726), pp. ii, v; *Daily Journal*, Friday 2 December 1726; *Parker's Penny Post*, Monday 28 November 1726.

10. Ragnhild M. Hatton, 'New light on George I of Great Britain', in Stephen B. Baxter, *England's Rise to Greatness, 1660–1763* (Berkeley: University of California Press, 1983), p. 236.

11. Nicholas Rogers, *Whigs and Cities: Popular Politics in the Age of Walpole and Pitt* (Oxford: Clarendon, 1990), p. 168.

12. Joseph Mitchell, 'Peter: An Heroi-Comical Poem', in *Poems on several occasions* (London, 1729), pp. 377, 373. On Peter in political satire see Julia V. Douthwaite, *The Wild Girl, Natural Man, and the Monster: Dangerous Experiments in the Age of Enlightenment* (Chicago: University of Chicago Press, 2002), pp. 21–2.

13. Mitchell, 'Peter: An Heroi-Comical Poem', pp. 373, 374; Paul Langford, 'Swift and Walpole', in C. Rawson, *Politics and Literature in the Age of Swift* (Cambridge: Cambridge University Press, 2010), pp. 52–60; *Mist's Weekly Journal*, Saturday 7 January 1727. See Harris, *London Newspapers*, p. 114.

14. *The Northumberland Monster: Or a true and perfect relation* (London, 1674).

15. Philip M. Soergel, 'Agnes Bowker's Cat, the Rabbit Woman of Godalming, and the Shifting Nature of Portents in Early-Modern Europe', *Studies in Medieval & Renaissance History*, 3rd ser., 4 (2007). p. 271; William E. Burns, *An Age of Wonders: Prodigies, Politics, and Providence in England, 1657–1727* (Manchester: Manchester University Press, 2010), p. 187.

16. Abel Boyer, *The Political State of Great Britain* (December 1726), p. 602; Gibbs, G. C., 'Boyer, Abel (1667?–1729), lexicographer and journalist, *Oxford Dictionary of National Biography* (Oxford: Oxford University Press, 2004). http://www.oxforddnb.com/view/10.1093/ref:odnb/9780198614128.001.0001/odnb-9780198614128-e-3122 (accessed 14/6/18).

17. *Mist's Weekly Journal*, Saturday 7 January 1727. On nation, race, and monstrous births see Lisa Forman Cody, *Birthing the Nation: Sex, Science, and the Conception of Eighteenth-Century Britons* (Oxford: Oxford University Press, 2005), pp. 136–40.

18. Earl of Peterborough to Jonathan Swift, 29 November 1726, in Jonathan Swift, *The works of Jonathan Swift, with notes historical and critical*, edited by J. Hawkesworth and others (Edinburgh, 1778), p. 30.

19. Jonathan Swift to Henrietta Howard, 27 November 1726, in *The Correspondence of Jonathan Swift*, ed. H. Williams, 5 vols. (1963–5), Vol. 3, pp. 187–8. Quoted in Cody, *Birthing the Nation*, p. 131. See also J. H. Plumb, *Sir Robert Walpole: The King's Minister* (London: Cresset Press, 1960), p. 104; Matthew Kilburn, 'Howard, Henrietta, countess of Suffolk (c.1688–1767)', *Oxford Dictionary of National Biography* (Oxford: Oxford University Press, 2004); online edn, Jan 2008. http://www.oxforddnb.com/view/article/13904 (accessed 2/4/15).

20. Ronald Paulson, 'Putting out the Fire in Her Imperial Majesty's Apartment: Opposition Politics, Anticlericalism, and Aesthetics', *ELH*, Vol. 63 (1996), pp. 89–90, 93, 96. Paulson says *The Punishment* was announced in the *Daily Post* on 3 December and announced as now published in the *Daily Post* of 27 December 1726: 'Putting out the Fire', p. 80.

21. Paulson, 'Putting out the Fire', p. 80; Harris, *London Newspapers*, p. 114.

22. *The Craftsman*, Monday 24 April–Friday 28 April 1727, pp. 1–2.

23. Harris, *London Newspapers*, p. 116.

24. *The Craftsman*, 20 May 1732, p. 1. *The Craftsman* was published from December 1726. Michael Erben, 'Amhurst, Nicholas (1697–1742)', *Oxford Dictionary of National Biography* (Oxford: Oxford University Press, 2004); online edn, Oct 2009. http://www.oxforddnb.com/view/article/446 (accessed 1/4/15).

25. *Daily Courant*, Saturday 27 May 1732.

26. See Vladimir Jankovic, 'The Politics of Sky Battles in Early Hanoverian Britain', *The Journal of British Studies*, Vol. 41, No. 4 (2002), pp. 429–59; Ian Bostridge, *Witchcraft and its Transformations c.1650–1750* (Oxford: Clarendon, 1997), esp. pp. 131–47.

27. Lorraine Daston and Katharine Park, *Wonders and the Order of Nature, 1150–1750* (New York: Zone Books, 1998), p. 343.

28. Thompson, *Whigs and Hunters*, p. 197; Lawrence E. Klein, 'Liberty, Manners, and Politeness in Early Eighteenth-Century England', *The Historical Journal*, Vol. 32, No. 03 (1989), pp. 583–605; Markku Peltonen, 'Politeness and Whiggism, 1688–1732', *The Historical Journal*, Vol. 48, No. 2 (2005), pp. 391–414.

29. Stephen Hague, *The Gentleman's House in the British Atlantic World, 1680–1780* (Basingstoke: Palgrave Macmillan, 2015), p. 28; T. P. Connor, 'Architecture and Planting at Goodwood, 1723–1750', *Sussex Archaeological Collections*, Vol. 117 (1979), p. 185; Carole Fry, 'Spanning the Political Divide: Neo-Palladianism and the Early Eighteenth-Century Landscape', *Garden History*, Vol. 31, No. 2 (2003), pp. 180–92; Simon Schaffer, 'A social history of plausibility: country, city and calculation in Augustan Britain', in Adrian Wilson, *Rethinking Social History: English Society 1570–1920 and its Interpretation* (Manchester: Manchester University Press, 1993), p. 129.

30. Richard Hewlings, 'Chiswick House and Gardens: Appearance and Meaning', in Toby Barnard and Jane Clark (eds), *Lord Burlington: Architecture, Art and Life* (London: Hambledon, 1995), p. 149.

31. Hewlings, 'Chiswick House and Gardens', p. 110; Christopher Hussey, 'Goodwood House—II, Sussex', *Country Life*, 72, 16 July 1932; P. Connor, 'Architecture and Planting at Goodwood, 1723–1750', *Sussex Archaeological Collections*, Vol. 117 (1979), pp. 186–7.

32. The house was still partly under construction at this time. The Historic England entry for Clandon Park dates the house 1725–31, and the design as *c.*1713. See https://historicengland.org.uk/listing/the-list/list-entry/1294591. The old Tudor house would have been demolished by 1726.

33. Barbara Duden, 'Remarks of a Historian of Women's Bodies (à propos the History of the Greek Orders of Columns by Joseph Rykwert)', *RES: Anthropology and Aesthetics*, Vol. 47 (2005), pp. 247–50; Margaret Healy, *Fictions of Disease in Early Modern England: Bodies, Plagues and Politics* (Basingstoke: Palgrave Macmillan, 2001), pp. 3–4; Soergel, 'Agnes Bowker's cat', p. 273.

34. Roy Porter, *Bodies Politic: Disease, Death, and Doctors in Britain, 1650–1900* (Ithaca, NY: Cornell University Press, 2001), p. 61. These ideas are based on the work of the literary scholar Mikael Bakhtin, also discussed in Séverine Pilloud and Micheline Louis-Courvoisier, 'The Intimate Experience of the Body in the Eighteenth Century: Between Interiority and Exteriority', *Medical History*, Vol. 47 (2003), p. 467; and Kevin Stagg, 'The body', in Garthine Walker (ed.), *Writing Early Modern History* (London: Bloomsbury, 2005), pp. 209–11.

35. Peter Elmer, *Witchcraft, Witch-Hunting, and Politics in Early Modern England* (Oxford: Oxford University Press, 2016), pp. 274–5, 285–90; Bostridge, *Witchcraft and its Transformations*, pp. 131–51.

36. Daniel Defoe, *The Political History of the Devil* (London, 1726), pp. 387, 388; Daniel Defoe, *A System of Magic* (London, 1727), p. 216, quoted in Bostridge, *Witchcraft and its Transformations*, p. 138.

37. On Moredike see Elmer, *Witchcraft, Witch-Hunting, and Politics*, pp. 276–8; Bostridge, *Witchcraft and its Transformations*, pp. 134–5. On Wenham see Mark Knights, *The Devil in Disguise: Deception, Delusion, and Fanaticism in the Early English Enlightenment* (Oxford: Oxford University Press, 2011), pp. 2, 240.

38. Bostridge, *Witchcraft and its Transformations*, p. 109.

39. Owen Davies, *Witchcraft, Magic and Culture, 1736–1951* (Manchester: Manchester University Press, 1999), quote at p. 7. On the Act see also Barry, *Witchcraft and Demonology*, p. 175.

40. Barry, *Witchcraft and Demonology*, pp. 169–70, 258–63; Davies, *Witchcraft, Magic and Culture*, pp. 8–9, and pp. 274–5 for rates of continuing prosecution.

41. Davies, *Witchcraft, Magic and Culture*, pp. 11–14. Quotes from *Round About Our Coal-Fire: or Christmas entertainments. Containing, Christmas gambols, tropes, figures* (London, [1730]), p. 24.

42. Lorraine Daston, 'Marvelous Facts and Miraculous Evidence in Early Modern Europe', *Critical Inquiry*, Vol. 18, No. 1 (1991), pp. 93–124.

43. James Blondel, *The Power of the Mother's Imagination Over the Foetus Examin'd. In answer to Dr. Daniel Turner's book, intitled A defence of the XIIth chapter of the first part of a treatise, De morbis cutaneis* (1729), p. i.

44. Daniel Turner, *De Morbis Cutaneis. A treatise of diseases incident to the skin*, third edition (London, 1726), pp. 155, 177.

45. James Blondel, *The Strength of Imagination in Pregnant Women Exam'd*, pp. 9, 11; James Blondel, *The Power of the Mother's Imagination Over the Foetus Examin'd. In answer to Dr. Daniel Turner's book, intitled A defence of the XIIth chapter of the first part of a treatise, De morbis cutaneis* (1729), pp. i, 5; 4. Daniel Turner's book was, *A discourse concerning gleets [. . .] To which is added, a defence of the 12 chapter of the first part of a treatise De morbis cutaneis, in respect to the Spots and Marks impress'd upon the Skin of the Foetus, by the Force of the Mother's Fancy: containing some remarks upon a discourse lately printed and entituled, The strength of imagination in pregnant women examin'd, &c. Whereby it is made plain, notwithstanding all the Objections therein, that the said Imagination in the Pregnant Woman, is capable of maiming, and does often both mutilate and mark the Foetus, or that the same, as he insinuates, is not a vulgar Error. In a Letter to the Author* (London, 1729).

46. Blondel, *The Power of the Mother's Imagination* (1729), pp. 4, 6, 2. On the continuation of the theory of the maternal imagination and the Toft case, see Paul-Gabriel Boucé, 'Imagination, pregnant women, and monsters, in eighteenth-century England and France', in Rousseau and Porter's (eds), *Sexual Underworlds of the Enlightenment*, pp. 86–100; Jenifer Buckley, *Gender, Pregnancy and Power in Eighteenth-Century Literature: The Maternal Imagination* (Basingstoke: Palgrave Macmillan, 2017), pp. 39–80; Philip K. Wilson,

Surgery, Skin and Syphilis: Daniel Turner's London (1667–1741) (Amsterdam: Editions Rodopi B. V., 1999), pp. 113–48.

47. Rowland Jackson, *A physical dissertation on drowning* (London, 1746), p. 2.

48. Advertisement for display at the Rummer, Fleet Street, London, *c.*1736. British Library: N.Tab.2026/25 (42). For other displays at the Rummer and nearby venues, see Walter Thornbury, 'Fleet Street: general introduction', in *Old and New London: Volume 1* (London, 1878), pp. 32–53. *British History Online* http://www.british-history.ac.uk/old-new-london/vol1/pp32-53 (accessed 14/6/18).

49. Jenifer Buckley, *Gender, Pregnancy and Power in Eighteenth-Century Literature: The Maternal Imagination* (Basingstoke: Palgrave Macmillan, 2017). On Voltaire see Lorraine Daston and Katharine Park, *Wonders and the Order of Nature* (London: Zone, 2001), p. 330.

50. Bernd Krysmanski, 'We See a Ghost: Hogarth's Satire on Methodists and Connoisseurs', *The Art Bulletin*, Vol. 80, No. 2 (June 1998), pp. 292–310; See Jane Shaw, 'Mary Toft, Religion and National Memory in Eighteenth-Century England', *Journal for Eighteenth-century Studies*, Vol. 32, No. 3 (2009), pp. 321–38; Todd, *Imagining Monsters*, p. 102; Daston and Park, *Wonders and the Order of Nature*, pp. 334–43.

51. *St James's Chronicle or the British Evening Post*, 4–6 July 1769.

52. *Gazetteer and New Daily Advertiser*, Saturday 23 September, 1769; *St James's Chronicle or the British Evening Post*, 11–14 July 1761; *Public Advertiser*, Saturday 4 January 1777; *St James's Chronicle or the British Evening Post*, 23–5 February 1762; *Public Advertiser*, Monday 20 June 1763; John Trusler, *Chronology; or, the historian's vade-mecum. Wherein every remarkable event in ancient and modern history, is alphabetically recorded, and the date affixed* (London, 1786), p. 172. On the persistence of the miraculous, see Jane Shaw, *Miracles in Enlightenment England* (New Haven: Yale University Press, 2006), p. 177.

53. Daston and Park, *Wonders and the Order of Nature*, p. 361. On the politics of rational knowledge, see Simon Schaffer, 'A social history of plausibility: country, city and calculation in Augustan Britain', in Adrian Wilson (ed.), *Rethinking Social History: English society 1570–1920 and its Interpretation* (Manchester: Manchester University Press, 1993), p. 150.

Chapter 9

1. Surrey History Centre (SHC): Parish Registers for Godalming (St Peter and St Paul). Elizabeth was baptized on 4 February 1728. John was baptized on 3 October and buried on 2 November 1729.

2. Todd gives no reference for this statement.

3. *The London Journal*, Saturday 19 August 1727; Parish records of St Peter and St Paul of Godalming, 1763, viewed on microfilm: Surrey History Centre. The reference to Toft being displayed at Richmond's house is discussed in

mentioned in Dennis Todd, *Imagining Monsters*, p. 37; *London Chronicle*, 20–2 January 1763.

4. Lisa Forman Cody, '"The doctor's in labour, or, A new whim wham from Guildford"', *Gender and History*, Vol. 4 (1992), pp. 172–96; S. A. Seligman, 'Mary Toft—The Rabbit Breeder', *Medical History*, Vol. 5 (1961), pp. 349–60; Barbara Stafford, *Artful Science: Enlightenment Entertainment and the Eclipse of Visual Education* (Cambridge, MA: MIT Press, 1994), p. 5.

5. Clifford Pickover, *The Girl Who Gave Birth to Rabbits: A True Medical Mystery* (Amherst: Prometheus Books, 2000), p. 156; Programme details for 'Rogues' Gallery' London Weekend Television programme on Toft: 3122, Godalming Museum; Colin Bytheway quoted in *Surrey Advertiser* article, 'Radio 4 airing for lurid "I gave birth to rabbits" tale', 24/4/2011: in Mary Toft's, folder 1, Godalming Museum.

6. Hilary Mantel, *The Giant O'Brien: A Novel* (New York: Picador, 1998), pp. 83–4; Proposal, 6 June 1993: Box 6, MN6o The Giant O'Brien, Hilary Mantel papers, Huntington library. See also Box 5 MN45 Notebook and Box 6 MN56 Notebook. On O'Brien, see K. D. Reynolds, 'Byrne [O'Brien], Charles (1761–1783), giant', *Oxford Dictionary of National Biography* (Oxford: Oxford University Press, 2004). http://www.oxforddnb.com/view/10.1093/ref:odnb/9780198614128.001.0001/odnb-9780198614128-e-4270 (accessed 5/6/18).

7. Emma Donoghue, 'The Last Rabbit', in *The Woman Who Gave Birth to Rabbits* (London: Virago, 2002), pp. 1, 12–13.

8. John Whale, *Waterloo Teeth* (Oxford: Carcanet, 2010), pp. 11–12.

9. Mukesh Verma, 'The human epigenome and cancer', in Muin J. Khoury et al. (eds), *Human Genome Epidemiology: Building the Evidence for Using Genetic Information to Improve Health and Prevent Sisease*, 2nd edition (Oxford: Oxford University Press, 2010), p. 551. For a summary of work in this area see Douglas Almond and Janet Currie, 'Killing Me Softly: The Fetal Origins Hypothesis', *Journal of Economic Perspectives*, Vol. 25, No. 3 (2011), pp. 153–7; Gwen Latendresse and Sandra Founds, 'The Fascinating and Complex Role of the Placenta in Pregnancy and Fetal Well-being', *Journal of Midwifery and Women's Health*, Vol. 60, No. 4 (2015), p. 362.

10. Jeffrey S. Gilbert, Christopher T. Banek, Ashley J. Bauer, Anne Gingery, and Hans C. Dreyer, 'Placental and Vascular Adaptations to Exercise Training before and during Pregnancy in the Rat', *Am J Physiol Regul Integr Comp Physiol*, Vol 303, No. 5 (2012), pp. R520–R526; Diana W. Bianchi, 'Prenatal diagnosis through the analysis of fetal cells in the maternal circulation', in Aubrey Milunsky (ed.), *Genetic Disorders and the Fetus: Diagnosis, Prevention, and Treatment*, 4th edition (1979; Baltimore: Johns Hopkins University Press, 1998), pp. 931–51. On the foetal origins thesis see Laura C. Schulz, 'The Dutch Hunger Winter and the Developmental Origins of Health and Disease', *Proceedings of the National Academy of Sciences*, Vol. 107, No. 39 (2010), pp. 16757–8; Almond and Currie, 'Killing Me Softly'.

11. Katie E. McGhee and Alison M. Bell, 'Paternal Care in a Fish: Epigenetics and Fitness Enhancing Effects on Offspring Anxiety', *Proceedings of the Royal Society B*, 7 November 2014, 281 (1794); James P. Curley, Rahia Mashoodh, Frances A. Champagne, 'Epigenetics and the Origins of Paternal Effects', *Hormones and Behavior*, Vol. 59, No. 3 (2011), pp. 306–14; Haotian Wu, Lisa Ashcraft, Brian W. Whitcomb, Tayyab Rahil, Ellen Tougias, Cynthia K. Sites, and J. Richard Pilsner, 'Parental Contributions to Early Embryo Development: Influences of Urinary Phthalate and Phthalate Alternatives among Couples Undergoing IVF Treatment', *Human Reproduction*, Vol. 32, No. 1 (2017), pp. 65–75.

12. Jocelien Olivier, Floor Heesch, Anthonieke Afrasiab-Middelman, Janneke Roelofs, Marloes Jonkers, Elke Peeters, Gerdien Korte-Bouws, Jos Dederen, Amanda Kiliaan, Gerard Martens, Dirk Schubert, and Judith Homberg, 'Fluoxetine Administration to Pregnant Rats Increases Anxiety-Related Behavior in the Offspring', *Psychopharmacology*, Vol. 217, No. 3 (2011), pp. 419–32. See also Tie-Yuan Zhang, Rose Bagot, Carine Parent, Cathy Nesbitt, Timothy W. Bredy, Christian Caldji, Eric Fish, Hymie Anisman, Moshe Szyf, and Michael J. Meaney, 'Maternal Programming of Defensive Responses through Sustained Effects on Gene Expression', *Biological Psychology*, Vol. 73, No. 1 (July 2006), pp. 72–89; Vivette Glover and Thomas G. O'Connor, 'Effects of Antenatal Stress and Anxiety: Implications for Development and Psychiatry', *The British Journal of Psychiatry*, Vol. 180, No. 5 (2002), pp. 389–91.

13. Gwen Latendresse and Sandra Founds, 'The Fascinating and Complex Role of the Placenta in Pregnancy and Fetal Well-being', *Journal of Midwifery and Women's Health*, Vol. 60, No. 4 (2015), pp. 360–70; Krisztina D. László, Tobias Svensson, Jiong Li, Carsten Obel, Mogens Vestergaard, Jørn Olsen, and Sven Cnattingius, 'Maternal Bereavement during Pregnancy and the Risk of Stillbirth: A Nationwide Cohort Study in Sweden', *American Journal of Epidemiology*, Vol. 177, No. 3 (2013), pp. 219–27; Dennis K. Kinney, Kerim M. Munir, David J. Crowley, and Andrea M. Miller, 'Prenatal Stress and Risk for Autism', *Neuroscience & Biobehavioral Reviews*, Vol. 32, No. 8 (2008), pp. 1519–32.

14. These comments are based on a meeting with NHS reproductive medicine researchers and clinicians (14 June 2016).

15. Latendresse and Founds, 'Fascinating and Complex Role of the Placenta in Pregnancy', p. 368. Quote from Almond and Currie, 'Killing Me Softly', p. 15.

16. The comments in this and the next paragraph are taken from a meeting with midwives (14 November 2016).

17. Yves G. Ville, Kypros H. Nicolaides, and Stuart Campbell, 'Prenatal diagnosis of fetal malformations by ultrasound', in Aubrey Milunsky (ed.), *Genetic Disorders and the Fetus: Diagnosis, Prevention, and Treatment*, 4th edition (1979; Baltimore: Johns Hopkins University Press, 1998), pp. 750–811.

18. Jennifer Evans and Sara Read, '"before midnight she had miscarried": Women, Men, and Miscarriage in Early Modern England', *Journal of Family*

History, Vol. 40, No. 1 (2015), pp. 3–23; http://www.miscarriageassociation.
org.uk/support/marking-your-loss/ (accessed 23/1/17).

19. Amanda Vickery, *The Gentleman's Daughter: Women's Lives in Georgian England*
(London and New York: Yale University Press, 1998). On historic fears see
Sharon Howard, 'Imagining the Pain and Peril of Seventeenth-Century
Childbirth: Travail and Deliverance in the Making of an Early Modern
World', *Social History of Medicine*, Vol. 16, No. 3 (2003), pp. 367–82; Herman
Roodenburg, 'The Maternal Imagination: The Fears of Pregnant Women in
Seventeenth-Century Holland', *Journal of Social History*, Vol. 21 (1988),
pp. 701–16; Roger Schofield, 'Did mothers really die? Three centuries of
maternal mortality', in L. Bonfield et al., *The World We Have Gained: Histories of
Population and Social Structure* (Oxford: Basil Blackwell, 1986), pp. 230–60;
Adrian Wilson, 'The Perils of Early Modern Procreation: Childbirth with or
without Fear?', *British Journal of Eighteenth Century Studies*, Vol. 16 (1993),
pp. 1–19.

20. These comments and those in the next paragraph are based on an interview
with an NHS consultant midwife and a clinical psychologist who work
with women experiencing birth trauma (19 July 2017). On tokophobia,
see 'Sixty Seconds on...Tokophobia', *BMJ*, 18 September 2018: https://
www.bmj.com/content/362/bmj.k3933/rr–1 (accessed 15/11/18). On the relationship between discourse and practice in childbirth, see Denis Walsh,
Amina M. R. El-Nemer, and Soo Downe, 'Rethinking risk and safety in
maternity care', in Soo Downe (ed.), *Normal Childbirth: Evidence and Debate*,
2nd edition (Edinburgh: Churchill Livingstone, 2008), pp. 117–27; Denis
Walsh, 'Childbirth Embodiment: Problematic Aspects of Current Understandings', *Sociology of Health & Illness*, Vol. 32, No. 3 (2010), pp. 486–501.

PICTURE ACKNOWLEDGEMENTS

1.1. Reproduced by permission of Surrey History Centre.

2.1. The Miriam and Ira D. Wallach Division of Art, Prints and Photographs: Print Collection, The New York Public Library. Accessed September 12, 2018. http://digitalcollections.nypl.org/items/bb7aa360-e8f3-0130-c126-58d385a7bbd0.

2.2. The Miriam and Ira D. Wallach Division of Art, Prints and Photographs: Print Collection, The New York Public Library. Accessed September 12, 2018. http://digitalcollections.nypl.org/items/bb7aa360-e8f3-0130-c126-58d385a7bbd0.

3.1. Wellcome Collection. Reproduced under the terms of the Creative Commons Attribution 4.0 International license (CC BY 4.0). https://creativecommons.org/licenses/by/4.0/.

3.2. The Miriam and Ira D. Wallach Division of Art, Prints and Photographs: Print Collection, The New York Public Library. Accessed September 12, 2018. http://digitalcollections.nypl.org/items/bb7aa360-e8f3-0130-c126-58d385a7bbd0.

3.3. The Miriam and Ira D. Wallach Division of Art, Prints and Photographs: Print Collection, The New York Public Library. Accessed September 12, 2018. http://digitalcollections.nypl.org/items/bb7aa360-e8f3-0130-c126-58d385a7bbd0.

4.1. Heritage Image Partnership Ltd / Alamy Stock Photo.

4.2. Wellcome Collection. Reproduced under the terms of the Creative Commons Attribution 4.0 International license (CC BY 4.0). https://creativecommons.org/licenses/by/4.0/.

4.3. The Miriam and Ira D. Wallach Division of Art, Prints and Photographs: Print Collection, The New York Public Library. Accessed September 12, 2018. http://digitalcollections.nypl.org/items/bb7aa360-e8f3-0130-c126-58d385a7bbd0.

4.4. By permission of University of Glasgow Library, Special Collections.

5.1. By permission of University of Glasgow Library, Special Collections.

6.1. Wellcome Collection. Reproduced under the terms of the Creative Commons Attribution 4.0 International license (CC BY 4.0). https://creativecommons.org/licenses/by/4.0/.

6.2. Wellcome Collection. Reproduced under the terms of the Creative Commons Attribution 4.0 International license (CC BY 4.0). https://creativecommons.org/licenses/by/4.0/.

INDEX

Note: Figures are indicated by an italic "*f*" following the page number.

For the benefit of digital users, indexed terms that span two pages (e.g., 52–53) may, on occasion, appear on only one of those pages.

INDEX